DEVELOPMENT, PSYCHOPATHOLOGY, AND TREATMENT TECHNIQUES ACROSS THE LIFE-SPAN

DEVELOPMENT, PSYCHOPATHOLOGY, AND TREATMENT TECHNIQUES ACROSS THE LIFE-SPAN

A Psychoanalytic Perspective

Ivan Sherick, Ph.D.

International Psychoanalytic Books (IPBooks)
New York • http://www.IPBooks.net

Development, Psychopathology, and Treatment Techniques
Across the Life-Span: A Psychoanalytic Perspective

Published by IPBooks, Queens, NY
Online at: www.IPBooks.net

Copyright © 2020 Ivan Sherick

All rights reserved. This book may not be reproduced, transmitted, or stored, in whole or in part by any means, including graphic, electronic, or mechanical without the express permission of the author and/or publisher, except in the case of brief quotations embodied in critical articles and reviews.

ISBN: 978-1-949093-86-5

AUTHOR'S COMMENT

Having the three former books under one cover makes them more accessible and available for integration. For example, in the book on development, interest may be in further investigating the oedipal years. The reader can then go to the book on psychopathology and peruse the section on childhood manifestations to learn about obsessional and hysterical symptoms originating during the oedipal stage. Next the reader can review the book on psychoanalytic technique to see if there are comments relevant to understanding and dealing with conflicts originating during the oedipal years but being revived during adolescence and adulthood. The same opportunity will exist for other issues.

Dedication

This book is dedicated to my wife, my children and their spouses, and to my grandchildren

TABLE OF CONTENTS

Book I: Introduction to Child, Adolescent & Adult Development

Introduction 1

Part 1
1. The decision to have a child 9
2. A new born and first-time parenting/Oral Phase 13
3. Infertility; multiples & adoption 23
4. The toddler years/Anal [Urethral] Phase 35
5. The preschool years/Phallic Phase 45
6. Day care 63
7. The Oedipal years 67
8. Psychological disturbances of the early years of childhood 79
9. Latency 97
10. Divorce: Helping children cope 109
11. Sex education, media exposure & after-school enrichment ... 113
12. Sexual abuse 119
13. Pre-adolescence 121
14. Early adolescence 125
15. Middle adolescence 135
16. Late adolescence 145

Part 2

17. Young adulthood 151
18. Homosexuality 155
19. Middle-age 159
20. Grand parenthood 165
21. Old age 169

Part 3

22. Obtaining professional help 175
23. Representative list of topics discussed in each chapter 179
24. Recommended readings 183

Book II: Introduction to Understanding Psychopathology

Preface 193

1. Essential Concepts in Understanding Psychopathology 195
2. Life Events and Psychopathology 205
3. Basic Biological Functions that May Be Drawn into Mental Conflict 215
4. Natural Strengths Interfered with by Mental Conflict 221
5. Diagnostic Categories 223
6. Childhood Psychopathology 229
7. Adolescent Psychopathology 239
8. Adult Psychopathology 245

Postscript 257

Representative List of Topics 259

Recommended Readings 261

TABLE OF CONTENTS

Book III: Psychoanalytic Technique with Children, Adolescents, and Adults

Preface 267

Part 1
1. Psychoanalytic Concepts of Development............................271
2. Psychoanalytic Model of the Mind.. 275

Part 2
3. Referral..281
4. Evaluation 283
5. Recommendation.. 287
6. The Frame 289
7. The Beginning of an Analysis 293
8. Establishing Working Alliance 297
9. Resistance 300
10. Transference.. 306
11. Real Object, Developmental Object, & Transference Object 310
12. Countertransference 312
13. Interpretation 315
14. Acting Out 324
15. Limit Setting 326
16. Ways of Bringing Material... 332
17. Comings & Goings 339
18. Role of Education 341
19. Work with Parents 344
20. Goals of Psychoanalytic Treatment.................................... 348
21. Working Through 351
22. Termination 353

Part 3
23. Brief Clinical Illustrations.. 359

Part 4
24. Other Schools of Psychoanalysis 377

Part 5
25. The Widening Spectrum of Psychoanalytic Treatment......... 383

Part 6
26. Dealing with Illness & Death 387
27. A Professional Will 389
28. Planned Retirement by the Analyst...................................... 390
29. Negative Therapeutic Reaction 391
30. "Soul Murder".. 392
31. Diversity 393

Part 7
32. Postscript 397

Representative List of Topics 401

Recommended Readings 407

Acknowledgments

My education began with the writings of Sigmund Freud, the founder of Psychoanalysis. His daughter, Miss Anna Freud, the founder and Director of the Hampstead Clinic in London inspired me as a student at her Clinic. Erna Furman's writing on early childhood development and Peter Blos, Sr.'s on the complexities of adolescent development have enriched me.

Numerous supervisors have assisted me and there have been many colleagues that I have discussed psychoanalytic child development with. I am grateful, also, to my supervisees and students who have challenged me to be organized and articulate in my exposition of psychoanalytic views on development. Thanks to Drs. Peter Blos, Jr., and James Heitler for reading an earlier version of this manuscript and making helpful suggestions.

My wife, Judie, has taught me a great deal about parenting. I am eternally grateful to her. Finally, my children Chaya and Dan, have given me the opportunity to be a parent and grandparent to wonderful grandchildren. I am also eternally grateful to all of them.

Introduction to Child, Adolescent, & Adult Development:

A Psychoanalytic Perspective for Students and Professionals

Ivan Sherick, Ph.D.

Introduction

My aim is to offer an introduction to the topic of development of the mind. I will consider this development over the lifetime of an individual. There will be no formal references in the text, although I will provide a list of recommended readings at the end. To help a reader relocate a subject I will provide a representative list of topics discussed in each chapter at the end. My focus is limited to the Western culture that I am familiar with. Clearly, my thinking has been formed by experiences communicated by former teachers, supervisors, colleagues, scholars, etc., to whom I am indebted, but what I offer is my own personalized synthesis of it all. The topic of the mind is so complicated that any one book cannot do justice to it.

My particular orientation is not a popular one in the present day. I am a psychoanalyst, having experience with patients of all ages. If you are in training to be a mental health specialist your program may de-emphasize a psychodynamic approach. It could be that psychoanalysis is a perspective about development of the mind that you are not familiar with. My doctorate is in clinical psychology and my internship was with adult patients. Even so, during graduate training I sought out child focused practicums. My postdoctoral training was at Reiss-Davis, a former psychoanalytically informed child guidance clinic in Los Angeles. I then completed the training in child psychoanalysis at the Hampstead Clinic in London, under Miss Anna Freud's directorship. After graduating, I completed training in adult psychoanalysis at the Michigan Psychoanalytic Institute in the USA.

I bring a developmental and ego psychological perspectives into my clinical and teaching efforts. What do these perspectives mean in simple terms? By a "developmental" perspective I mean that I do not lose sight of the continuity of a person, pulled forward by an inherent developmental force, from childhood through adulthood and into old age, as well as the timelessness of experience in the human mind. A developmental perspective looks backward and looks forward. I am interested in the interaction of the environment with an individual's maturing inherited potentialities, and the psychological and learned aspects of the mind, resulting in personal experience. Out of this interaction, the mind develops. I also attend to the psychological developmental tasks that we all must deal with at different stages of our life. While continuity is fundamental, it is not all-inclusive. Maturational changes – some physical (like puberty) and some mental (like changes in cognition) that affect ego capacities – will introduce non-linear discontinuities that can be transformative in their consequences. Also, unpredictable environmental experiences can lead to identifications and transformative outcomes.

By an "ego psychological" perspective I mean that the human mind is faced with conflicting demands, some unconscious, and expends effort to avoid mental pain and to maximize pleasure. It is this complicated, but real and valid, view of development that I hope to bring to your attention. The predominant focus will be on child and adolescent development but I extend my observations to the whole lifespan.

I hope my particular psychoanalytic perspective will be helpful to you. If you are a graduate of a psychoanalytic institute I hope you will find my views stimulating enough to further your reflection on issues about development. While there are many valuable contemporary contributions to psychoanalysis, they need to be integrated with more classical contributions. This is a task that I have not taken upon myself in this manuscript. I have, however, referred to the concepts of mentalisation and attachment insofar as I believe they are derived from our existing theory of child development and extend our understanding of the development of the mind. When considering child development, I focus mainly on the comprehensive developmental insights particularly derived from the writings of Anna Freud. In my judgment they are immensely valuable and I believe if we lose sight of them we will lose much that is helpful in working with children and parents. Currently such views, in my opinion, are neglected in the contemporary psychoanalytic literature and rarely cited. My hope is that in my introduction to these concepts I succeed in underscoring their continued usefulness. I rely on Peter Blos, Sr.'s formulations about adolescent development that also are in this tradition, as is the ego psychology perspective of psychoanalysis that I employ.

Psychoanalysis, in general, is disparaged in films and many non-psychoanalytic professionals in the field discredit it. They may discredit it but they often will take components of it into their own practices and theories without attribution as to its origin. They will say that psychoanalysis is like an extinct insect frozen in amber. The latest neuroscience evidence, however, supports much of what Freud theorized at a time when modern technology such as MRI was not available to allow electro-imaging of the brain. Additionally, empirical research underscores the efficacy of psychodynamic psychotherapeutic approaches based on psychoanalysis with patients.

What I am presenting is my personal view of a psychoanalytic perspective on development. You should know that psychoanalysis is not a unified theory and is in flux. There will be psychoanalysts who might disagree with some of what I say. I have tried to be practical and focus on the concerns most young professionals have about their patients and those brought by parents in consultations about their children and about their parenting. The stages of adulthood will also be considered from becoming a parent to old age.

I will try in what follows to introduce you to how this particular psychoanalyst views development in language that is intelligible. When technical concepts are used I will explain them in language that is more comprehensible but still able to convey the nuances and complexity of the concept. My purpose in including theory about a model of the mind and about psychological conflict is to help you understand how an analyst conceptualizes the workings of the mind. My hope is that it will allow you to appreciate not only your patient's mind, but also your own. Having a theory is like providing you with a flashlight as you enter a dark cave in which are the most extraordinary paintings and carvings created by ancient people. The theory can help you to know what to look for and how to understand what you see. Development is complex, so rarely do simplistic linear formulations suffice as causative explanations. Instead, we think of outcomes as usually being multi-determined.

For the most part, I am focusing on normal development but will diverge my focus to "psychopathology" when I think it might be helpful. As a psychoanalyst, when I think of "normal" I am not thinking of ordinary or conventional or obedient. Insofar as mental conflict is ubiquitous, the normal individual is also " normally neurotic." "Neurotic" for a psychoanalyst is not a pejorative term. All of us, to a lesser or greater degree, are neurotic.

The book is organized in a description of stages of development that roughly follows chronological age. These stages of development are characterized by familiar epochs in the lives of people, e.g., newborn, toddler, preschooler, school age, middle school student, teenager, young adult, middle age, grandparent, and old age. These stages also inter-relate with "phases" of development that psychoanalysts distinguish by the kinds of personal issues and conflicts characteristic for that particular period of development. I will relate a descriptive stage and corresponding psychoanalytic phase to one another in non-technical terms. Interspersed will be a variety of topics that concern professionals insofar as they impinge upon a child's development, e.g., divorce. I have tried to address these topics at the stage of development when parents usually consider them, but in real life it is not so orderly and predictable.

Often I will refer to parental attitudes and concerns insofar when discussing a child's development it is impossible to do so without considering parents. There are no children without parents (adult caregivers). Almost all children develop in the context of a family. The parenting skills of mothers and fathers, or lack of them, have major consequences for a child's development. As a professional dealing with children you will need to deal with their parents. You will be asked to give parental guidance. Sometimes an interpretation to a parent about their parenting will be a timely intervention. If you work only with adults, your patients will recount memories of interactions with their parents. Your knowledge of child development and parenting issues can inform your work with adults and be helpful to you as a psychodynamic therapist or psychoanalyst.

The book is divided up into three parts. Part 1 involves what we call childhood and adolescence. The second, Part 2, involves the young adult years through old age. Part 3 has to do with obtaining professional help. I hope you find in these pages something of value to help you understand your patients whatever his or her age. I include a list of topics discussed in each chapter as a guide to the contents of the book. I conclude with a section of recommended readings.

PART 1

Chapter 1
The Decision To Have A Child

Partners can benefit from taking the time to know each other better in an intimate relationship without the added responsibilities of attending to a newborn. A true partnership can evolve with each member feeling equity has been achieved. Issues of career, life style, avocational pursuits, etc., can be consolidated more or less by young adults who have committed themselves to each other and are ready to consider parenthood as a new stage of being adult. Thus, entering parenthood does not depend solely on giving birth to an infant but entails a mental change in how you view yourself, your partner, and a child you will care for, as well as the relationships between the three of you.

It makes intuitive sense to me that a couple does not rush into parenthood. Parenthood can be postponed these days with awareness and availability of birth control measures. Of course, postponing the decision, beginning with the current practice of getting married later in age, can introduce issues of infertility that seem more frequent in contemporary times than in the past. Issues of infertility, adoption, and couples of the same gender becoming parents, are increasingly present and I will devote a chapter to them later on.

Once conception occurs it will not be "business as usual." The future mother needs to attend to the specific health needs of her new pregnant state. She will find herself increasingly imagining, first, the fetus growing within her own self-boundaries, and, second, as a being outside of her. But it will take a period of time, if ever in some cases, that the child-to-be will be felt to be a separate and autonomous person outside of her own personal boundaries. A first-time mother may find herself worried about the well being of her fetus and will need the support of her spouse.

For some men, their wives' increasing preoccupation with the unborn baby may feel threatening, and they may feel rivalrous with the unborn baby. If he recognizes this he may feel embarrassed or even guilty. The expectant father may have doubts about his capacity to be an economic provider, the traditional role of males. If they cannot talk openly about this to their wife, perhaps they can to a male friend.

Some expectant fathers can be envious of their pregnant partners. It is rare, but sometimes men have simulated symptoms of being pregnant, e.g., experiencing morning sickness or weight gain. This virtual pregnancy is known as "couvade." Most men are unaware of the link to their wife's pregnancy. Those who recognize the connection may not want to speak openly about such thoughts but it would be helpful to them if they could. They may feel ashamed or embarrassed, believing such thoughts and feelings not to be masculine.

Together the couple will need to prepare the "nest," the nursery area for the yet to be born baby. Family and friends will need to be told about the expected baby, and the choice of a name will be considered. What would seem to be matter-of-fact actions can, for some couples, become stressors. For example, rivalries with siblings, dealing with too intrusive or indifferent future grandparents, and extended family expectations about names can complicate what ordinarily is a time of happiness and increased feelings of self worth.

Likely, the motive to become a parent has a biological, evolutionary component. The survival of the species depends upon it. The early doll play of young girls supports a proposition of an inborn tendency to parent. Likely, some of this play will be the young girl's doing with her dolls what her mother did with her. It's hard for a male to empathize with a pregnant woman but not impossible. The feeling of being fertile and nurturing a new future person that will grow inside of you, must be a powerful motive to become a parent. For the male to feel he has contributed to this, must allow for a similar feeling of creativity. To express a generative need is part of the stage of parenthood. A derivative of this generative need, an attitude that is consolidated in the young adult, is being creative in life and the sense of being productive in a career. Presumably, for some young adults, the idea of nurturing a child and exposing them to ideals that could allow them to mature into individuals that a parent could feel proud of, serves as a motive.

A wish to be like one's own parent likely plays a role in the decision to try to conceive. This wish to use one's own same-gendered parent as a model, if realized, results in a modification of the mind's image of one's self. The result of such an identification is sort of an unconscious expansion of one's self image. Identifications are not necessarily intentional, nor always adaptive. A boy who is scared of his harsh unaffectionate father could identify with him and act the same way in the future when he becomes a father. You can see how intergenerational problems can get transmitted. Identifications, however, need not be based only upon fear, but can also be based on emulation, e.g., admiring a nurturing father, so our boy grows up to be one too.

In some instances there may be less noble aims, likely unconscious ones that motivate becoming a parent. A potential mother or father may have unmet goals in their life and may unwittingly aspire for their unborn children to accomplish what they could not so they can have vicarious pleasure. Often this motive can have an invidious outcome because the child's uniqueness regarding talents and interests is ignored. The result is disappointment for all concerned.

It is difficult for a young adult to get their mind around issues of mortality, but such concerns are ubiquitous, albeit kept out of consciousness for many. A child carrying your DNA that looks like you allows for an illusion of immortality. In some instances, a couple may unwittingly conceive to distract themselves from a failing marriage and with the hope of rescuing it. Fortunately, most children are conceived with the best of intentions and are welcomed into an orbit of love and future promise.

As parents enter parenthood, they best not to think of it in an idealized manner. Being a "good" parent is not being a "perfect" parent. Perfection is a fiction when it comes to the complicated job of parenting. Good parents do not succeed in making their child invulnerable to life's trials and tribulations. I am fond of the Greek myth of

Achilles. Recall how his mother dipped him in some magical water to make him invincible. To do this she needed to hold him by one ankle lest he drown, this area of his body remaining vulnerable and the eventual site of a fatal injury. It is impossible to shield children from every untoward experience. Becoming a "good enough" parent means facilitating children to become self-reliant and self-fulfilled within their own potential. This way they will do their best with untoward events and develop personal resilience.

Let me address the issue of co-parenting between spouses. Certainly men are more involved in direct childcare than they were two generations earlier. They change diapers, they participate in bottle feedings, they may be the one who responds to the nighttime distress calls of their child, etc. Likely, this is a response to feminism which enabled men to re-evaluate masculinity. Men discovered that nurturance and masculinity are compatible.

Chapter 2
A New-Born & First-Time-Parenting/Oral Phase

Have you noticed new parents gazing at their baby? From the expression on their faces you can surmise that they are in wonder that the adorable being is their child. He or she looks like them and/or the partner. They notice the beautiful hands and feet and a wonderful complexion. A baby will bring parents much pleasure but also being a parent will be a challenge.

One of the first questions parents might ask you, as an expert, is should the baby sleep in the parental bedroom in the parental bed or a separate bed, or in a separate bedroom? I know that having the family sleep together in one bed has been gaining in popularity in recent years. I, however, do not advise it, mainly for two reasons. The first is based on safety. I would be concerned all night about inadvertently rolling over onto the infant and suffocating it. Secondly, the issue of privacy would be a concern, especially as the infant gets older. Privacy issues would apply to both instances, either where the baby sleeps in the parental bed or in a separate bed in the parents' bedroom. Spouses usually seek resuming sexual intimacy soon after childbirth and the presence of the infant in the bed could make this burdensome. As the child gets older, excluding him or her would be based on the rationale that witnessing the parents engaging in sex will be over-stimulating and not beneficial to the child.

Having the infant in a nearby room of its own makes sense because the child and mother will need to accommodate themselves to becoming physically separate from each other. Often parents will choose expediency in deciding where to have the infant sleep. After all, night time feedings will be more easily achieved if the baby is physically present and sleep will be less disturbed if you only have to roll over to feed. Expediency, however, is usually never the correct choice in parenting. Taking the time even if inconvenient always turns out to be prudent.

Infants will benefit for their entire lives if they learn how to soothe themselves. Sleeping in the parental bed makes this less likely to occur. Infants who find a finger to suck or a soft doll or blanket to handle are being masterful and adaptive. In the long run, their tolerance for frustration will benefit. This is the ability to tolerate an unmet need for increasing durations of time. They will be able to calm themselves sufficiently until the mother appears. They will be able to put themselves to sleep. Later on it will not be necessary for a parent to be in bed with them until they fall asleep or to introduce extreme measures like taking them for a ride in a car to induce sleeping. The thumb to suck becomes a substitute for the nipple and the sucking satisfies the non-nutritional component of sucking, providing pleasure for the so-called oral needs of the infant (more about this later).

A valued soft doll or blanket in the crib has been termed a "transitional object" insofar as it is thought to represent in the mind of the baby aspects of him or herself and also of the major care-giving person they are involved with, usually the mother. It is as if the thing valued represents a transition from a focus for gratification on the self and internal world to the external world. For example, the scent may contain remnants of mother's perfume as well as scents from the baby's own saliva. The satin edge of the blanket may feel like mother's skin. A child will rub the satin edge on their cheek or will finger it, behaviors reminiscent of nursing at the breast. A transitional object usually does not appear to be valued by the baby until around at least six months, a point in the child's life that he or she is sorting out what sensations and perceptions are part of them and which are part of the surround. Some parents have difficulties with their baby having a transitional object insofar as they want their child to be soothed by them and not by an inanimate object or part of the baby's own body such as a thumb. It is best for parents not to remove a transitional object by hiding or throwing it away as this will be very upsetting to the baby. The transitional object usually fades away in importance as the child grows older.

It is always difficult for parents to know at what point they should intervene when their infant is crying. After all, the newborn seems so helpless. There are no hard and fast rules here, insofar as each parent's tolerance differs as does each baby's. But there are some guidelines. First, a baby will not die from crying which likely is an unconscious primordial fear of a parent. Recall that the aim is for the infant to learn to console itself. If a parent is too quick to intervene one cannot expect a baby to attain self-consoling behaviors. My sense is that through trial and error parents will learn their child's threshold for becoming inconsolable. Parents need to pick up their children and assist them to become consoled. Intuitively, a parent will lengthen the period of delay of intervention, as the child gets older and more capable of tolerating frustration and being self-soothing.

Spouses need to support each other during these early days of parenthood, especially first-time parents. One should keep in mind that there is a learning curve for new parents and most will become competent for the task. A grandmother, sibling, or friend who has been through it can be a mentor.

Some infants are prone to a digestive distress known as colic. It starts in some infants from birth and lasts often until three months of age, but for some infants it is extended in duration. Infants experiencing colic are often crying and appear to be inconsolable. It sometimes helps if a parent holds them in an upright position, so their eyes are open, swaddled, and firmly against your own body. But for some infants nothing seems to calm them. Some parents, in a frantic effort to calm them and to help them sleep will put babies in an infant bed secured in an automobile and drive around the neighborhood. The motion of the moving car seems to help. It's easy to feel incompetent when your baby seems inconsolable despite your best efforts. Parents need to be aware that the cause of colic is not their responsibility. This is one condition that infants truly "grow out of." Spouses need to support one another during such times.

The choice to nurse or bottle-feed needs to be made. It is likely the choice was made before the birth. It is important that mothers not be made to feel guilty by others if they choose contrary to what is thought to be better. Besides the obvious nutritional needs that a mother must satisfy, consideration is also paid to the mode that will best satisfy the need for intimacy for a nursing couple. Whether nursing or bottle-feeding, this is an opportunity for mother and baby to gaze into each other's eyes and to establish a unique bond or attachment. Intuitively, most caregivers will treat these occasions as special, not an opportunity to speak on the phone or watch television.

This bonding is the foundation for empathy, for sensing what another separate individual is feeling, and facilitates coming in touch with what you, yourself, are feeling. Recent research suggests "mirror neurons" in primates like monkeys. If so, they may also be discovered in humans. Essentially, this means that the same area of the brain is activated when two primates are interacting in an involved emotional manner. It is as if the brain constructs an experience of the other person in the same part of the brain for the same self-experience. Presumably this neurological event underlies empathy. A corollary of this is that we infer that as the newborn ages, he or she feels "emotionally held" when his or her mother is emotionally attuned with it. This emotional attunement is an important foundational requirement for the developing sense of self. When a mother "mirrors" her infant she is helping the child process feelings. She essentially mimics the infant's feelings on her own face or with a vocalization that conveys an understanding to the infant of their own feelings. In this way we speak of the infant's mental self or space as expanding.

If one observes a nursing mother and her baby, one cannot but be impressed with the sense of reciprocity that includes pleasure and intimacy. Out of this physical experience is the birth of a psychological experience, the beginning of a sense of self and eventually of "other." If the infant places its finger in mother's mouth perhaps we are seeing the origin of play?

From birth to approximately the first two years of life the infant is developmentally engaged in the so-called "oral phase." Please keep in mind that when I give approximate ages when phases appear that individual differences results in some variation, and that phases overlap, i.e. one phase may begin when another is still present. One particular phase is the most influential or dominant in the mind of the child during a particular time period.

Let us return to the oral phase. What this means is that inborn physiological needs exist that become psychophysiological when they make specific demands to be satisfied upon the immature mind of the infant. When these needs go unsatisfied the infant experiences frustration and in reaction to this unpleasant feeling, anger. It is satisfying to suck and by the time teeth appear, to bite. If either of these component oral needs, during many instances, is either frustrated or gratified too much, derivative oral behaviors or oral personality features can become permanent characteristics or signature traits of the person. What is "too much" deprivation or gratification will differ for each person, likely based upon inborn biological factors such as the "strength" of an instinct (need). Most of us have some "permanent" derivative features from each phase of development, based upon multiple determinants.

Please keep in mind that personality traits are formed by multiple determinants. Personality features of being overly pessimistic or optimistic may have as one contribution, respectively, deprivation or over-gratification of the first part of the oral phase (sucking). Examples derived from the later biting stage of the oral phase would be sarcasm (deprivation) and being tenacious (over-gratification). We all know adults who portray such features as characteristics of their personalities.

Healthy derivatives also appear in adult lovemaking, e.g., as part of foreplay (kissing, sucking and gentle biting). Such observations and the psychoanalyses of adults suggest that pleasure from sucking and biting is sexual in quality. Biting also satisfies an aggressive urge. At this early age both sexual and aggressive urges are intertwined. If you have ever seen a toddler express a loving feeling towards a newborn, a kitten, or puppy, you know you have to be there to supervise lest the toddler can hurt the recipient of their affection.

The aim of an urge can be either active and/or passive. If active, the aim is to act upon another; if passive, the aim is to be acted upon by another. An example might be to bite (active) or to be bitten (passive). When both active and passive aims co-exist, we call this conflict ambivalence. One side of this conflict within the mind likely will be unconscious. This type of ambivalence is hard for us to intuit. Our evidence is based on the clinical psychoanalyses of people of all ages, and on our understanding of fairytales that express such universal themes. The fairytale "Little Red Riding Hood" is relevant for the oral dynamics we are examining. A child's behavior, both interactive with you or privately within their own mind, may be examples of these dynamics. A young child may wish to bite you and even express a wish that you try to bite them, like two kittens at play. Or the child may want to take turns being a wolf that is trying to blow a house down to catch the occupants and eat them.

Let us consider thumb sucking. It usually starts around two to three months of age in a consistent way. Not all children do suck their thumb. It is a natural way for the baby to satisfy the psychophysiological need to suck. It is a way for the infant to soothe itself when frustrated or falling asleep. During the activity of thumb sucking, part of one's own body satisfies and brings erotic pleasure to a sexually sensitive area of the body, the oral cavity. Thumb sucking bothers many parents. They prefer that they soothe the baby. For others there is concern about future orthodontic needs and expenses. Most importantly, the baby should not be shamed or scolded for thumb sucking. Many babies that choose to thumb suck reduce their interest in this activity once they progress into the next phase of instinctual drive expression. Some children will persist for a long time (into the fourth year) because of an oral fixation and they or their parents may need professional help. In a later chapter I will discuss what I mean by a "fixation." Introducing a pacifier does not allow an infant to discover its own method of self-soothing.

During these early months, children will become increasingly aware of themselves and of the world. They will benefit from all their senses, gradually building up in their mind an internal representation of the animate and inanimate world. We now know that newborns are more capable of seeing and hearing the world, than we thought, from day one. Newborns are able to distinguish intonational sounds from each parent's language from each other and from the language of others. Hearing mother's sounds helps with affect regulation. The child looks at things that mother points to, gradually building up a group of external referents in connection with their particular relationship. The child who looks does not look at itself, the looker, but the child who speaks hears itself, the speaker. Hence, seeing likely objectifies while speaking and hearing involves intrasubjectivity. These two senses help build up an "object" (an "other") and a "self." (In psychoanalysis we call the person one loves or hates an "object" to distinguish the person from the self, the "subject." It is not meant to dehumanize a person.) Infants do not recognize themselves in a mirror until the second year.

It is via the mouth that much of the world is first experienced by the newborn. Everything seems to end up in the infant's mouth. Eventually the fingers enter the mouth and they will help the baby to explore. The child's hand will be very important in helping to distinguish oneself from non-self. At first, the hand is likely a thing like other things that are seen and felt. It is only with one's own body as a thing, however, that the infant can simultaneously experience both touching and being touched. Delay of gratification will also aid the infant to distinguish between self and the environment. If gratification is not immediate it must be coming from "out there." With time, a particular "other", the mother, or caregiver becomes a psychic image. Gradually, the boundaries of the body will consolidate and a rudimentary body image will be established by the end of the first year. Many experiences of gratification and frustration will contribute to a differentiation between a remembered gratification, a memory, and an actual gratification, a perception.

Between the second and third month the baby will reliably smile at the sight of significant caregivers. I say "reliably" smile because you will likely see evidence of smiling earlier but you cannot be confident that it is meant to be a social awareness response and not a reaction to an intestinal stimulus. Nothing gives parents more pleasure than the smile of their baby in response to their own smile. Perhaps second to this pleasure is the time the baby first says a "word" like "Ma" or "Da." This usually occurs around the sixth month. Also, other milestones are sitting up (around six months), standing up (around ten-twelve months), and the first step (around ten-twelve months).

It is important to keep in mind that each child is different and the chronological age when behaviors first appear will differ, so that parental worry that a child is abnormal in almost all instances is unnecessary. If the delay is very significant a pediatrician will bring it to a parent's attention. Parents differ as to which behaviors they reinforce and it is likely these will progress at a more rapid rate than others. In some instances a behavior may develop in a precocious manner. For example, if parents are particularly invested in language they will make a bigger deal out of the child's utterances while more athletically inclined parents might reinforce signs of motoric agility. In any case, most children grow up to be "well rounded" individuals having the basic equipment to benefit from educational and other kinds of experience.

It is very important to understand that a parent's psychic reality, the subjective internal image of one's child, **is** the objective reality that impinges upon the child and to which he or she must accommodate. It is, as if, an unconscious image is treated as equivalent to a perception. For example, if a parent continually imposes an image of their own sibling upon that of their child, the child may grow up and have personality characteristics like the parent's sibling. A child's personality can become a self-fulfilling prophecy. Another way to say this is that expectations we have of a child influences how we react to that child, as well as effecting how the child feels about itself and behaves. A parent can exaggerate strengths and/or weaknesses of a child. The less objective is the view of one's child the more likely problems can arise.

A baby will benefit from routines. Children thrive on routines and become disrupted by the unpredictable. This is not to say that spontaneity is bad. The showing of affection is always beneficial and cannot be scheduled. But eating and bedtime, for example, are the kind of routines that are helpful to schedule. When babies build up expectations and these prove true it contributes to a trustful sense of the world as predictable and gratifying. The child's sense of reality and reality testing are enhanced. Reality testing establishes a concept of cause and effect and later helps in making choices. Recognition of the principle of cause and effect also underlies rational thinking. I hope I am conveying to you that the future development of a child can benefit from a firm foundation.

This topic leads me to digress for a moment and talk about issues more pertinent to an older child. I hope this digression further helps you to see the continuity of development and the importance of looking to the past to help understand the present and the future child. Older children need to be given appropriate choices. Choices are best when limited and succinct. For example, they can choose doing their homework either before or after bathing. Threats should not be made and are unnecessary if the choices are appropriate. Choices are presented positively, not negatively. A negative choice would be to say if they do not do their homework they will not be allowed to watch television. This wrongly focuses on watching television. A child could elect not to do their homework and forgo watching television. Establishing limits enters here insofar as children learn natural consequences have a connection to their choices. Thus, if they bathe and want to watch television but have not finished their homework a natural consequence will be that they will not be able to.

Paying careful attention to limits early on in the child's life will have important implications down the road. If limits were allowed to be disregarded from the beginning, one cannot introduce them later on and expect the misbehaving older child to give them any credence. When no limits are set, children become scared of their own powers. Their parents are the ones they depend upon to protect them from their own powerful urges and if parents fail them in this manner, children get anxious. Parents need to learn the difference between discipline and punishment.

Discipline is when the parental aim is to help the child establish internal regulations to help control intense feelings and focus on the desired outcome. This usually involves talking to the child and processing the sequence of events of which the parent is disapproving. A good criterion for setting limits is always safety of the child, not arbitrary ones established to underscore the authority of the parent. But what is the consequence to the child of their misbehaving? A natural consequence is parental disapproval. Children want very much to be approved of by parents. Not to be approved of diminishes their security and as they get older results in guilt. We distinguish between healthy guilt and neurotic guilt. It is appropriate for the older child to be motivated by healthy guilt when they do not live up to reasonable parental standards of behavior, and later internalized standards.

Neurotic guilt could involve feeling contrite for something imagined but not committed.

The aim is not to instill guilt but to help the child internalize a moral compass to help them regulate intense feelings and imperative urges. With very young children, of course, processing the errant behavior often cannot occur verbally. We must keep in mind, however, that even young children have receptive language comprehension before they have expressive language. That is, they can understand long before they can make themselves understood. A stern "No" will suffice for the very young. Parents best aim to communicate clearly to children, regardless of their age, that it is the behavior you disapprove of, not them as a person, whom you love. Sometimes a consequence for older children may need to be the withholding of a privilege that they have abused. For example, withholding computer time if the child has spent more than the agreed upon time on it the day before. I rarely see the sense in "time outs" when young children are sent to their room for misbehaving. First of all, the physical separation can create anxiety for some children. Also, the parental expectation that the child will "think" about what happened likely only rarely takes place. Instead the child angrily distracts him or herself. Having the child sit quietly within sight of the parent makes more sense. I will discuss neurotic guilt later.

When parents punish a child for a transgression they are expressing their anger and disappointment towards their child and wish to hurt the child. Usually, they feel their authority as an adult and parent has been disregarded and this evokes anger. The angry parent often chooses a consequence that has no connection to the child's transgression. As a parent, we feel guilty to recognize our anger towards our child whom we love. I think it is very important that parents accept that they can harbor an angry wish towards a loved child. I say this early in this exposition and emphatically because unless parents can accept and acknowledge this they will have difficulties in setting limits. They will have trouble distinguishing limits from an angry expression. They will also feel they are "bad" and feel relentlessly guilty. They may react by being extremely "nice" to the child. Every parent is capable of being physically abusive or even sadistic towards one of his or her children. I say this because in the unconscious part of the mind, even something as horrific as an infanticidal fantasy may reside. But there is a **world of difference** between having a wish or fantasy and enacting it. Hopefully, it is the exception and not the rule that parents enact their anger physically. Of course, even a rare instance is once too many. More likely, parents use their words to shame or humiliate a child towards whom they are angry. This, too, is unnecessary and can be injurious to a child's psyche.

Let me return to our infant. From birth, infants demonstrate intense feelings. Likely some feelings are inborn so that there is a readiness for the feeling to be manifested if the releasing stimulus is present, e.g., a loud noise will cause a startle. From birth onward the infant gradually learns to regulate feelings with the help of his caregivers. Parents gradually learn to discriminate the meaning of different distress cries their infants' present. One cry may mean hunger (thirst), another pain, and yet another feeling cold. With experience, a mother will learn that when her infant appears to be angry it could be that he is really distressed about something that is not being effectively communicated to the infant. In the first few years of life, children have few words to convey how they feel. Hence, they may say they "hate" when a better descriptor might be " don't like." By helping children label their feelings parents help them become better communicators and regulators of their feelings. This labeling of feelings by parents begins in the first year of life. You can observe mothers intuiting the feelings behind their infants' expressions and offering names to them.

During these early months a gradual differentiation will occur between mother and her newborn. Mother's self-boundaries which once included the baby growing inside of her, must now allow for the baby to be separate and outside of her own self. For mothers the unity at first was both biological and psychological. Intellectually, mothers know this but emotionally this takes time and mothers differ as to how long. For the child there is the same evolution but it's beginning was biological. We presume that awareness of the mother is at first based entirely on need satisfaction and only gradually evolves into a psychological connection. We then speak of a social awareness. The awareness of mother, the "other," we presume is initially based on "parts" of her, e.g., the rhythm and timbre of her voice, the quality of her touch, her scent, her smile, the sound of her gait, etc. We call these self-other moment's "part object" experiences. Later, they will be experienced as "transitional phenomena" (see below). With repeated such part object experiences a whole object experience is built up, probably towards the end of the second year. The child's sense of self apart from its caregiver is a gradual process.

As indicated above, much of it occurs in the context of interactions with its caregiver, in most instances its mother. There are countless interactions of caring involving feeding, bathing, dressing, playing, cuddling, reflections about feelings, etc., wherein the mother serves as a "mirror" for the child. We will talk more about this later in Chapter 5 when we speak of mentalization. I do not mean to sound mystical, but it is in mother's gentle touch, the lilt of her voice, the smile in her eyes, and other demonstrations of responsiveness that contribute to the infant's sense that itself is an entity, or being. Also, the bodily experiences and perceptions of its own body, mentioned earlier, as well as interactions with the rest of the world contribute to the infant's emerging sense of identity, of differentiation out of an undifferentiated state of being. While a differentiation is occurring, a parallel process of "being with" is also ongoing. The infant gradually feels an attachment to the caregiver. An essential aspect of the developing attachment being an emotional attunement of the infant's feelings to those of the maternal object conveyed via her touch, voice and facial expression.

Mention should be made of postpartum depression that affects a minority of women. The time of onset varies after the birth of the newborn. Mothers feel depressed or sad, easily given to crying without apparent cause. This condition is likely caused by the hormonal changes during pregnancy and is usually short-lived. After some weeks or a couple of months it seems to pass and the mother feels more like her usual self. Because of these feelings, some of these women feel guilty because they believe they have not been as attentive to their infant as they would have liked. This maternal guilt might be considered healthy insofar as the mother has not been able to function as effectively as she hoped even if not responsible, and it motivates her to be responsive once again to her child. If the guilt is severe and long lasting then it is no longer healthy. A spouse can be very helpful by being supportive and stepping in to give their partner respite during this trying time.

Chapter 3
Infertility, Multiples, & Adoption

Infertility

Infertility can be an insufferable experience for some couples that have made the decision to become parents. A sense of inadequacy and failure can diminish feelings of self-worth. An infertile couple finds it difficult to be around friends or family that have children and who ask about their intentions to become parents. Fortunately, modern science and medicine can be of help with techniques to maximize chances of fertility or to artificially cause insemination by laboratory means. This is expensive and most often not covered by medical insurance. Those who have the financial means are fortunate.

There are different arrangements, e.g., the eggs may be harvested from the female of the couple or from a surrogate and similarly with the sperm. the egg can be fertilized *in vitro* in a laboratory or via intra-uterine insemination. The fertilized egg then can be implanted in the female partner or in a surrogate mother. Or intra-uterine insemination can take place, if possible. Of course, regardless of the arrangements there will be intense feelings. Even if it is each partner's own egg and sperm there will be regrets that conception did not occur naturally. But at least in this case, one can be reassured that the child is your "own" with your DNA. Nevertheless, an infertile partner must deal with the fact that a surrogate was necessary. It's not inevitable that this has to become a major issue for the infertile member of the couple. It will, however, be a reality about which each parent will have feelings. It is better to talk openly about these feelings with a partner than to suppress them.

What do parents tell children conceived unnaturally when they are older and inevitably ask questions about their birth? Professionals do not have sufficient experience yet with this population to be of much help with guidance. My own sense is to tell the truth about the conception. This would be told in the context of how important it was to become a parent and how sought after the child was. If there was a surrogate involved either as a donor or carrier of the fertilized egg, my inclination is to delay imparting this information until the child is older, e.g., at least until 8 years of age and preferably until adolescence. My reason for this has the same rationale as delaying the facts of adoption, if possible, until the child is older, which I will discuss later in this chapter. I do think that a parent should elevate a donor sperm or egg to the status, respectively, of a biological father or biological mother, when talking to a child. Intuitively, I assume this would help children, if inclined, to fantasize about their biological parent. It is through such mental processing that a child will be able to integrate the facts of their conception.

A word about miscarriages is in order. How to treat a woman who has miscarried a pregnancy has changed the last twenty years. My impression is that prior to that time, professionals did not give it the consideration that it is due. It was believed to be a disappointment but not a significant loss for a woman. We know better now. It is imperative that spouses, relatives and friends not trivialize the loss. A prospective mother that miscarries needs to be allowed to mourn her unborn child. Every pregnant woman has fantasies of the unborn child and these will need to be mourned as well. A memorial service of some kind is recommended by some professionals to assist in the process. A woman who miscarries may irrationally blame herself and feel guilty. One young mother, already caring for a toddler, felt relieved after the miscarriage because she realized with hindsight that she was unprepared for a second child. But the relief in its wake brought feelings of guilt thinking of the miscarried "baby."

A woman, who miscarries, along with her spouse, is often encouraged by others to get pregnant again as soon as possible. I think this is best delayed until sufficient mourning for the miscarried fetus has occurred. Often a new child is conceived or adopted to replace a child that was born, lived awhile and then dies. If there is a rush to get pregnant again, the possibility of the new baby to become a so-called "replacement child" exists. A replacement child is at risk insofar as the identity they adopt likely will be that of the fantasized unborn child or of the child that died. Parents that have insufficiently mourned unconsciously encourage the assignment of this identity. The replacement child can grow up with an inauthentic self-identity that is not a firm foundation for dealing with the world. A replacement child may feel unattached to his or her self. Essentially, the child is being asked to identify with a dead child in order to feel alive. Of course, this is an impossible task. If a mother has not sufficiently mourned, the intense grief experienced will interfere with her ability to bond with her newborn child. It is impossible to imagine the grief experienced when a child dies. It is difficult to put an exact duration on what is "sufficient mourning," because it is so individual, but I would think in the range of six months to one year. Sometimes, parents adopt a child to be a replacement and the same concerns apply here, too.

A premature birth is another particularly stressful time for parents. There is the loss of a fantasy of a full term birth. The new mother may feel reactively depressed that she has not been able like other women to carry her baby for the full gestation period. The experience may cause her to feel diminished in some way. She irrationally may wonder if she is "less than a full women," or good mother. Also, the neonate may need to be put in an incubator for a period of time so that the mother will be unable to hold her newborn causing her to feel deprived of this basic need. If a premature infant needs to be incubated, arrangements usually can be made in most neonatal ICUs for a parent to visit and to talk and even touch or encourage sucking and feeding of the baby. Such interventions can foster a developmental attachment for both baby and mother. A healthy attachment facilitates developmental progress. If the infant is very premature its health or even survival will be uncertain and worries about it succumbing may exist. Parents will need to be very supportive of each other during this trying period until the baby is "out of the woods."

Multiples

As a result of artificial insemination, births of multiples are becoming more frequent. This results from the implanting of more than one fertilized egg in the uterus to insure success. Parents may elect not to reduce the number of implanted eggs for different reasons. The ordeal of the process following months or years of infertility may be a determinant to "get it over with," or there may be religious objections to a reduction. This is so even though they know intellectually that reducing will benefit the viability of the remaining implanted fertilized eggs. Reduction to these parents will feel the same as an objectionable abortion.

Professionals have had experiences with multiple births prior to the introduction of artificial insemination. Our experience, however, usually does not go beyond triplets. Twins are not that uncommon, while triplets are infrequent naturally. There is the possibility of identical or fraternal twins or triplets. "Sororial" is a contemporary term denoting multiple births of non-identical girls. When the twins or triplets are identical there are many psychological challenges. Individuality needs to be contended with. At a deeper level, one's sense of identity needs to be forged. Who am I? What is my essence? What makes me unique? After all, there is another person who not only resembles you, as a sibling might, but is identical to you. Only a few people can tell you apart. Some identical twins relish this and conspiratorially play games with people pretending to be the other twin. Presumably there is a sense of power that they experience. Other identical twins hate the fact that he or she is not unique and mistaken all the time for his or her twin. Fraternal or sororial twins need not deal with this. They must deal with sharing the limelight on birthdays. Competitiveness and cooperation struggle with each other. The competition might even extend to who was born "first." There is the close bond that is possible between twins or triplets that potentially brings a lifetime of companionship and support. Sometimes, being separated from the twin can be difficult. Sleeping arrangements may need to consider this. Twins may insist upon sleeping in the same room.

I need to digress here and speak about a tragic event, the death of a child. This topic, of course, can be introduced at any age in an exposition of development. An ultimate loss for an identical twin can be the death of the other twin; it can be experienced as the death of a part of one's self. Of course, the age of the surviving twin will determine the manner in which parents help the survivor cope with the loss. If the death occurs during childbirth, parents may believe the surviving twin need not be told of this happening and keep it a secret. We know from experience that family secrets (see below) are "malignant" and that it is better to talk about them when it is believed a child can comprehend the content and associated feelings and process them.

The death of a child is a terrible tragedy for parents, regardless of the age of the child. Parents need to allow themselves to mourn. During this period of grieving they will be internally focused and have difficulties attending to the external world. If there are other children, especially young ones, or newborns in the case of a surviving twin, this will be a hardship for the children. If the surviving children are older, they, too, will be dealing with a loss. In addition, they will be dealing with the temporary "loss" of their grieving parents. This is a time when relatives and friends can be especially helpful to step in and be surrogate parents. Sometimes professional help may be needed to help a family deal with a death of a child.

It is frequently observed that twins will complement one another in skills. One twin may be gregarious while the other is reticent. The reticent one may be academically advanced while the other is average, and so on. I doubt that this is consciously decided upon but is unconsciously negotiated by the twins over years of interactions. It is as if there is "unconscious" communication between the twins. This communication is based on empathy and familiarity with each other's feelings and inclinations. Analogous is how long-timed married spouses often end each other's sentences or use excessive pronouns insofar as they anticipate what is being said and who is being talked about.

Parents of twins or triplets have to deal with the practical problems of providing care for more than one child simultaneously. The greater the number of multiples, the more difficult the task. Imagine feeding triplet newborns, all of which could be thirsty or hungry at the same time. The participation of the father is essential and grandparents can also lend a hand. The early infancy period presents a strain, but there are others as the children mature. The financial costs with multiples are more than with a singleton and this can be a burden. When twins or triplets are identical, parents must decide whether or not to maximize this or minimize this. They can dress them alike or differently, part their hair on the same or different sides, etc. Then once school starts do parents lobby to have them in the same or different classes? Parents might consider allowing the twins or triplets to decide this issue, or participate in the decision-making. They may elect to start out in the same class but later revise this decision as they make separate friends.

Adoption

Adoption is not an easy decision for most couples. For those who adopt for ideological reasons it is easier. One is motivated by humanistic ideals to provide a family for an orphan or hard-to-adopt child. When the motive originates because of infertility it is more complicated. The infertile couple must deal with their infertility, as discussed earlier, and with the common fantasy that they are taking away or even stealing someone else's child, albeit an irrational fantasy. The child may have become adoptable because it was born to a single mother. The adoptive mother (or parents) may attribute, unconsciously, the "bad" behavior of the biological mother to the baby, who is then thought of as the "bad seed" of a sinful (unmarried) or delinquent mother.

Older children who are adopted may have trouble bonding with their adoptive parents and are at risk if this cannot be accomplished. They may have bonded already with a surrogate or foster caregiver and this will be broken because of the adoption. The child may react with anger towards the adoptive parents who are perceived to be the cause of the loss. If the adoptive couple has biological children, there will likely be feelings that need to be attended to by the parents. Biological children may wonder why their presence was not sufficient to satisfy their parents. While adoption can be difficult, for reasons like the above, often it can be successful and bring great satisfaction to all concerned.

A major task for both the adoptive parents and adopted child is to feel that the newcomer is an intrinsic part of the family. This is why I think it is a mistake to tell a child from birth it was adopted, or to maintain so-called "open adoptions" where the biological parent

(s) are involved in the life of the adopted child, or to immerse children adopted from foreign cultures in enrichment programs acquainting them with the culture of their origin. While well intended, I think these agendas are all misguided. There are professionals, however, who think otherwise. I think all of the above complicate an adoptee's task of feeling fully integrated and a part of the adoptive family. This achievement is necessary for later individuation to take place and its absence has major implications for the developing personality of the child, which will be discussed in Chapter 7.

I advise not telling the child until it is older, if this is possible. Often it is impossible because friends, relatives and acquaintances talk openly about the child's adoption. Adoption across racial lines also makes this impossible. Ideally, my minimum age would be eight. At eight years of age, for most youngsters, there occurs a major maturational cognitive change, a shift from sensory-motor to concrete operations. This is a change from simple perceptual and motor responses to the world to a more rational, organized and conceptual way of engaging things and people in the surrounding world. A child's ability to comprehend a parent's personal narrative will be easier at this older age.

I wish to distinguish my advocacy of delaying disclosure of the fact of adoption from what is called a family secret. With the latter there is no intent to tell the facts ever to the child, whereas I am guided by the intention of delaying the telling until a more propitious time. A family secret is in the context of shame, whereas my rationale is the capacity to understand and maintenance of a sense of "family-belonging."

Most adoptive parents elect to tell adoptees they were adopted from "day one." The explanation is in the context of how much they were "wanted" by the adoptive parents. If the child is of a different race from the adoptive parents then withholding the knowledge of adoption cannot be accomplished. If this is so, a parent can help a child by being truthful about the facts when the child becomes curious about their biological parents. This can be difficult for some adoptive parents who feel they are the "true" parents of the child and they may feel discarded and competitive with the biological parents. But such curiosity is natural, especially for an adolescent or young adult contemplating becoming a parent him or herself. There are agencies that can be of help to an adoptee with such a quest. Biological parents differ as to whether or not they welcome contact with the child given up for adoption. For many it reawakens all the old feelings long since buried that were felt at the time of giving up their baby for adoption. Some reunions are successful, while others are not. When they are successful adoptees will feel enriched by having new people in their lives. In instances where it is unsuccessful a new felt rejection must be dealt with. Sometimes the adoptee discovers a full or half biological sib that was not given up for adoption. This is particularly hard to reconcile with one's own personal history. The "family romance" fantasy, discussed fully in the chapter below dealing with the Oedipal Complex, is an additional potentially complicating and confusing factor for adoptive children, and another consideration of mine for opposing open adoptions.

More and more partners of the same gender are either adopting or, in the case of a lesbian couple one partner seeks artificial insemination. Again, we have insufficient experience with such couples or their children to offer much advice to these parents and their children. The obvious question is "What are the effects upon a child to have both parents be the same gender?" What if you are a boy and have two mothers or a girl having two fathers? We have an *a priori* hunch that it will be confusing. I think that such a couple, usually well educated and informed according to existing demographic data, go to lengths to expose their children to adults of each gender. In this manner, children can learn about the various gender roles in our society and have opportunities to identify with an adult of the same gender as their own. Presumably, the parents help their children process questions and concerns about being different from peers. In recent generations, divergences in life style and ethnic and racial origins are not infrequent so children from these backgrounds are now considered less exotic.

Chapter 4
The Toddler Years/Anal [Urethral] Phase

The toddler period roughly begins when a child starts to be able to walk, albeit uncertainly to begin with. Children differ as to when this happens but usually by twelve months of age a child will start to get around, toddle, in an upright position without holding onto to things like furniture. Earlier children are able to crawl or scoot around but the advent of upright locomotion introduces a "new world" to them. Secure in the foundation of an attachment to their parent, they feel more comfortable to venture forth into this new world, leaving the fond embrace of mother or father.

Look upon the face of a toddler who is toddling about and you see exuberance and joy. For a parent to see a toddler standing upright and moving about without holding on is equally a joyous occasion. But it is also a sad one for **both** parties. For the parent, her or his little baby is growing up. There is a feeling of loss connected with another sign of separateness. For the toddler the joyful expression can disappear after a fall or when he or she realizes that mother or father is not standing alongside. Toddlers may need to return to the side of parents to touch them, sight not being reassuring enough. This simple fact is also very profound. All of us from early on must come to terms with acceptance that each new acquired skill results in a mini-loss insofar as a parent will no longer be there to do the task for you or with you. Every child needs a mother to leave and in the process establishes a sense of his or her own individuality or identity. For some this accumulative feeling of loss proves too much and they reassert their dependency and take on a characteristic immaturity. Separation becomes a major issue for these children. It is helpful to young children to alert them when you are leaving the room and reassure them you will be returning very shortly. "Fred, mommy is going to the bathroom and will be back very soon."

Parents, predominantly mothers who are usually more involved with daily care, intuitively know this, so they allow for the autonomy to occur gradually. For awhile they will do things for toddlers, after awhile they allow toddlers to try to accomplish tasks for themselves while they are close by smiling approvingly and supportively, and then they allow toddlers to do tasks independently. Toddlers notice the gleam in their parents' eyes as they increasingly act autonomously. This progression allows for the toddler to feel reassured and to develop a beginning sense of competence.

But toddlers are still very helpless in many ways and naturally need an adult to care for them. The human animal differs from many other animals that must have more inborn readiness skills and faster maturation in order to survive predators. The human animal will go through a long apprenticeship before he or she can adequately independently take care of him or herself. Parenting is a long-term job. This long-term dependence of the human child on its caregiver is coupled with a likely perception of her as omnipotent. The young child does not want to relinquish this omnipotence that he can imagine he shares by virtue of not being completely separate from the caregiver (mother). Hence, the ambivalence about becoming autonomous.

The toddler will begin to give verbal signs of self-awareness and a sense of identity. For example, they may refer to themselves by name, "Johnny want," and soon they will refer to themselves as "I." Sentences of a rudimentary kind are spoken, expressing demands. Parents will try to be very alert to decipher their child's early words. The readiness to use language is inborn and children acquire the dialect of their caregivers. Sometime during the toddler period children seem to recognize themselves in a mirror.

What is conveyed during the toddler period and following months is that toddlers are very willful. Setting limits is an essential parental assignment during these months. Issues of safety guide most parents. A child may not be able to do something autonomously but will insist on doing it. If attempting some motor act, like going down a step, can be accomplished safely, most parents will tolerate it, allowing their child to experience the pleasure and honing of a skill. Parent need to recognize shaming is not the way to control their child. Taking the time to explain in terms that the youngster can understand is important. Remember, even at this young age children understand more than they can verbally communicate. They are guided by a resolute tone to understand their parent opposes an action.

Parents do well to treat their toddler respectfully. Even though the toddler has not much language they are beginning to understand the emotional intent behind words. Manners are taught by example. Parents who talk to their children politely are more likely to have well-mannered older children who will have the social awareness to treat all people civilly and with courtesy.

Some children are more active than others. Temperament seems to be inborn. If parents are basically passive and placid and their child is similar, this is a more compatible arrangement than if the child seems to be active and persistent. In the latter instance, parents will need to accommodate to their child's temperament. This is more realistic than to expect it to be the other way around. Some parents find this difficult. Some children are easy to please and the day with them seems seamless going from one activity to another. With other children, transitions are not easy, they are hard to satisfy and do not easily accept a substitute gratification if the one they seek is unavailable. Such children are challenging to even an experienced mother, so a mother best be forgiving of herself if she is finding such a child to be a challenge. It is helpful to young children to give them a "heads-up" that a transition will soon be taking place. "Sarah, very soon you will have to stop playing and get dressed to go to "play group."

The so-called "anal phase" of development will likely begin and overlap with oral urges by the age of two, more reliably by two and one half, and can be prominent until the child is nearly four years old. This phase of drive development is inborn, like its predecessor, and also has an urgent quality for expression. It is this that fuels the willfulness of the older toddler (two year old). Whereas earlier, the mouth, or oral cavity, seemed to be the child's focus of activity, now the anus becomes the focus. The time of toilet mastery is upon us. We prefer toilet "mastery" to "training" because the aim is to help a child develop a sense of mastery over bodily urges, not to feel like an automaton responding to a stimulus. The sense of mastery over bodily urges is important and begun at this early age will be consolidated in adolescence. That is, it takes a long period of time before a child feels more confident that they have some semblance of control over desires or urges that are originally physiological but take on a psychological coloring, too, e.g., hunger, sexual needs, etc.

The first stage of the anal phase includes a quality of expulsive elimination to the psychophysiological urge to defecate. The young child is deriving pleasure from expelling its feces with great destructive force. In the second stage a toddler will obtain pleasure by exercising withholding and control over its bowel movements. Later on in the process of toilet mastery the child becomes aware that elimination of body products seem to provide pleasure not only to him or herself but also to the parent. Most parents make a "big deal" when the child eliminates. They smile and praise the toddler. The elimination of stools takes on the quality of a gift from the child to the parent. But it is confusing to the child insofar as the gift is flushed away and disappears. Older children may become defiant and are ambivalently cooperative in complying with the parent's requests they deposit their gift in the toilet and not in their diaper. This ambivalence spreads to the way they treat their parents, showing affection and hurting them in close succession. The child responds to its stools in a concretized fashion. I mean by this that the stools are treated like family members. The biggest are said to be the daddy, with the smallest being the child, with the mommy in between.

The pleasure the child takes in withholding and then finally eliminating its stools has an erogenous or sexual quality. We know this from the analyses of adults and from self-reports from adults honest enough to remark about the pleasurable feeling of a well-formed bowel movement. The inborn erogeneity of the buttocks and anus is topic that we all are socialized to be very private about, unlike the erogeneity of the oral zone which is more acceptable and is permitted to be publicly acknowledged, such as via kissing, or even implied in eating something succulent, or drinking something sweet and warm.

The pleasure derived from anality is not only erogenous; it is also derived from aggressive urges. The admixture of the two drive expressions is called "sadism." Sadism evolves into pleasure obtained from controlling another person or from causing others pain. The pleasure in controlling another person originates in the pleasure in controlling one's stools. Temporarily, children may be sadistic towards insects or pets. Most children are socialized not to be sadistic.

It is **essential** at this point to make a distinction between "wishing" and "wanting." **Another way to put it is to distinguish "thoughts" from "deeds." Psychoanalysts do not equate the two.** As stated earlier, there is a world of difference between having a sadistic wish (thought or fantasy) and enacting the wish. So to say all children are capable of a sadistic thoughts is not to say that all children are sadists. But we do know, unfortunately, that the human species is capable of such behavior. An example would be the atrocities committed by the Nazis against humanity. When sadism turns against the self we call it "masochism," a pleasure derived from suffering (psychologically or physically) or surrendering to another's will. Fantasies of a child being beaten may be present in derivative form in latency age children. Fantasies involving coercion and submission regarding sex wherein one is perpetrator and/or recipient (sado-masochism) may be present in adults. Recall my earlier comments about active and passive aims in instinctual expression.

It is difficult for most adults to accept that children can have base instincts like sexual and destructive ones. We prefer to think of children as 'pure' and innocent. We must recognize that the human species is part of the animal kingdom. We are now civilized but our basic animal needs still exist in us, albeit for the most part not in the conscious part of our minds. Children must be taught to be civilized. As "domesticated" animals of the highest degree (we prefer "civilized") we usually are far removed from the jungle and hold ourselves to humanistic ideals. The uncivilized urges residing in the unconscious part of our mind may come out in our dreams and fantasies, and in transformed ways via the creative arts, but usually not in actions. Recent research suggests that in the latter half of the first year, babies prefer to look at or reach for things that help rather than have hindered.

Does this suggest an inherent morality? Perhaps, a biological inherent trend having to do with survival that culture needs to reinforce.

Let us return to our toddler. In general, toilet mastery should not be rushed. Patience and support of the child is very much called for. Children will differ as to how cooperative they will be in the process. It seems to have some connection to how innately strong the anal drive is. If it is not very strong then they will not be so insistent that they be in command of when and how they gratify its expression. If it is a strong urge they will struggle to express it and defy the parent's cajoling them to be "clean." It is with the latter child that a parent needs to avoid a control battle. Such a child will come around and comply at his or her own pace, albeit with some children not till around the ages of four to five. The rewards of becoming clean and identification with older peers and friends will eventually result in toilet mastery for almost all children. It is the rare child who is encopretic, a syndrome where a child soils indiscriminately as to time and place. I will have more to say about establishing toilet mastery in Chapter 8.

Parents during the earlier oral phase were faced with the same issue about having a child transform the manner of gratification with regard to weaning either from the breast or bottle. Some children compared to others have a strong urge to suck while other could care less. For parents, their own history of nursing (sucking) and toilet mastery will be unconscious determinants in how easy or difficult it will be for them to traverse their child's seeking of pleasure of these early inborn drives. I could state this for each developmental phase that your child passes through. Parents who are aware of their own "hot spots" or "buttons" may avoid making inappropriate demands or providing inappropriate indulgences that their child either cannot meet nor is seeking regarding the expression and eventual regulation of early childhood drives. A parent might "insist" that a less than two year old child use the toilet (deprivation.) Or a parent might delay encouraging their child to use a "potty" even though they are overtly displaying curiosity (indulgence). Such inappropriate demands or indulgences (either too much deprivation or gratification) lead to vulnerabilities in their child around which later neurotic conflicts can form. We call these vulnerabilities fixations. There seems to be an inverse relationship between the strength of an inborn component instinct and the quantity of deprivation or indulgence to result in a fixation (complemental series). Later in Chapters 5 & 8, the nature of neurotic conflicts will be discussed.

Towards the end of the anal phase, interest in urination comes to the fore, so a focus on the anus is shared with the urethra. This marks a phase called the "urethral phase." Boys take pleasure in their urinary stream. Did you ever see a boy around four or five or even older given the task of using a hose to water the garden? Often there is sheer delight. Remnants of this pleasure can be seen in the derivative pleasure some boys later take in spitting. Girls like to look at their urinary stream too and are sometimes envious that boys can stand and urinate and that a boy's urinary stream is more forceful than their own.

Adults often inappropriately tickle children and the outcome often is a need to urinate on the child's part. Children when excited will often urinate presumably because the excitement has become sexual in quality. Because of immaturity of their genital systems, urination occurs, and not ejaculation for boys, and not vaginal lubrication for girls.

As mentioned earlier, during the later toddler months, there is a growth spurt in speech and language sophistication. This acquisition of an inborn readiness will result in more effective communication between parent and child. Parents from then on will continually be telling their child to "use your words."

The more this is successful the more likely frustrations will not mount for both children and parents. This is a gradual process and parents must be patient. As a child gets older the ability increases to employ mental processes ("defenses") that will help in reducing the intensity and imperiousness of needs. With greater mental maturity more complex thinking processes become available. If a child can daydream gratification, thereby deriving partial gratification, a substitute for an unavailable desired source of gratification might be more acceptable to the child. The use of action as a means of communication is readily available to children and will be so through adolescence. It is only gradually that symbolic thought and words can replace action as a preferred mode of communication. Internal thought is a form of trial action insofar as different outcomes can be considered and one chosen that is expected to end with a desired outcome that is adaptive and in the best interests of the child or adolescent. For some children action feels more real or authentic because it is irrevocable while thought is silent and changeable.

The more children can use words to discharge feelings, the less reliance on somatic, bodily channels of expression. Bodily means of expression of feelings might be via aches and pains, perspiration, diarrhea, hyperactivity, etc. Preferred means of bodily expression of tension is noticeable very early in a child's life and will be retained for most of a person's life. Some adults when stressed are more likely to get headaches, others to get diarrhea, still others to sweat, and so on. Differentiating somatic feelings, e.g., hunger or pain, from emotional feelings, e.g., sadness or anxiety, is a gradual process not achieved in a reliable way till the early Latency years. We will speak more about the various mental maneuvers that the mind employs when we consider the Latency phase of development in Chapter 9.

Children love to run around nude during their early years. Perhaps you remember the exhilaration yourself when you were a late toddler or early preschooler? Adults are often uneasy about allowing this. Perhaps, there is a worry about easy access to masturbation or to elimination in the wrong places? Nakedness is a natural inclination for the child. Exhibitionistic pleasure and delight in unrestrained motility seem to be involved. Alas, children do need to be socialized and to learn that modesty is the norm of civil society and this childhood pleasure will need to be given up. They can learn this without being shamed and will accommodate themselves to this expectation of society. Displaying one's body and looking at another's seems to be inborn desires that bring pleasure for all people. With time such desires evolve into concern about attractiveness, adornment and physical fitness. Regretfully, our culture has capitalized upon this and has commercialized vanity to the point that some teenagers and adults are preoccupied with how they look to others. With a minority, dieting can become a pathological enterprise. I will say more about this when I consider the stages of adolescence.

Children at this age do not easily share toys with other children. Also they may grab something being held by another toddler. At this young age they are self-centered and it will take some learning before they can share and tolerate the frustration of "taking turns." They engage in "parallel play," whereby the activity they are engaged in can be the same one that another toddler is busy with but there does not occur interaction between the two toddlers. This, too, will change during the latter pre-school years.

Chapter 5
The Preschool Years/ Phallic Phase

Preschool requires the child to deal for a period of time with a teacher, an adult different from his or her parents. Up till entry into preschool most other adults dealt with in the absence of parents likely have been relatives. A baby sitter may be an exception but this encounter usually is within the familiarity of the child's home. I advise that mothers or fathers be present when a 2 year old has a preschool experience and that it be only for a few hours a couple of times a week. I hold this as an ideal, maybe unrealistic in most families and I will discuss day care in the next chapter. The majority of two year olds are not ready to spend a lot of time away from their mothers. Children must have the capacity to evoke and sustain an internal image in their mind of the mother or other significant caregiver. The image needs to be sustained even when they have a physical or psychological need in their parent's absence, or when the need is fulfilled. When such needs exist and a parent is absent the evocation of anxiety followed by rage or apathy is likely. The stability of the mental image of the parent must be able to withstand the rage and not be obliterated. If it is unable to be sustained, intense anxiety will follow. This capacity usually occurs reliably around 36 months. We call this capacity the establishment of object constancy. Essentially the process involves being able to feel the presence of a real person in the external world to now "inhabit" the inner world. A prominent psychoanalyst has termed this a "presence in an absence."

It is not that unusual in a preschool setting to see a youngster carrying a valued blanket or soft animal. You know from our earlier discussion that we call such things transitional objects. You will recall we call them such because the child is transitioning from self-investment to self-other differentiation. We conjecture that transitional objects are experienced as both as an aspect of the self and of the part object (in most instances the mother). We conjecture that the child is feeling the loss or absence of the soothing maternal figure and uses the transitional object to try to conjure up the experience of her presence, e.g., the mother's scent, in her absence. Usually, such transitional objects wither away in importance, as the child gets older. Some parents, however, prefer that their distressed child seek them out for comfort. Parents are advised to let this process occur naturally and not to expedite it by throwing away the transitional object. This can be vey upsetting to a youngster. In some instances an older child or even an adult can lapse into a reverie type mood when listening to music or smelling a particular scent, etc. Such phenomena create a transitional mood. We conjecture that at such moments an individual is feeling a primordial emotional connection to an early self-other experience for which there is no words.

A sophisticated nursery school will accommodate itself to the dependency needs of the children and will introduce a graduated separation period of parent and child. What this means is that parents may be in the same classroom with the child for a period of time, perhaps days, then in the building so that if their child becomes inconsolable they can be available. Once the child is comfortable transitioning to the teacher the parent should exit quickly. Parents need to accept at pickups that their child may ignore them for some minutes or become dramatically whiney as a punishment for "abandoning" them. I advise parents to try not to take it personally and soon such dramatizations will stop. Additionally, parents are encouraged to keep in touch with teachers so after the school day they can talk with their child about their experiences. Children react to the emotional moods of peers, so that if a child in their class is grieving the loss of a pet, it is helpful that parents are aware of this classroom news to make more sense of their children and to be helpful to them in processing the news. Towards the end of entry in preschool, a parent may start to feel uneasy about the transition to kindergarten, especially if it is a full day one. One's child is growing up and a parent will be dealing with the end of an era. Soon the child will be going out into the bigger community. Although more self reliant, the child is still very dependent upon his parent. Some children, too, start to anticipate the longer day away from mother, but they are usually eager for the move to "big school." These feelings will be revisited for both child and parent in the transition period from high school to college.

The three year old is usually dealing with the beginning of the so-called "phallic phase" of drive development, overlapping with the earlier onset anal and urethral phases. Remnants of the earliest oral phase will coexist, too. The phallic phase will last usually up until five or six years of age. The term "phallic phase" has been justifiably criticized because of its male focus but another label has not been commonly accepted. "Phallic" originally was proposed because it was believed that both boys and girls seemed to think of themselves as boys during the early part of this phase. This notion has been modified in contemporary psychoanalytic thinking. We now believe that girls value and are interested in their own genitals and the interior space that they have and boys do not. During the phallic phase, for both boys and girls, the genitals are a focus of pleasure. Masturbatory behavior begins and parents often admonish their children, "Don't touch yourself." The boy values his penis and becomes anxious that an injury to it could occur or he could have it taken from his body ("castration anxiety"). Some girls may believe they, too, once had a penis. Boys notice girls do not have a penis and in their egocentricity assume girls once had one like them which confirms their belief their own penis is in peril. Actually the term "castration" is a misnomer insofar as it refers to the testicles.

Boys behave like penetrating missiles, often hurling their bodies through space. Girls begin to play with dolls in maternal ways. Boys will build towers out of blocks and girls' build harbors suggestive of an inner space (the uterus?). At this early stage of the phallic phase, both genders are beginning to become aware of gender differences. They will notice that females have breasts and men do not, that males have facial hair and females do not, etc. In a few months, the phallic feelings will be elaborated to take into account gender differences and discriminative responses are manifested. This occurs with progressive entry into what is called the "Oedipal Phase," to be discussed in Chapter 7.

"Penis envy," a concept that describes and conceptualizes about feelings in young girls, once was believed to be ubiquitous in girls. It was conceptualized that girls wished that they had a penis and treated their clitoris as if it was a diminutive penis. We used to think that girls as they got older adopted total body narcissism as a compensation for the penis they lack. This could be achieved by later interest in fashion, body shapeliness, and via adornment, e.g., use of makeup and jewelry. As indicated above, we now appreciate much more that girls are interested in their vulva as the entrance to a valued interior space in which a baby might grow. Mothers should use the scientific names for female genitalia and distinguish the different anatomical parts. This will help demystify the girl's genitals that are harder to see than a boy's and subject to a greater sense of the "unknown." Boys, on the other hand, have always envied girls' abilities to have babies.

People ubiquitously envy what the other has and they do not possess. I believe as our culture has become less male-privileged, women have more pride in their gender and more self-respect. Mothers have modeled greater acceptance of their femininity, so that their daughters are more pleased with their genital differences, and penis envy is observed less and less. Women now have more opportunities than before regarding career choice and they are confidently and competently engaging in them. In previous generations, they may have agreed that many careers were privileges of men. For many women, however, careers outside the home have not been an issue. For these women, being a full time homemaker and caregiver is fulfilling.

The women's liberation movement has raised the consciousness of many women who were dissatisfied as to their intrinsic self-worth. Contemporary young fathers have become more involved in hands-on childcare than previous generations. Perhaps, this is a side effect of changes in women that has allowed men to re-examine masculinity and resulted in an adaptive way for men to deal with envy of procreation.

Infants seem to appreciate the mock affect of their parents, who, e.g., exaggerate surprise very early on to the delight of their infant. It appears to an observer that the infant understands it to be a pretense.

If you watch mothers with infants when they are calming their child you may notice them telling the child a story about themselves as a child being distressed and then calmed. The infant may even be pre-verbal but an observer gets a sense of comprehension on the infant's part. The infant begins to be calmed. As the child gets older he may use a story similar to one he has been told countless times with dolls and toy animals. This copying of mother's narrative may be the beginning of pretend play. While pretending in play seems to be available in the second year it stabilizes the following year for a child.

Up until three years of age, young children have had contacts with other children of limited durations, but now as a preschooler they have moved from parallel play to cooperative fantasy play with peers. During parallel play, we have noted how two young children playing alongside one another, perhaps with blocks, seem to ignore one another. Children in fantasy play can pretend and assign roles to each other and a plot is enacted. "You're the Daddy and I'm the mommy and you can be the baby." Peer relationships have to be dealt with. Dominance and submissiveness need to be negotiated and accommodated. Fantasy play will allow the child to pretend to be adults they experience in their life, e.g., the mailmen, policeman, teacher, nurse, doctor, father, mother, etc. Enactment of these roles helps children to sort out the multiplicity of relationships that they observe adult people to be engaged in. Also themes having to do with complicated issues like competition, monsters, heroes, etc., will be dramatized in fantasy play. Themes will deal with who is the "strongest" parent, who is the scariest "ghost," and whether "Superman" or "Spiderman" is the best hero. Incomprehensible notions to immature minds, such as "death," are enacted in play with peers and while still a mystery may become less scary. Toys and costumes increasingly are used as props and facilitators of the narrative.

Play helps children become aware of feelings and to label them, thereby allowing them to be more accessible and open to regulation by the child. Play originates as the child nurses and touches the breast or puts its finger into its mother's mouth. Perhaps the first toy is mother's nipple or a child's own fingers. As it evolves, play is a way children bring into conscious awareness scary feelings and accompanying thoughts in a venue that is different from the original scary one. Children customarily avoid being self-reflective about frightening experience or imaginings. In play what was scary or traumatic may not be altered but the stage on which it is re-experienced is different so that there can be abreaction (discharge of feeling) and integration of the experience in a manageable way. Many a young child after a visit to the doctor or dentist has pretended to be the professional examining a patient (another child or a doll). Hence, via playing and pretending children can turn a scary experience passively endured into an active re-creation in which they do the scaring. Such play helps them to become less fearful of imagined scary figures and less stricken by real ones.

Are there some toys that should be avoided? What I particularly have in mind is whether or not to select toys that are representative of weapons, usually given to boys, and Barbie dolls, usually given to girls. While I do not see the sense of giving toy weapons resembling real ones to children based on my value system that values the preservation of life rather than its destruction, I believe it is a misguided belief that violent play by a child encourages violence in later life. In most instances, children and not adults will select what they play out, and if they so choose they can pretend anything, e.g., a block, to be a gun or knife in an enacted scenario. They may be attempting in a pretend way to master something violent that they witnessed or heard about. But I caution you about concluding this is so insofar as they may be dealing instead with age appropriate internal issues that are temporary and get sorted out via such play. If violent enactments, however, were the only theme whenever they engaged in pretend play, then, I would be alerted to the possibility that something might be amiss for the child and I would try to engage him or her in conversation about their interest in such scenarios. If something is bothering a child a teacher's or parent's attentiveness and clarification may be supportive and may be even sufficient to help a child to resolve what is preoccupying.

For very young girls, an important consideration for me as to whether or not to provide your daughter a Barbie doll is that it is a representation of an adult, not a baby. A little girl wants to cuddle and mother a doll that looks more like her, not one that looks more like her mother. Hence, a soft doll would be welcomed. Often she uses the Barbie doll to represent an older girl or a mother. Barbie dolls have recently received a lot of media attention because it was the fiftieth anniversary of their introduction onto the market. Many people object to them because the doll portrays an image of women that conveys that conventional beauty is the ideal for girls to aspire to. Its popularity with girls is thought by some to underlay the self-consciousness of girls about their bodies' appearance. My own belief is that Barbie dolls do not cause this but are more a reflection of our culture's idealization of this image of women. I think that an array of different dolls can be provided to introduce divergences in body shape, appearance, and clothes styles to help girls to value themselves more. Also, mothers can be very helpful to their daughters in modeling acceptance of one's own body type and taste in clothes.

Many preschools include the topic of the life cycle in their curriculum. A child will learn that although leaves die the tree does not. They will learn that in the spring, new leaves grow from the buds on the trees. They will plant seeds and watch sprouts grow and then flowers appear and bloom. Then the flowers will wither and die. There may be an aquarium with fish. Baby fish will be born and some fish will die. Perhaps there will be hamsters or gerbils and also births and deaths. It is via these observations that children will be introduced to the topics of death and regeneration, making the former a little less mysterious and scary. Most importantly, there will be an adult who will be listening to a child's questions and helping to process the answers.

During these years a pet may be introduced into the family. Sometimes, parents wait until a child is old enough to be responsible for some of the care of the pet. This will not be until late latency years in most cases. In some families prior to having children, a couple will have a pet so when a baby joins the family a pet already is a member. A pet can be a very important companion for a child. The young child may be a little rough in showing affection towards the pet and an adult may need to be aware of this possibility and instruct the child. Other children may be too controlling of the pet. Children will use their pet dog or cat to express feelings that they are uncomfortable expressing towards others. Parents will need to be aware of this and educate their child about how the pet also has feelings. This is a good opportunity for helping children to regulate the expression of feelings. Parents need to be aware when getting a puppy that is not housebroken if their child is gaining toilet mastery simultaneously. The methods of toilet mastery will be different and confusing to the child. Adults can be harsh with their puppies. You certainly do not want to put the puppy's nose close to the mess it has made and say "bad Rufus!" within a young child's sight or hearing. Remember, too, a puppy has feelings.

Issues of self- esteem and a beginning sense of morality that began to be inculcated in the home are reinforced in the preschool setting. Sharing and taking turns and cleaning up your own mess are tasks that the teacher is helping the kids in her charge to consider and struggle with. The good teacher works to strengthen the parental bond and not to usurp it with regard to rules and expectations. The child will lapse often in efforts to be fair, generous, and truthful, because the "inner helper," i.e. the conscience, is not yet consolidated. The experienced teacher knows this and does not shame, humiliate or threaten the transgressing child. She, like a savvy parent, will help the child process events such as when Bobby grabbed Johnny's toy and the latter hit the former in retaliation. She is helping Johnny use his words to confront Bobby with the unfairness of his action and restrain from hitting him and thereby demonstrating what colleagues have felicitously labeled "emotional muscle." Self-expression within the confines of self-regulation is reinforced.

Helping children to process events, as mentioned earlier, beneficially begins in infancy. It is a multi-year process for the child to go from expressing feelings via the body, to fantasy, and then via secondary, higher-order symbolic mental functioning to abstract thinking. We now believe that children first have implicit knowledge about their bodily experiences. Essentially this is a non-verbal form of knowing. As children get older, explicit knowing augments experiencing. Memories based upon implicit knowing will be somatic and non-verbal (procedural memory). You may revisit a specific early childhood locale and become tense, start to sweat, and not know why because you banished the frightful image from your conscious mind. This is likely because you experienced something scary or painful before you even had words to label it. Some of these memories will involve early experiences of self-other (part-object) before language was used. Once you acquire words, memories, explicit memory, will include the words. "I remember being very young and being scared by a big dog here." The attaching of words, too, makes the memory more accessible to consciousness. Memories are organized into systems of procedural and explicit memories. This system is called the "mnemic" or "memorial system."

Separation and unavailability of the mother for the baby (deprivation) as well as mother's presence and responsiveness to the infant's needs (satisfaction) both promote memories. Eventually, a stable mental image of mother (object constancy) capable of being revived in her absence and during experiences of need and in the absence of need will be established. Repeated such experiences are involved in helping the child eventually to distinguish perceptions from memories, and outer from inner.

The establishment of a system of memories is an essential part of the mind. Subjectively, it might even feel as if they are one and the same thing. Memories allow for continuity and meaning to our lives. The past is compared to the present and the future is imagined in connection with the here-and-now. Sometimes memories can screen earlier or later memories. Remembering is not a simple matter, being influenced by feelings (e.g., recalling pleasurable events, usually more so, than un-pleasurable ones). Very frightening memories, traumatic in quality, are best affirmed as historical reality when sufficient conviction exists that this is so. There might be a tendency to insist on them being a subjective distortion of objective events. In some instances this could be so. Distinguishing the two can often be an important part of treatment. Traumatic memories are sort of frozen in time, often dissociated from feeling.

Helping children to think about their thoughts is invaluable in helping children to appreciate (likely sometime at the end of the second year) that they have a mind, and that others do, too, and that their mind and its contents can be different from others. "You see me smiling but you are not." This leads to what has been called the process of mentalization, a kind of self-reflectiveness or theory of mind. It helps children in the process of becoming separate individuals, i.e., to keep separate the internal representation of themselves from that of others. This facilitates empathy and relationships with other people. Awareness of others also having a similar capacity facilitates cooperative fantasy play. It also aids in the development of higher order mental functioning, e.g., fantasying or pretending. Another way to put it would be to say a child begins to appreciate psychic reality. If you know you have a mind, you can imagine events outside of your mind within your mind. "Mommy is in the car returning from shopping and she'll be here soon." Parents help their children engage in this process throughout childhood.

This cognitive development also heralds recognition for the child that they are capable of "private" thoughts that others are not privy to. Presumably, this encourages fantasying. It will take at least a couple of more years, maybe longer, before a child will abandon the idea that a parent(s) can read his or her mind. Parents, too, accept that their child is entitled to have private thoughts. For children to value the *privacy* of their mind and for parents to accept this, is linked to an emotional acceptance by both parties of the separateness of each from the other. With increasing age, the voluntary sharing of private thoughts with another person leads to intimacy. For some children and later as adults, having secrets is understood to be like having power and control over people with whom silence is used like a weapon. Establishing intimacy for some people is fraught with anxiety.

The ability to fantasize, in turn, is a way station to more symbolic and abstract thinking. Later on, when the child confidently knows the difference between real and pretend, fantasying particularly is an asset. During this mental activity, reality can be deliberately suspended. In a fantasy, a person can partially gratify any wish that is deprived in reality. A child can imagine riding a bicycle that he wished for but did not get as a birthday present. Frustration tolerance is not pushed to its limits. When children are excessively frustrated, the tension experienced from the deprivation tips self-regulation and major emotive disruption of functioning occurs. Often less mature functioning occurs along with anger.

The earliest fantasies, primal fantasies that likely are never accessible to the conscious mind, we speculate to involve bodily experiences having to do with physical closeness to mother who becomes the infant's object of desire. Once the infant singles out mother as the most important object, separation from her causes distress. We speculate that the infant, under the sway of oral impulses, orally incorporates the mother. This creates an unconscious feeling of union with mother.

Earlier, in Chapter 2, I talked about "psychic reality" and contrasted it to "objective reality." If this is not enough for people of all ages, especially children, to learn to distinguish, contemporary children (adults too) need to come to comprehend "virtual reality." This is computer generated simulated reality. Sometimes stereoscopic glasses add a three dimensional quality. How confusing it must be for a young mind to talk on the telephone with a family member. Where is the person the toddler or preschooler must be wondering? Now, imagine telecommunication on Skype, and add to the confusion.

It is important for young children to acquire a sense of predictability about their environment. If they have such, they will feel safe. Feeling safe is a basic need and connected to this feeling is the consolidation of the reality principle. An important aspect of this principle is knowing the difference between a perception and a thought, or as mentioned above, the difference between psychic and objective reality.

Characteristic of thinking during the early years is animistic thinking, a belief in magic. Thinking having a magical quality causes a belief that a wish or thought actually will occur. This is because of the child's irrational belief in the power of thoughts (omnipotence). This kind of thinking temporarily helps a child to deal with a feeling of relative helplessness. But if it persists, it can lead to serious difficulties. It is irrational to believe that thoughts directly cause actions. Belief otherwise will reduce initiative and being proactive. More so, an older child could feel responsible, for example, if in a fit of anger they wish a sibling to get hit by a car and this coincidentally happens. Serious guilt will follow.

Many parents inadvertently reinforce magical thinking in their well intentioned but misguided wish to keep alive the excitement of early childhood by the promulgation of certain myths. I'm thinking of myths such as "Santa Claus," and assorted portrayals of the supernatural. But it is present in numerous explanations of reality based on non-scientific, irrational thinking.

You might be thinking, "Come on, you're such a spoil sport. What harm can it do if a child gets some fun out of enchantment or a belief in miracles?" Fairy tales are forms of enchantment but they are presented to a child in the context of a conscious decision to allow for the suspension of reality to enjoy a story of pretend. I think you can contextualize explanations within the frame of imagination and pretend and still have fun. If they are not they should be, in my judgment, and questions for clarification that are asked by young listeners should be answered truthfully (factually). "Daddy, are fairies real?" "No son, we have fun pretending that fairies are real." I believe the same principle holds for stories about mythical characters like Santa Claus. When young children are told that heaven is a real place "up in the sky," they take it quite literally, along with portrayals of angels. If, additionally, a young child is told that stars embody people who have "died" but are not "really" dead and the twinkling is a proof of this, a young child's belief is reinforced about the impermanency of death.

Due to the tenuous hold on what is "real" and what is "pretend" for the young child, picture books with animals as characters that talk may cause confusion to a young child. Parents may have little choice insofar as most children's picture books are illustrated with animals. It makes more sense to me to illustrate the stories with pictures of people if its reality that you are trying to reinforce for young children. As they get older and the distinction is clear between the real world and "make believe world," imaginary characters will be fun.

Sometimes young children create imaginary companions whom they talk to and have seated next to themselves. Intelligent children are more likely to create such a companion. This does not mean that if your child has no imaginary companion that he or she is unintelligent. A child will often use the imagined companion to attribute to them their own behaviors unapproved by parents or their own early conscience. It might be a thought and not an action that is attributed. "Jimmy (the imagined companion) told me he wants to pull Becky's (sister) hair." The child will wait to see the parent's reaction. It is as if they are adaptively "testing the waters" via such a play. Parents can play along and not try to convince the child of the non-existence of the imagined companion. Doing so will only upset the child and serves no purpose. They might ask, "What did you tell Jimmy?" An imaginary companion gets less important as the child gets older.

Halloween is a difficult holiday for young children. It is becoming one of the major holidays in the States. The costumes and images are scary. Imagine taking a pre-school age child "trick-or-treating." You go up to a house with skeletons hanging from trees and jack-o-lanterns lit up on the porch. The door opens and a woman dressed as a witch opens the door. I'll wager that your young child will be frightened. Parents can try to bypass this occurrence by pre-arranging to only go to friends' homes, but probably have to pass houses decorated for Halloween to get there. I suggest having a party at home until the child gets older and understanding differences between pretend and real is consolidated.

Preschool is a time of learning through play but also helping children with cognitive skills. While cognitive skills should not be neglected, my bias is in favoring learning through play. I think that for the preschooler, play is a natural way for the intense feelings and bodily/mental urges to be expressed and controlled in a safe way. Also, ideas of conception, even if false, can be enacted. In a preschool environment cognitive skills are introduced such as learning to read and write. By the time children enter kindergarten, they have some rudimentary cognitive skills such as the ability to write their name, remember the alphabet, and read simple words. Preschoolers who are interested in reading will attempt to read signs they see from trips in the car or read words on the cereal box. Social skills are reinforced in interactions with peers and teachers.

I believe parents are beginning to teach "values" to their child from the very beginning of their life. If parents treat a child and others with respect, if parents are civil in dealing with others, if they are honest, if they persevere despite adversity, etc., then it is more likely that their child will adopt the same values. Parents serve as models, especially in their dealings with their child. Children eventually will internalize parental behavior and own it themselves and strive to realize these ideals. Other adults, e.g., relatives, teachers, coaches, religious leaders, etc., also serve as models.

For some parents dealing with teachers can be a problem. Insofar as their child, beginning in preschool, will have twelve or more years of schooling in which contact with teachers is likely, it is helpful to understand what might be the cause of the problem. For these parents feelings that arose when they were their child's age and they had to deal with teachers can be re-experienced. It is as if they are children dealing with adult teachers in the here-and-now. Understanding these unconscious repetitious phenomena from one's past, called "transference," might allow parents to get distance from their feelings and permit assuming a more adult role capable of advocating for their child, if necessary, vis-à-vis the teacher.

As a psychoanalyst I use the term "unconscious" a lot. This is because we contend that much of what motivates us is not in our conscious awareness. The mind is like an iceberg insofar as that which is conscious, i.e., in our metaphor, above water, is very little, while most of it is underwater. Despite being outside our awareness unconscious entities exert a motivational force on the mind. In some instances, bringing someone's attention to a thought or wish that they are unaware of may allow the person to become aware of it. In this case we speak of the thought or wish as preconscious. Primal images that were never conscious, in our theory preverbal, are unconscious. The majority of the constituents of the unconscious part of the mind are conceptualized as being thoughts (wishes, images, impulses, etc.) which were banished from consciousness and are blocked (repressed) and cannot re-enter consciousness except in a dream or the occasional daytime breakthrough of the repression barrier. Derivatives of unconscious impulses, images, ideas, thoughts, desires, and wishes, do enter our consciousness and it is these that we grapple with in every day life, in most instances in adaptive ways.

I now will introduce some more theory. I hope it will help you appreciate the complexity of a child's mind. The young child is still very much a creature of very strong drives and needs. In a psychoanalytic model of the mind, this is the part of the mind (Id) dominated by primordial inborn psychic needs that have biological bodily origins. These needs demand to be satisfied and the mind must deal with them. We call these needs by various names, e.g., instincts, urges, drives, wishes or desires. The two major drives are Eros (libido or sex) and aggression and their derivatives. Derivatives of these two major drives are numerous and account for much of motivation. Drives very early on seek external objects (people and/or things) in relation to which satisfaction is sought. The mind learns ways to control and regulate drives. Socialization, a process wherein children internalize societal values and learn skills, is one way to regulate intense inner drives and feelings. Societal values will dictate that the "raw" expression of a wish will be unacceptable. The wish will need to be modified or transformed to make it more acceptable. The child (really, the child's mind) may allow for a partial gratification in a day- or nocturnal dream.

In the psychoanalytic model of the mind we refer to the executive functions of the mind (Ego). These functions, (e.g., regulatory mental measures [defenses], perception, fantasying, judgment, reality testing, memory, etc.) comprise mainly the conscious part of the mind. The executive part of the mind "negotiates" with the inner and outer worlds. Our internalized moral code (both what is and is not allowed expression in action) and our standards (ideals) comprise another part of the mind (Superego).

The drives or desires are in conflict with the two major regulatory agencies of the mind, that comprising the executive functions and moral code. This conflict is what is meant when the term "mental dynamics" is used. Mental conflicts are **universal** and an on going feature of life. I will say more about this later in Chapter 8. We help our children get a good start in this life-long struggle by helping them to think rationally and to be adaptive. Adaptation involves being cognizant of both inner and outer demands and arriving at sensible and creative solutions to conflicts. A major achievement of the mind is when intense feelings can be transformed into signal feelings, like a yellow light alerts an auto driver to an impending red light so they take steps to decelerate. There is a special feeling that alerts the mind to the pressure of an unconscious desire demanding active expression. We call this anxiety. The mind, upon which the demand is felt, anticipates danger in the form of punishment if the desire is expressed openly. Principal **imagined** dangers that seem to be universal are loss of the object [abandonment], loss of the object's love [e.g., mother's love], castration, and loss of the love of the conscience [experienced as the feeling of guilt]. You can see these imagined dangers all involve a loss. To avoid these punishments becomes a strong motivation to keep forbidden desires contained in some way. Anxiety as a signal alerts the mind to keep a forbidden wish (desire) from consciousness, or transform it, or to control it by not putting it into action. This is not a form of problem solving, but rather a dynamic mental process, aspects of which are unconscious. When the mind is unable to heed anxiety as a signal, panic is felt. This regulatory process takes years to consolidate in the form of a reliable internal "firewall". When the danger is conscious and not imagined but real we speak of fear.

We help our children to transform intense drive aims that are unacceptable to society into more acceptable ones. We call the process of transformation of the aims of sexual urges sublimation, e.g., changing a wish to mess with feces into a wish to sculpt clay. We call the transformation of aggressive wishes de-aggressivization, e.g., changing a wish to destroy living matter by pulling leaves off of a plant into a wish to nurture, by pruning. In the preschool venue, sublimation is given a head start in the encouragement of creativity and play, e.g., in finger painting in lieu of playing with one's own body products. Aggressiveness in preschool can be directed into competitiveness or into its opposite, cooperation.

Another way to understand regulation and transformation of instinctual wishes is to comprehend how the mind must learn greater tolerance of the instinctual demands made upon it. This does not mean, "giving into" the demand. This is where regulation and transformation come into play. Complete non-welcoming of unconscious wishes is not the ideal. A harmonious equilibrium involves communication between the unconscious and conscious parts of the mind. Recognition of an unconscious desire will not scare a mind that appreciates the significant difference between a wish and an act. Rather than "exiling" unconscious desire from conscious awareness, acknowledgment is acceptable. Integrating unconscious wishes might mean giving expression to some form of them in creative endeavors such as art, sport, play, drama, poetry, prose, etc., or in a dream. A psychoanalytically informed education recognizes the instinctual side of Man and attempts to benefit from its vitality while "taming" it.

As a child gets older the regulatory agencies of the mind mature. The initial consolidation of the regulatory parts of the mind, usually by six years of age, allows for increased utilization of higher order rational thinking and moral values. Mentation, or the mental processes of the mind, evolves from a primitive organization (primary process) to a higher organization (secondary process). Essentially, this higher organization comes about by the linking of words to images of things. It is with words that the mind becomes capable of reasoning. This in turn enables the child to process and control wishes.

It is essential for parents to realize that they will serve as auxiliaries to the immature mind of their child for a number of years. They will be his or her allies to help the child cope adaptively with inner (desires) and outer demands (rules, values). As an auxiliary ego, parents will help insure that a lack of preparedness on a child's part does not result in the child feeling overwhelmed and consequently traumatized. As an aspect of a parent serving as an auxiliary ego, a child feels valued and appreciated. Basic needs for children when satisfied help to build up healthy narcissism.

I hope this digression into a description of this model of the mind is helpful to you. You can appreciate how complicated the mind of a child is and how it will take years to consolidate the mind's "firewall" and how parents will need to be patient, clarifying, and supportive of their child's efforts to become rational, reasonable, and adaptable young men and women.

Chapter 6
Day Care

In the best of worlds, only one parent would need to work to be able to provide financially for the family. There would be a child allowance from the government to encourage one parent to refrain from employment outside the home, or employers would allow employees to split a full time job with a colleague and maintain benefits, and guaranteed job retention and career progression would exist for extended parental leave. But these are not society's priorities and day care is a necessity. Unfortunately, in some families, because of financial necessity, both parents need to return to work before the child is really ready to separate for a long time.

There is a big difference between day care for a child beginning after a few days or weeks post-delivery versus after a child is two and a half to three years of age. Before approximately three years of age, a child can be prone to intense distress upon being separated from a parent, usually the mother. The inner representation of the care-giving parent may not yet have been securely consolidated in the child's mind. Thus, in the presence of a need, the absent parent temporarily cannot be securely substituted by an internal image of the parent, and a child will likely experience distress. A preschool that is aware of this will arrange for parents to be present, for children three years and under, either in the classroom or in the building to be summoned if their child becomes distressed.

During the first few months of an infant's life, it is the engagements of the mother with her infant that is essential to help her infant's mind develop. It is a mother's responsiveness to her infant's upset, when her infant in need is at its most alert state having been awakened from its somnolent state because of hunger or pain, that enables the infant gradually to learn that something outside of it reduces noxious feelings. The mother takes on a significance of special importance in the surrounding external world beginning in the second half of the first year and substitutes for her will have a different way of responding to the infant. These differences can cause confusion and upset. The child's mind is not sufficiently developed to cope with the distress. In a daycare venue caregivers will be responsible for more than one infant and will be unable to show the optimal attentiveness that an infant requires especially during the earliest months. Later in the second half of the first year and early into the second year it often is only the mother that the child desires and can be comforted by, despite the best efforts by devoted daycare caregivers.

Businesses vary in terms of the length of maternal leave that they grant their female employees or temporary leave for spouses whose wives have delivered babies or have adopted a child. The longer there is financed maternal leave, the more opportunity for the mother-child attachment to establish a foothold. Some countries also provide financial assistance to their citizens to take maternal leave.

While I have a bias against day care for children younger than three years of age, based on the reasons stated above, I recognize that practical realities make it a financial necessity. In some circumstances it may not be a financial necessity for a woman but rather a practical necessity for career circumstances. Many women derive great satisfaction from their careers. Given this reality what could make day care more attuned to developmental needs of children and parents? In some countries, e.g., France, day care centers are government supported. Training to become an early educator is a respected and well-paid career. This would be helpful in the States. Undoubtedly, many caregivers who work in daycare centers are devoted and loving parent surrogates. Many, however, lack knowledge about child development, although some are parents too. Smaller care-giver/child ratios would be desirable, but insofar as the enterprise of day care is a for-profit one it would need to be economical to build more centers. Insofar as my contribution is not politically focused, let me return to the psychological issues.

Before selecting a day care center, parents best visit some if possible, and select one where the children seem happy and the workers genuinely fond of them. Notice the ratio of caregivers to children.

If a caregiver is responsible for many children, it is unlikely that any one child will get sufficient personal attention. Is there a good balance between free/structured play and cognitive learning? Parent might choose to interview the director of the day care center to learn about the model of care of children practiced.

When a young child is absent from parents, providing them with photos of them that they can access during the time spent away can be helpful. Day care workers can refer to the child's parents now and again to underscore the parents' importance. The schedule of the parent can be known and mentioned and the child can be reassured that "Mommy is at lunch now and thinking of you." On some occasions the parent can be talked to on the phone (cell phones make this more possible). Parents can visit when possible so that the venue has their imprimatur on it for their child.

The old adage, "It's the quality and not the quantity that matters," is true. Parents need to maximize the quality of time spent with their children who are in day care. One-on-one time, if practical, is desirable. Parents can observe children at home. Are they eager to go to daycare or do they protest? Are they clingier than before starting day care? Are they having trouble sleeping? In other words, parents can be alert to evidence of tension, stress and conflict. If they see such evidence, a consultation with the provider and caregiver responsible for their child can be arranged. If their observations corroborate those of the parents, it can be asked what the day care workers intend to do to make the child feel more comfortable? Collaboration between parents and the surrogate caregiver is encouraged so that a child hears complementary things to reassure them.

Chapter 7
The Oedipal Years

During the years 3-5, a major developmental change occurs, sometimes beginning as early as the latter half of the second year. In our Western traditional intact families, Oedipal themes can be observed in the interactions of the child with parents, in play, in the child's reverie, sometimes verbalized with the intention to be heard by the parent, but also often in a disguised derivative way capable of being noticed only by the trained observer. What do we mean by Oedipal themes? The term is taken from a Greek myth where Oedipus kills his father, both unaware of their relationship, and then marries his own biological mother, both also unaware of their relationship, all in accordance with a soothsayer's prescient telling of the future. Oedipus afflicts self-punishment upon himself, blinding himself, when he learns the truth. Certainly this is a monumental tragedy. For our little boy or girl, while it can be very intense, it indeed is not so tragic. Nevertheless, the Oedipal experience for a child is a major step in development.

It is a time of **powerful** emotions for the child. It is also an opportunity, metaphorically, for the child to struggle with an internal "beast," the slaying of which, or more accurately, the domestication or taming of (desire and murderous feelings), leads to the early establishment of very significant internal regulatory structures in the mind of the child. By a mental structure, I do not mean an anatomical entity but a class of mental processes that are of very long-standing duration. The duration is long enough that essentially we think of it as permanent, although not immutable. Our metaphoric beast, however, never fully relinquishes its wildness and the child will need to struggle with it again, especially during adolescence. I need to acquaint you with some theoretical concepts that psychoanalysts have so that you can appreciate the complexity of the dynamics that a child's mind is engaged in. Remember, this is universal and much of it is engaged in outside of conscious awareness. While this is a difficult time for children and parents most traverse it successfully.

The boy might tell his mother he wishes to marry her, and the girl may say the same to her father. It is important to treat this seriously and not to convey that this is cute or stupid. This will be very hurtful to the young suitor. A sensitive parent will convey appreciation for the wish and add that he or she is already married to the child's father (or mother). Their child might respond back with "Daddy can go away." The flummoxed parent might say something like "Won't you miss Daddy (or Mommy)?" The boy might say "Yes," or maybe "No." Likely, the conversation will change subject, at least for the time being.

The same scenario might be played out with dolls or in play with peers and then it might go unnoticed by the parents. Teachers, child therapists, and child analysts have observed the narrative, respectively, with students and child patients. Psychoanalysts also have heard a version of this story from countless adult patients discovering or recollecting memories from early childhood. The theme enters into much of ancient Greek epics and modern world literature too. So why is it that the narrative is often derisively dismissed by most people? My hunch is that this is because the Oedipal dynamic involves intense and taboo parenticidal and incestuous wishes and feelings from our distant past (childhood) that we all want to keep locked away in the unconscious part of our minds. Also, sexuality in particular, and drives in general, are diminished in importance as motives in generating behavior by some modern psychoanalytic theorists. I believe that this is wrong.

Let us return to our young boy and girl. The Oedipal drama involves a triangular relationship, the child and both parents. This is a mental change from a relationship with a single parent. Prior to this development the complexity of triangular relationships was beyond the cognitive capabilities of the child's mind. The mind has to deal with complicated wishes and feelings simultaneously towards the mother, father, and self. This is a lot to deal with. Also, the picture is not as straight forward as portrayed in the above-imagined conversation between the boy or girl and the parent of the opposite sex. To complicate circumstances, the parent felt to be a rival is also a parent that the child loves and needs. These are the ingredients for universal mental conflict.

Sigmund Freud was the first observer who saw the significance of the Oedipal Complex for mankind. He also accepted the scientific observation of a few contemporaries who proposed the unpopular formulation that Man is a mentally bisexual animal. Both genders are mentally inborn with a readiness to express bisexual tendencies. We refer to these traits as masculine and feminine.

For each individual there is a predominant tendency. The majority of men and women are heterosexual, but we infer each gender has a less prevalent or weaker attraction towards the same gender. After all, boys love their fathers and girls love their mothers. We infer that for boys who are dealing with Oedipal desires, the love for mother (positive Oedipal Complex) during this period is more intense than the love for father (negative Oedipal Complex) and for girls the opposite (also divided into "positive" and "negative") is true. Nevertheless, this results in the universal developmental mental conflict addressed above.

I need to expand upon the nature of the love felt for the parents during this period. It is sexual in quality. Yes, little children are not pure and innocent but have a sexual life. The sexual life of children is **different in content** from that of adults. With regard to the pleasure, however, it is the same quality, albeit of a lesser quantity. We can all observe young children touching their genitals (masturbating), not with the vigor of an adolescent, but still the same activity. The childhood notions of sex are different from that of adults. How babies are conceived is based on limited knowledge and personal bodily experiences that have had a quality of erogenous pleasure, such as eating or defecating. Theories of sex between adults are based on a child's previous experiences and misunderstandings, such as believing the moans and noises emanating behind closed parental bedroom doors as suggestive of an attack or fight between the parents. This deduction is colored by the attribution, to the imagined scenario behind closed doors, of their own sadomasochistic wishes (deriving pleasure by inflicting pain/being the recipient of pain, or controlling another person/being under another's control).

As mentioned above, children's sexual theories are based upon bodily experiences of their own, so that conception might, e.g., be based upon eating something. Children have experienced that their abdomen can get bigger after a full meal, much like a pregnant woman's belly. They may have a little scientific knowledge that can be distorted, e.g., that sperm are involved but may believe they are deposited in the mouth. They may have been told that father deposits a seed into the mother to fertilize her egg. They know that seeds develop and grow into plants. This can lead to belief that you can get pregnant if you eat something. If that is the case they too can get pregnant, regardless of their gender. They may have been told the seed comes via the father's penis. If the child is a boy, he, too, has one but all he has experienced is urine coming out of his penis. Hence, he could deduce that urination is involved in "making a baby." I think you "get the picture." Even if children have been told the facts, they prefer their own theories.

The predominant wish for the Oedipal boy is to give mother a baby and the Oedipal girl wants her father to give her a baby. But there can exist for many children a less prevalent and intense wish to have a baby with the parent of the same sex. Please keep in mind our earlier discussion, when we spoke of orality, of passive and active aims of wishes. Hence, children both want actively to produce babies for others and want passively to have babies produced in them.

The classical theoretical formulation is that for both genders the initial wish is to produce a baby with mother, with the girl switching over to the father following disappointment with the mother who is held responsible for depriving her of a penis. As mentioned earlier, this theory regarding the girl has for the most part been modified, at least with regard to the idea that the disappointment is a severe narcissistic one about not having a penis. We now know that most little girls are pleased with the genitals they have and the "inner space" (uterus) that boys do not have. Some little girls would prefer both a penis and a vagina. It is more likely, I believe, that it is the mother who is the initial figure towards whom wishes for a baby are directed because she is the predominant caregiver for girls. The girl switches to her father because of an inborn biological readiness to do so. Weaker inclinations towards the same sexed parent are present due to an inborn bisexuality.

When a boy wishes to eliminate his father, in order to have exclusive prerogatives with his mother, he becomes anxious because he believes father will retaliate. A son believes his father will become aware of his patricidal wishes. This dynamic (castration anxiety) is mostly or exclusively unconscious. Boys manifest this anxiety by frequently touching their genitals probably to reassure themselves, or by seeking reassurance by going to the bathroom supposedly to urinate, but an opportunity to handle their penis. During this phase boys (and girls) often will notice people with physical deformities in a crowd. In the mind of the boy a physical deformity is a derivative of castration anxiety. A boy is anxious even if his father is the least threatening and enlightened of fathers. This is so, we believe, because the boy unconsciously attributes to his father his own wishes to castrate his parent (to take away the source of his imagined power and prerogatives) and imagines retaliatory punishment. The boy's mind employs this mental maneuver (projection) because of the anxiety ensuing from the conflict of ambivalence between opposing loving and hating feelings directed at father. But getting rid of hostile wishes in such a manner is not very adaptive and the attempt boomerangs.

The father as rival likely originates at an earlier time, during the latter part of the oral phase when father is perceived to interrupt the physical closeness between mother and infant. We can only speculate that a father is experienced by both boy and girl infants as an intruder that interrupts the emotional intimacy with their mother. As a child matures and fantasies become more sophisticated, a fantasized elimination of the father as an intruder can be accomplished. Later in adolescence during experiences of unrequited love we wonder if this primal feeling is revived and adds to the agony of unattainable love. Primal fantasies of merging with mother are unavailable to consciousness. However, insofar as we believe that timelessness is characteristic of the Unconscious we wonder if such fantasies enter into dreams and offer some gratification to a victim of unrequited love.

The situation for the girl is more complicated. It cannot be that the loss of a penis as punishment for competitive and matricidal feelings can be a threat. Most girls have already acknowledged the absence of a penis. The loss of mother's love, however, can be a felt threat. For both sexes the discomfort can be so intense that they retreat from Oedipal dynamics.

Some children regress to earlier ways of relating. There is a tendency for children under stress to regress temporarily to earlier levels. We see it when children are tired or sick. At each earlier level of development there are vulnerable spots (fixations) because of earlier experiences that may not have been traversed smoothly and these act like magnets to draw the inner life of the child back to them. Here an observer looks "backwards" in time to understand present day behavior. Both drive expressions and ways of relating will be colored by earlier experiences. Immature ways of relating to parents and immature behaviors to obtain gratification may come to the fore. Sleeping may become disturbed as the child's dreams are immersed with the struggle that has been retreated from.

This can be a stressful time for parents and children. If handled well by parents it need not be permanent and the child can get back on a progressive course. Sometimes professional help for the family is prudent. It is also possible for a child to avoid Oedipal stress via fleeing to the next developmental level. However, if this is a result of avoidance it is unlikely it is progressive or that the child lingered long enough in the Oedipal stage to benefit from it.

An imagined threat of genital injury for a boy and loss of love for a girl, act as strong motivators to move out of the troubled waters of the Oedipal phase. Some modicum of reality intrudes and children realize with some narcissistic hurt and disappointment that they really cannot rival their parent for the exclusive love of the other parent. They realize they are children and not adults. They envy the privileges and skills of their adult parents. This is another determinant of the partial dissolution of the Oedipal Complex. I say "partial," insofar as it is doubtful that the Oedipus Complex is ever completely obliterated. Typically, both boys and girls have struggled for years with loving and hating feelings for beloved and depended-upon parents. As mentioned above, we speculate that from very early on father is experienced as an intruder interrupting the intimacy of the infant with its mother. The insidious feeling of jealousy has its primordial origin in this struggle. Because of various mental maneuvers to weaken and/or disguise demands for action made by conflicting wishes, around the end of the fifth year a child can get distance by repressing Oedipal wishes, i.e., relegating them to the unconscious part of the mind and guarding against their re-entry into conscious awareness.

Correlated with this repression is a partial identification with the parent of the same sex, the main rival and therefore potential threat. It is partial because the identification is with the conscience of the parent. So, in place of forbidden Oedipal desire for the mother, by identifying with father's superego, the male child has internalized the representation of societal moral standards, the "shalls" and "shall nots." One of the "shall nots" is a prohibition against patricidal and incestuous desires. We might say "father," in this respect, represents the demands of reality. Earlier, boys have identified with the paternal figure in what we call a masculine identification. We could say this is an early ego ideal type of identification. Ego ideals are akin to ideal selves that the child aspires to and are changeable. It is a task of late adolescence for achieving an integration of the disparate self-ideals that exist. Boys have also identified with their mothers early on. In part this might be with the "active" mother, i.e., the care-giving mother, but they also might identify with the more passive aspects of mother, what is traditionally labeled as "feminine." There is more acceptance of feminine qualities in males and masculine qualities in females, and the current generation is less threatened by transgender behavior than previous ones.

Another consequence of feeling Oedipal defeat is for the boy again to identify with his father as his ego ideal, that is, the self he would like to become. After all, father is mother's choice over him. A girl can deal with Oedipal defeat in a similar fashion. Father chose mother over her and gave mother a baby. Taking her mother as her ego ideal that she strives to be like can help her deal with her wounded narcissism as a result of feeling defeated in her oedipal strivings.

In a valued relationship with another person a likely constituent of the mental representation of the relationship is identification with the person. In an identification a self representation is modified to be like a part or the whole of an object representation. Initially there is a sameness between the self and object representation along with their drive (libido/aggression) investments. With further mental processing (internalization) a depersonification of an identification can occur, making it less personal. Thereby, an identification can be re-organized (transformed) to a different level into a mental structure that may unexpectedly enrich a child's mind. However, it is not uncommon for children to identify with whomever severely frightens them; we call this identification with the perceived aggressor. This is an instance of non-linear discontinuity in development that may become a non-enriching transformation. While identificatory processes are ongoing, object relationships continue, e.g., as with a child and its parents.

One consequence of the part identification with the conscience of the parent of the same gender for the oedipal child transitioning into Latency is that this rudimentary agency of the mind employs the very aggression and libido directed at the parents now towards the self. Thus, when the child's thoughts and/or behavior goes against moral codes, condemnatory guilt is now felt by the child; and, when the thoughts and/or behavior is in accordance with inner standards, the child feels love from his conscience. In its early state the conscience has links to the unconscious drives (wishes), which contributes to its tyrannical and absolutist quality, as well as to reality. As a child gets older, however, the conscience can become less linked to the unconscious drives (wishes) and become less rigid, more compassionate and maturely organized. This part of the mind, only rudimentary up to now, becomes like an inner policeman, an "inner helper" or moral compass to help the child control powerful drives. Insofar as it is usually the parental figures with which the Oedipal drama unfolds, they are the models whose consciences are identified with in this process of partial Oedipal Complex dissolution. If the parents are morally corrupt, these are the standards identified with by the child. Fortunately, the conscience is not immutable beyond all possibility.

Girls find it easier to identify with their mothers than do boys. Boys always are longing for maternal closeness, but are very conflicted about it. Mother's femininity is not easy for them to identify with. They may identify with aspects of mother that are active. Girls recognize mother to be the same gender and aspire to be physically like her as they mature. Her generative powers are emulated. Girls have identified with their mothers all along as ego ideals (feminine identification). Identifying with her conscience is a part of the process of dissolution for the girl of Oedipal desires for the father and matricidal urges directed at mother.

In instances where families are not intact, such as after death or divorce, or with households having single parents, Oedipal dramas can still unfold, albeit with greater difficulty. The mind of a child is very creative and the pressure brought upon it by unconscious desire is very strong. Solutions are sought and created in fantasy, if necessary. Sometimes an elder sib, an aunt or uncle, or a teacher is drawn into an imagined triangle. Of course, an imagined triangle is not as compelling as a real one, so we can expect this Oedipal narrative to be convoluted and maybe not as intense.

For children where the Oedipal Complex is not experienced, this is a disadvantage because of a reduced opportunity for progressive development of the mind, i.e., the internalized conscience. An example might be a child so engrossed in earlier pre-Oedipal issues because of a broad and strong oral fixation that Oedipal issues cannot be reached at the expected chronological age. For most children, the Oedipal Complex will be revived with puberty, and there is a second chance for children of all familial circumstances, to resolve it more thoroughly. Regrettably, a child with strong pre-Oedipal fixations will still be at a disadvantage when Oedipal issues are re-visited in adolescence. To use a metaphor of Freud's, because of the multi-fronts at which they are waging a war against conflicted oral, anal urethral and phallic wishes, many battles will be lost and retreats will take place. There will be few, if any, troops to wage war at the Oedipal stage. Under these circumstances, the Oedipal struggle will be only a small skirmish. Some children have such massive fixations in pre-Oedipal phases that the Oedipal struggle is not engaged in by the mind. In such instances progressive developments will not be experienced. The mind will be arrested and express itself in a primitive quality devoid of moral and other regulatory restraints.

With the partial dissolution of the Oedipal Complex, a fantasy known as the family romance can be enacted in a child's play, or expressed in a dream. The theme appears in world literature, often in fairy tales.

The family romance usually has its onset during the Latency years where an educated observer can see it in derivative form in the play of children in the early stages of Latency. Sometimes this fantasy may even be in the conscious awareness of a child without an appreciation by the child of its meaning. In the family romance fantasy a child entertains the notion that he or she is not living with his or her biological parents but with adoptive parents. It seems to owe its existence to disillusionment with parents stemming from disappointment of Oedipal wishes. One's biological parents are imagined to be of a higher station, or social class, or even from royalty. In this manner, the real biological parents are devalued, insofar as Oedipal wishes have gone ungratified, and the imagined parents are idealized to deal with the narcissistic hurt.

In instances when a child really has been adopted, and is aware of this fact, the family romance fantasy is modified. A blood relationship to the adoptive parents is imagined in the fantasy. The real biological parents are imagined to have kidnapped them or that in the hospital there was a mistaken kinship assigned to them. This is an attempt to cut the tie to the real biological parents. Hence, the real biological parents are devalued to deal with the fact and resultant narcissistic hurt that they gave up the child for adoption. Adoptees who are products of open adoptions have to contend with family romance dynamics that only adds to the child's potential confusion, in addition to the other issues alluded to earlier.

Another unconscious fantasy, seen in some adult men, having its origins in disappointment in their Oedipal desires, is what we term a "rescue" fantasy. Essentially, the male imagines rescuing a "fallen" or "needy" woman (the mother in disguise who has chosen his father over him) and giving her a child like himself, thereby being his own father to himself.

The Oedipal years of their children can be very stressful for some parents. Most parents support the emancipation of their children, albeit it some with mixed feelings. Earlier, I pointed out that as a child progresses through their life and passes through phases of development, a parent's own vulnerable "hot spots" can be rekindled. If a parent experienced an intense Oedipal phase in their own childhood, they might re-experience such thoughts and feelings. A father might become competitive with his son for the attention of his wife, or make veiled castration threats to his son evoking the boy's castration anxiety. Some parents act immodestly around their children, so that nudity is commonplace. If a spouse is away, a parent might not object to an adolescent sleeping in the parental bed. Such actions are over-stimulating of children, and get them excited and usually anxious because of imagined reprisals. Adequate means of discharging the excitement are not available. As a general principle, exposing children to parental sexual intimacy should be avoided.

    Censorship by parents of over-stimulating sexual and frightening violent themes in movies and on television is called for to protect children from feeling overwhelmed. They may already feel so because of inner thoughts and feelings and adding to this does not make good sense. Here parents may take a lot of "heat" because their child's friends may be allowed to watch such programs and movies. Likely, censorship will be incomplete insofar as a child may be exposed to inappropriate content in a friend's home. Perhaps a child can talk about it afterwards so parents can be of help. Here, the value of having a good communication with a child cannot be over-stated. Children whose parents endeavor to engage them in processing their confusing and scary thoughts and feelings are truly fortunate. The written word is less problematic, insofar as children can take the time to ponder and process what they are reading before going onto the next page. Literature should also be appropriate to the child's level of comprehension.

Chapter 8
Psychological disturbances of the early years of childhood

As you read this section, please keep in mind that while a parent and child may be struggling with a developmental issue or a particular behavior, we do not mean to convey necessarily that the struggle is considered pathological or that the difficulty is being elevated to a diagnosable level. Most struggles are temporary if dealt with in a reasonably appropriate manner by parents. What follows is a description of the common problems that parents become aware of from birth through the teenage years of their child. Some of these problems have their onset generally in connection with a particular stage of development but may continue into the next contiguous stage or beyond. I will try to make it clear from my exposition as to what age child I am talking about. It is beyond my focus to consider autism.

Developmental Interferences

When parents introduce expectations that are inappropriate to the developmental age of the child, i.e., where the child has not the capabilities of satisfying them, the parents are introducing a developmental interference. This can be experienced at any chronological age of childhood. The child will experience unnecessary stress. For example, over-stimulating a child and then expecting him or her to go to sleep is not an expectation that can be satisfied by the child. Or if a parent expects a fifteen-month-old toddler to be compliant with toileting expectations, this is unrealistic. If the parent gets impatient and angry it impacts the young toddler in a deleterious way. If this is typical and happens a lot we have the potential conditions for a cumulative trauma. Single instances of this kind of inappropriate parental impatience do not seriously hurt a child but repeated ones "add up" and can result in trauma. When a single instance of a very unpleasant experience is so severe it is traumatic, an experience we label as a shock trauma.

Earlier, we defined trauma as an experience where a person feels unprepared and overwhelmed to deal efficiently with the amount of stimuli impinging upon the mind. Such experiences have negative consequences for a child in its ability to regulate feelings, among other things. When traumatized, children usually display behavior indicative of a significant disruption of psychic equilibrium. Later in this chapter we will discuss what we mean by developmental conflict, psychoneurosis, and delinquency.

Sleep Problems

Usually, the first manifestation of a "problem" that parents encounter is difficulty putting a young baby to sleep. Parents become very stressed about this for two reasons. Firstly, they believe correctly that the child needs to sleep for its wellbeing. Secondly, the baby's sleeping is a respite for the parents to attend to their own chores and needs, including sleeping or grabbing a nap. Infants differ as to their degree of fussiness. Some are easy to satisfy and seem to naturally and almost seamlessly fall into rhythms of sleeping and being awake. But others seem to find this rhythm impossible to achieve. Some infants suffer from colic and seem to be inconsolable and impossible to fall asleep (see Chapter 2). By trial and error, parents hope to find the panacea that will allow them to overcome future periods of difficulty in this arena. For the most part, the majority of children eventually fall into a cycle (usually by six months) that fits into their family's life style. But problems of sleep will arise again and again, usually temporarily. Sleeping seems to be a bodily activity prone to disruption during periods of stress. As adults we know that to be true. Also, as a child progresses through different developmental stages the issues of each particular stage can contribute toward sleeping disruptions, e.g., a child struggling with toilet mastery can be afraid of soiling while asleep.

A major problem is when parents react to temporary disruptions in ways that could lend the problem to become a permanent one. Parents are not "bad" if they become impatient with a child that will not easily fall asleep. It can be difficult for all parents. To lighten things up, I will introduce a bit of humor into a distressing topic. I will tell you of a *New Yorker* cartoon on the subject. It shows a husband and wife in bed bandaged up to look like mummies. The caption is, "This should keep Emily from running to our bed every time she has a bad dream." Obviously, this strategy is not advised.

A more pernicious problem is when parents' marital problems get played out in a child's bedroom. It is not uncommon for spouses that are unhappy with each other and avoiding sexual intimacy to exacerbate their child's sleeping problems, e.g., by not conveying clear expectations that their child sleep through the night and not come into the parental bedroom. Another issue is the transgenerational transmission of trauma. For example, a parent as a young child may have been exposed to his or her own parents engaged in sexual intercourse (primal scene) and traumatized because of the misinterpretation of the scene as a violent one with one parent inflicting harm onto the other. When grown up the parent, unwittingly, i.e., unconsciously, could arrange for his or her own child to witness the same act. This child can be traumatized and a sleep problem could ensue.

When someone of any age intends to go asleep he or she are essentially disengaging from the outer world and withdrawing into the inner world. I am describing this in a subjective way. If this is valid, it does not make sense for daddy to come home from work and to stimulate his baby in a vigorous playful way and for the parents then to expect a seamless transition to sleep. We are sympathetic to the father who takes the first opportunity of his day to be playful with his newborn, but it is not in the best interests of the child that the play be vigorous or a long duration. Infants need their sleep and to postpone it until after the 11 p.m. television news is not in a baby's best interest. My impression is that infants and children of all ages stay up too late, because parents find it easier not to deal with it. Eventually, out of exhaustion, the child falls asleep. What about the benefits of allowing a baby to discover a way to sooth him or herself and put itself to sleep? Insofar as infants benefit from routine, as discussed earlier, parents need to create reliably the best possible conditions required to promote falling asleep for their infant.

It is not unusual after a family vacation in which sleeping arrangements often are not typical, for young child to have some sleep difficulties. Such problems ordinarily are temporary if parents can help the child process recent events. They understand that the vacation sleeping arrangements deviated from the usual routine and may have been scary or over-stimulating for their child, especially if the family slept together in the same room or even in the same bed.

Putting an infant to sleep, beneficially, is a moment of quiet bonding between a mother and baby, especially if breastfeeding. It's an opportunity for gazing at each other, to sing a bedtime lullaby, for bodily contact, and other warm fuzzy things. I do not advise getting into bed alongside the baby for reasons already stated. Older children like to be read to or to be told a story in bed prior to going to sleep. Parents can select an appropriate non-scary book from the vast literature or make up a story. If a story is made up, choose fictitious people so as to allow for distance to enable a child to listen. The story can include a theme of the day's experience and can include resolution of an experience that was trying for the child. Helping child to process the day's events that may not have been assimilated is useful. Otherwise, the event could enter a young child's dream.

Dreams of an upsetting nature can disrupt a child's sleep. We believe that dreams serve the purpose of wish fulfillment. Many of these wishes are not acceptable to the conscious mind. The mind of a neonate is not mature enough to dream in this fashion. We do not confidently know what constitutes a newborn's dream. A preschooler likely dreams much like an adult but some dreams are likely re-experiencing the events of the day that were intense and not processed. The more mature mind disguises a wish sufficiently so that it can get past the mind's sleeping censorship and be expressed in the dream and gain partial gratification. When the disguise has not been sufficient, and the mind's censor has caught enough of its presence in the dream to become alert, the dreamer can awake with a fright. This is a so-called "nightmare." Other nightmares are simply the inclusion in a dream of a frightening image. Parents will be alerted, either by a cry, footsteps, or pleas, "Mommy (daddy), wake up!"

Comforting will follow and putting the child back to sleep will be necessary. Expediency will dictate allowing the child to crawl into bed with a parent. Even though inconvenient, parents are advised to take the child back to their own bed and sit alongside them until they are consoled enough to go back to sleep. In the morning parents can give the child an opportunity to speak about the dream if recalled. Children can be reassured that a dream is not real. Learning the difference between pretend and real is acquired gradually and likely is attained securely by the five year old or earlier by a precocious child. A scary dog is not hiding under the bed and monsters and ghosts do not exist. If the nightmare's content is remembered and involves a frightening theme parents can help them to understand it within the limits of their cognitive capacities and psychological readiness. Here the parents' intuitive grasp of their child's readiness to process upsetting experiences will serve them well.

It is the rare child, fortunately, that walks while asleep, oblivious to safety concerns and hard to console because they are still asleep. Professionals know little about sleepwalking, and can offer little comfort to parents, except to underscore the need to secure their child's safety, e.g., putting a gate at the top of the stairs. Sleepwalking, however, usually does not become a permanent feature when it occurs.

A word should be mentioned about the faulty connection made by some children between death and sleeping. To a child, both resemble each other. If a child views a dead relative in an open-coffin memorial service the dead person will appear to the child to be asleep. Unfortunately, some parents may even compare being dead to being asleep. This erroneous explanation connects up being dead with the natural state of sleeping. It could cause falling asleep to be scary to a child. A child can be informed that when one is dead one has no feelings whatsoever evermore, but when one is asleep one is alive and does feel and wakes up refreshed.

Separation Problems

Separation issues are ubiquitous in childhood. Indeed, they underlay sleeping problems. The youngster temporarily must withdraw his emotional investment in the parent(s) and turn it inward in order to fall asleep. For some children this is difficult because of an insecure attachment to their parent(s). Contemporary psychoanalysis has identified the different types of attachment that young children are able to establish with maternal figures. We have underscored the ingredients that help secure a secure attachment. Most mothers are aware of making eye contact, not being intrusive, being in rhythm emotionally, modulating the intensity of their affect, reflecting on their child's affects and moods, etc, all of which contribute to a secure attachment with their infant. There are many empirical studies detailing the consequences for different types of attachment upon the relationship between a child and parent, as the child gets older. The bonding or attachment experience starts from day one but its consolidation is not achieved probably until 3 years of age. These principles of development were discussed earlier (see Chapters 2, 4 & 5) when we talked of the experience of "being with" involving emotional attunement, and the gradual consolidation of the capacity to maintain an internal image of the maternal figure, the one who is comforting and need satisfying, in the presence of a strong need, or a gratified need, but in the absence of that figure. We call that capacity object constancy. "Object" because it is not the self ("subject") and "constancy" because of its permanency. It is a real achievement the first time the child is able to manage a sleepover at a friend's house. This is so, even if the child insists on taking along their transitional object. Children able to do so feel securely attached and bonded with their parent(s).

As every parent knows, young children often can be clingy and react with upset when baby-sitting arrangements are made until they become familiar with the baby-sitter. Parents, understandably, are hesitant to arrange to have baby-sitters that are not relatives because of fears of the person's suitability, unless they have thoroughly vetted the person. Assuming the person is safe, it's a good idea for children to become comfortable with people other than members of their nuclear family. Of course, parents help children to be wary of strangers, whom they have not vetted, in unfamiliar settings. Probably this caution should begin when your child is a toddler.

Hospitalization of a child involves a separation in the context of pain and discomfort. Your young child's resources will be greatly taxed. This is an occasion where a parent must insist that they be with a child twenty-four hours a day as long as the child is an inpatient. Most hospitals are sophisticated about the psychological needs of ill children and their parents to know the correctness of this request and they grant it. Hospitals were not always this accommodating.

Parents wonder at what age they can have an extended vacation without the children? Usually, arrangements are made with a relative, like grandparents, to look after the children. It is preferable that the relatives temporarily move into the child's residence so that the child need not have to deal with unfamiliar surroundings at the same time as dealing with their parents' absence. This is more important the younger the child. For many children, by three years of age such a separation is viable. A stable inner representation of the parent usually has been achieved, enabling them to tolerate their parents' absence as long as their needs generally are satisfied. For many children, the upset follows their parents' return. This may appear counter-intuitive to the parents. It is as if they mobilized their defenses while the parents were gone but with their reappearance they can let down their guard. It is also a way of "paying back the parents." Yes, children can be vengeful, making their parents feel what they felt.

The ultimate separation, of course, follows the death of a parent. Professionals used to think that children were unable truly to grieve until adolescence when the natural tendency is to disengage from one's parents. Observations, however, suggest that even young children can mourn and can accept a substitute parental caregiver who satisfies their basic biological needs. With time they can bond with the substitute, too.

Toilet Mastery

Parents can pick up indications of readiness on the part of their child to begin the process of toilet mastery. Such readiness can begin from around two years onwards. Do not expect, however, that such readiness means that older toddlers necessarily will achieve toilet mastery quickly. Expressions of curiosity may occur about the toilet or about the toileting activities of their parents. There might be a spoken wish to be "like" mommy or daddy when it comes to using the toilet. Some children let you know they are ready because they become squeamish about messes and wish to have their bodies, especially their hands, clean. They may object to eating finger-foods because they dislike dirtying their fingers. They may express a desire to wear pull-ups or underwear instead of diapers.

At the beginning of toilet mastery a child-size portable toilet can be introduced. Children feel more secure if their feet touch the floor than if they dangle. Many children have a fearful approach to the toilet. They are afraid of falling into the toilet, the sound of the flush scares them, and disappearance of the stool makes them anxious. Parents need to be patient, supportive and reassuring.

After awhile, a child presents their bowel movements as "gifts" to the parent. It is experienced as part of him or herself and it is confusing when a parent seems so pleased that a child has deposited it in the toilet but then flushes it away. An explanation that everyone disposes of stools in this manner may remove the self-reference for your child. The focus should be on the child's self control over their body's products, its feces, expressing pride in the child's own achievement. Because the aim is mastery and not training, I propose not to begin toilet mastery till the toddler is at least two-and-a-half years old. Sphincter control is likely not mature at least until that age. Sometimes younger children can be toilet-trained but it is not mastery and instead it is a stimulus-response behavior.

A minority of children fails to become toilet mastered, even up to around puberty. Some children may have achieved and then lost toilet mastery. These children have a condition known as encopresis. These children soil their underpants and hide them. Soiling may occur because they try to withhold their feces but then fail to do so. Assuming there are no physical reasons, e.g., problems with the integrity of the sphincter, the causes can be multiple due to psychological conflict. The dynamics underlying the condition, e.g., could be due to an attempt to hold onto and control mother, symbolically by holding onto feces that become concrete representations of her. Consultation with a professional is warranted if a child is five years old and still soiling.

Bladder control in the daytime is usually achieved before nighttime control. Sometimes the latter is accomplished but then control is lost during a time of stress and later regained. Wetting at night can sometimes be prolonged in duration. If a child is still wetting by age six (enuresis), I suggest a consultation with a professional. If nocturnal bladder control has been achieved but then lost because of acute stress the prognosis is more favorable than if it has never been achieved. When lack of bladder control extends over years, the psychological meaning of the inability to control this body function can take on additional individual meaning specific to each developmental phase it extends into. This multiple meaning is what complicates the prognosis insofar as to eliminate the symptom all of the meanings may need to be processed by the child.

The advent of nighttime pull-ups that now allow for absorbency but discomfort being wet should help. Children may wish to regulate the body function more effectively once they are physically uncomfortable from being wet. Most children know the negative social consequences of wetting, especially diurnal wetting, and make efforts to deal with it. Soiling among older children is more rare and may unconsciously have to do, as mentioned above, with the stool being treated like a person that a child wishes, concretely, to hold onto because of an insecure attachment. Parents can be reassured that almost all children will have achieved bladder and bowel control by the time puberty is reached. This late age may offer little consolation to most parents.

Eating Problems

Eating difficulties seem to be a common concern of parents. With the newborn, breastfeeding, if chosen, can be a difficulty for some women. For some women, nipples can hurt, baby's sucking response may be weak, and milk production may be minimal. We have discussed the issues coloring a decision to nurse or bottle-feed. Weaning and how and when to do it needs to be considered. The child may communicate a readiness to wean by showing less interest in the breast or bottle. Often, getting bit on the nipple becomes a motivator for the mother to consider weaning, as the child's teeth start to erupt and interest grows in more solid foods.

In our culture, nursing rarely extends beyond a year and a half in duration. Mothers become embarrassed when a two or three year old publicly asks to nurse. There are some mothers who are very insistent on the benefits of extended periods of breastfeeding. This is based, in our culture, on the psychological advantages for mother and baby, and less so for nutritional gains. There are groups such as La Leche that advocate for the practice. My own observation is that in many instances it is extended more for the mother's needs than for the child's. A major difficulty is that the mother's breast is not the best venue for the resolution of anger directed at mother once a child gets teeth.

When children enter the period when toilet mastery is starting, certain foods are avoided that can remind them of their body products. They do not like the color or dislike touching the food. They are beginning to erect defenses against a natural interest in their eliminated body products and this tendency generalizes to things that are similar in looks. Becoming clean is a conflicted goal so touching finger food can become conflictual. Use of utensils will take time to master. It's a good idea to let children "mess" with their food earlier, during their first two years, insofar as pleasure doing so can reinforce pleasure in eating and interest in foods.

There are more and more reports of eating disorders among school age children, especially among girls, a problem of endemic proportions among adolescent girls and young adult females in our culture. There is so much emphasis in the media on a standard of slimness for women, especially, that girls become very conscious of their weight. They diet to an extreme causing a psychophysiological condition called anorexia nervosa. Sometimes the eating disorder takes on the characteristic of binge eating followed by purging, what is called bulimia. Both are much more prevalent in adolescence and I will discuss the topic again later in Chapter 15.

School age kids can become vegetarian or vegans, usually temporarily, but for some, the beginning of a life choice, especially if reinforced by parental inclinations. More commonly, children develop food fads and/or food avoidances. It is common for children to dislike vegetables, much to the consternation of parents. Eating a balanced meal becomes a family creed and many a family meal can be an unpleasant experience for all when the child refuses some foods despite parental admonishments.

Eating habits are established early in life. Parents need not pressure children to eat. They should provide healthy foods and let their toddler self-regulate what he or she consume. It may take a child as much as twenty times to eat a particular kind of food before they decide they like it. Parents can have confidence that a child ultimately will eat in a growth promoting way. Parents can encourage adventurousness about what can be eaten but not insist upon it. What one tries to avoid is a power struggle. Children will always win to no one's benefit. All that struggles promote are children choosing to eat only a limited range of foods. Parents should not be expected to prepare a different meal for each child. But parents can plan menus that take into account the different tastes of children compared to adults. That way every meal will be more acceptable to all concerned. When it is not a family meal, it makes sense to prepare macaroni and cheese rather than cordon bleu. Parents can be reassured that most children broaden their tastes as they get older.

Parents are models for their children. If they overeat, eat unhealthy foods, and buy "junk food," it is likely that their children will copy them. This may be one determinant for the presence of an increase in obesity in children.

Learning Problems

Parents want their children to do well in school. This is the foundation for later achievement and competence. Teachers are much more aware these days that children differ as to learning styles. Underachievement, in some instances, in the past may have been the result of educational expectations that children conform to a method of teaching incompatible with their learning style. In such circumstances children get bored. This recognition makes teaching more difficult but modern teachers are being trained to accommodate their methods to the broader range of learning styles. While this makes intuitive sense, and experienced teachers espouse the existence of different learning styles among children, the evidence from empirical research does not support this viewpoint. The latest research suggests that varying the type of material to be learned results in a more lasting effect on the brain. It is like providing more neural connections for the material. An analogy would be an athlete mixing strength, speed and skill exercises in his or her workouts. It seems to me, however, that motivation to learn would be greater if the learner experienced the learning via a sensory mode believed to be a strength rather than a weakness. Thus, it would appear that the jury is still out on this.

Many elementary school aged children are given the diagnosis of ADD or ADHD, which connote, respectively, attention deficit and attention deficit/hyperactivity disorders. These children are then put on stimulant drugs that have a paradoxical effect, namely, they seem to calm the recipient. My own impression is that these diagnoses have been over applied and too many children have been put on a drug regimen whose long-term side effects are unknown. I believe that inattention and hyperactivity describe behaviors that can have different underlying causes. Professionals have not made these distinctions enough. Presumably, there are some children with such behaviors whose central nervous systems are functioning abnormally to cause these disruptive behaviors. These children benefit from a drug like Ritalin. I contend, however, that a majority of these disruptive children are manifesting these behaviors because they are anxious or that their particular learning styles are being ignored. For those children who are anxious, supportively listening to them may be sufficient, and if not, then psychotherapy and not drugs, may be more potent. For those who are bored or disregarded by educational methods, then a master teacher consulting to the classroom teacher might be the answer. Drugs are expedient and are not a good model, except as a last resort, for children in a culture where recreational drug taking is commonplace.

Sibling Rivalry

I was not sure under which section to put my thoughts on sibling rivalry. This was partly because it is so ubiquitous. It also can be life long, so it could be addressed under different age periods. Siblings have only one set of parents and they do not usually like sharing them. If you are an only child you may be wondering why is this so. As an only child you have wished, maybe even cajoled your parents to have another child. You have thought it would be great to have a playmate and a lifetime companion and friend who has shared common experiences. There is truth to these sentiments. It is also true, in families with more than a single child, that a sibling has likely harbored, not necessarily consciously, rivalrous thoughts and maybe even wishes to get rid of another. Siblings often think the other receives preferred treatment from a parent.

While this belief may be greatly exaggerated, it often can have some truth. Parents like to believe that they love all of their children equally and maybe consciously they do, although I do not know how you can quantify this to prove or disprove the assertion. In any case, unwittingly a parent may have feelings and thoughts about a child that may not have originated with that child but instead with someone from their own past. This phenomenon is called transference and is universal. It happens with everyone in our lives. You may, for example, transfer feelings originating with a parent or sibling onto your boss. Hence, parents do treat each child somewhat differently. Recognizing this, parents can make deliberative efforts to try to be fair.

One sib may envy another's being older, taller, having blue eyes, being more slender, wearing teeth braces, developing breasts earlier, and so on and on. Or the focus could be on talents or athletic skills, or on intelligence for academics, or on social skills and so on and on. Envy breeds resentment and wishes to sabotage. Competitiveness between siblings will not necessarily vanish in future decades as they age. Emulation, however, is also possible. A sib can vow to be just like an admired other sib in some respect.

Extended family dynamics are often dominated by sibling rivalries that extend over many years in duration. These feelings may be just beneath the surface but are able to ignite at extended family gatherings, e.g., the legendary reunions at a Christmas dinner or after the funeral of a family member. It is not uncommon for siblings to fight over the disbursement of family heirlooms, memorabilia, furniture, etc., after both parents are deceased.

How are parents to deal with sibling rivalry? I think that first they have to recognize it and acknowledge it. Parents can endeavor to be fair and this may considerably reduce sibling rivalry, especially among older sibs who have acquired some insight. In my view, being fair does not mean providing the same for each child or arranging the same enrichment for each child. Each child is an individual with unique needs, skills and talents. Children are capable of recognizing this reality and are able to appreciate parents doing so, too. But being fair in setting limits, showing affection, disciplining, and so on, may not be perceived to be so, despite a parent's best efforts. As the children get older they can be encouraged to settle their differences directly with each other, and not use a parent as an intermediary. Some children will gravitate towards one parent to try to get them to support their grievance and get them as an advocate to lobby on their behalf with the other parent in family disputes. Spouses can avoid this and present a united position in many instances. They can, at least, agree that the older children settle their differences directly with one another.

Developmental Conflicts

A developmental conflict is unavoidable and even can be beneficial for a child because of the growth promoting consequences of a successful struggle with the conflict. An example of this kind of conflict is the Oedipal Complex, discussed in Chapter 7. Its reappearance in later developmental phases, discussed below, reintroduces conflict and another growth promoting opportunity. Childhood is a time of many fears, but these are not disorders. They are a result of limited cognitive abilities of a child to understand an experience or maybe even inborn in some instances. They are usually temporary and respond well to clarifications and explanations offered by an adult. Fears of thunder, e.g., may be inborn and have to do with evolutionary genetics. Phobias, on the other hand are fears that are part of so-called psychoneuroses.

Psychoneuroses

Psychoneuroses are symptoms that result from maladaptive resolutions of mental conflict. Sometimes they are transitory and/

or stage (phase)-limited, although sometimes psychoneuroses can endure over a number of years. I need to present some theory here. These conflicts occur within the mind when competing and contradictory demands are made upon it. Originally, conflict was between the child and the parent as representative of the external world. The wish for candy causes a demand (in our model) to be made upon the mind to act in order to satisfy this desire. A parent may thwart a child's desire for candy. This is an external conflict. After many similar interactions, a representation of a prohibiting parent is internalized. Now conflict can be between the wish for candy and the internalized representation of the prohibiting parent. We call the collection of prohibitory images the conscience. The child's mind (in our model, specifically the executive part) will feel anxious, and must mediate between desire and internal and/or external prohibition. The solution, in our example, might be for the child to secretly stash candy away and consume it when the parent is absent and later to feel guilty, or consume it if the conscience can be seduced into leniency by a rationalization. Or the child might never again eat candy. All these solutions can become symptomatic and are maladaptive and neurotic. This simplified example is what we mean by neurotic conflict.

"One-shot" instances usually do not result in neurotic conflict except if traumatic. The prerequisites for the formation of a neurosis require sufficient mental structures, as illustrated in Chapter 5 in our model of neurotic conflict. Recall, a mental structure is a collection of mental processes of unlimited duration of existence. An example of a structure would be a mental agency such as the conscience. When psychoanalysts use the term symptom we mean a behavior that is a compromise between a wish and a defense. In other words, a symptom is the compromise between a wish and adherence to the constraints of reality (as represented by an internal regulatory structure). The symptom when analyzed contains elements traceable back to the components of the neurotic conflict, namely, wish, defense, and usually guilt. You can decipher these in the behavior of a child who secretly stores candy. The development of psychoneuroses requires that at least the phallic-oedipal phase has been reached.

There are different kinds of classes of psychoneuroses based on typical dynamics [conflicts] and symptoms, e.g., phobias, anxiety hysteria, hysterical conversions, anxiety disorders, and obsessive-compulsive symptoms. In childhood, psychoneuroses are often mixed, i.e., having symptoms reflective of conflict from different levels. Insofar as my focus is not on psychopathology, I will present descriptions of the different neuroses in a brief manner.

In phobias, a classical example would be an anxiety that a particular kind of experience will result in injury or death. Analysis will reveal that the fear of death is symbolic of injury to the body, in concrete terms, castration. The thing imagined to cause the injury is a displacement from a significant figure, e.g., father. So a boy may fear horses that will bite him, instead of father injuring his genitals. In anxiety hysteria there is a repression of Oedipal wishes in an attempt to avoid conflict. The mind is unsuccessful despite employment of phobic or obsessive defenses. The mind of the child remains apprehensive that repressed wishes will return to consciousness and anxiety can be intense. If repression has to be assiduously maintained it can spread and a pseudo-stupidity can result as a symptom. In hysterical conversion, there is also repression of Oedipal wishes and ensuing conflict, as the mind converts the conflict mainly to a somatic symptom. Abdominal pains can be a symbolic hysterical equivalent of labor pains resulting from a girl's competitive wishes towards a pregnant mother. In an anxiety neurosis there is a free floating anxiety that may at times feel like panic. In obsessive-compulsive neurosis, Oedipal wishes and fantasies are not acceptable to the conscious mind, causing guilt and anxiety. There is a regression to an anal-sadistic level and this augments the guilt already felt. Magical thinking, characteristic of the mind during the early years, along with a whole host of defenses is employed, resulting in the obsessional and compulsive symptoms. An example might be a child who has to rearrange the bed's pillows repeatedly before being able to go to sleep. If the child does not "get it right" he or she will feel anxious. Presumably, the arrangement has to be a perfect and specific as a way to ward off some imagined dreaded event. In neurotic depression, depressive feelings are reactive to events like a disappointment or loss (e.g., a separation or ending of a relationship).

These feelings are not thought to have a biological etiology. The depressive feelings can be accompanied by anxiety. In many instances unconscious guilt feelings underlie the depressive feelings. An important dynamic is an unconscious symbolic meaning of the experienced loss. For example, a person might get a job promotion but become depressed because they have lost a less desirable position, which satisfied a need to be punished for perceived Oedipal triumph. You can see that the evolution of psychoneuroses often involves Oedipal dynamics.

A type of dynamic therapy, e.g., child psychoanalysis, is the treatment of choice for these disturbances. Parental involvement is part of this intervention. Such interventions can be of great help. Parents need to insure that they are referred to a properly trained child analyst. I will discuss this further in Chapter 22.

Delinquency

Delinquency describes behavior that is due to a poorly consolidated inner morality, or conscience, or the consequence of one that is modeled on sociopathic adults. Healthy guilt cannot be utilized to help regulate urges. The delinquent child takes whatever he or she wants without feeling guilt or later contrition. Their only regret is getting caught. Sometimes such behavior can look delinquent but the underlying cause may be an attempted resolution of a mental conflict, i.e., the child may be seeking to be punished as a neurotic compromise between desire and prohibition (neurotic delinquency). We will say more about this when we discuss adolescence.

Super-Intelligence

It may seem counter-intuitive to you that such a section is included in a chapter dealing with early childhood disturbances. Being very intelligent ordinarily is considered an asset, but, regretfully, it can include a particular risk. In the case of **very** intelligent children, a keen precocious social awareness can occur before the mind is developed sufficiently to be able to regulate intense drives and feelings. Because of their sharp awareness, these children are very sensitive to nuances of social judgment that less intelligent children ordinarily are unaware of. I am thinking here about normal exuberant, noisy and crude behavior of young children that many adults can find intrusive and unacceptable. A potential consequence for these children is to experience external disapproval. They begin to have an expectation of disapproval and a general inhibition can result. They will not be able to capitalize on their keen intelligence in the interest of social adaptation and will be awkward in relating to others. Some of these children in school resort to clowning as a neurotic maneuver to disarm imagined disapproving peers or adults. Sensitive parenting can be very helpful to such a child. Parents can help these children to use their keen intelligence to process their feelings.

The opposite sort of imbalance is also possible. That is, some children who are very intelligent may have precocious egos demonstrated in creative and imaginative fantasying, advanced understanding of the external world, but their internal ego controls and "inner policeman" (conscience) may be delayed, perhaps because of the inability of their parents to set limits. Such children may have difficulties in impulse control and could have difficulties in complying with classroom expectations of decorum.

Chapter 9
Latency

Latency for the majority of children extends roughly from age six through ten. Hence, it coincides with entry into primary school and ends with the advent of the earliest signs of puberty, what we term the "preadolescent years." The term latency is meant to convey that the powerful drives or urges of the preceding years, especially the Oedipal years, have receded and their power *vis-à-vis* the executive part of the mind, have been diminished. While the balance of power has shifted, it is not true that the latency child can "forget about" sexual and aggressive wishes throughout latency. One only has to observe boys touching their genitals, what has been felicitously termed "pocket pool," to appreciate that sexual (libidinal) drives do not disappear, or to see the meanness of a group of latency age girls against a peer that has been banished from the group to recognize that aggression also has not expired. This biphasic development of the ascendency and retreat of the strength of drives is uniquely human.

The role of the Latency Period of development is to consolidate gains and prepare the child (the mind) for the onslaught of puberty. That is, with puberty, the drives strengthen in power and are once again in ascendancy vis-à-vis the part of the mind that directs executive functioning (e.g., judgment, reasoning, etc.), the negotiator between the inner and outer worlds. With puberty, maturation of the genitals and reproductive system takes place and genital drives demand to be gratified. With puberty, such drives can potentially be discharged and gratified in mature ways, unlike earlier in age. However, drives from earlier phases, what are termed pre-genital ones, the oral, anal, urethral, and phallic drives, are also strengthened and clamor for expression. This renewed strength of the drives threatens the defenses set up against their expression. So, the mind of the pubertal child has to have been reinforced in its defenses and coping skills *vis-à-vis* the drives during latency to withstand the surge of drives in puberty.

By withstanding we essentially mean for the mind to have developed a resistance to regression. Under the pressure of the drives, the child (the mind) could succumb to the expression of less mature ways of gratifying them if the executive part of the mind was not reinforced. The strengthening of the conscience is another attainment of the latency years. Recall, it was internalized in a more completed manner, reinforcing a primitive conscience, at the time of the dissolution of the Oedipal Complex, resulting in entry into the Latency Phase. Together, the executive component of the mind and the conscience, ally themselves against the strengthened drives of puberty. It is analogous to the strengthening of levees after a strong hurricane that breached them so that hopefully this will not happen again when another even stronger hurricane occurs.

The standards of groups that latency age children affiliate with help support the internalized but still relatively weak conscience. Groups such as the Cub Scouts, Brownies, athletic teams, can provide a code of ethics and standards of sportsmanship that help to strengthen the conscience. Children engage in competitive games and are very cognizant of the rules of the game that they adhere to, so that cheating is frowned upon. During the latency years religious training may also begin for some children and this, too, strengthens the immature "inner helper" of early childhood. Educational efforts in school also encourage ethical choices.

With the relative weakening of the drives, the mind can pay more attention to reality and mastery over it. Latency is a time to focus on and learn about the world. Around age eight there is a significant change in the formal properties of thinking, from immature to more mature. It is no wonder that the beginning of formal education coincides with entering Latency for most children. Amassing knowledge about the world allows children to feel more comfortable outside of their nuclear family. Adults that are not relatives, such as teachers, librarians, coaches, clergy, can be related to. Further information about the world can be imparted to young minds and thereby expanding their familiarity with the world even further. However, latency age children continue to identify with aspects of their parents in various ways. Via identification (internalization) they broaden their repertoire of interests and skills and thereby enrich the strength and competency of their egos. Latency age children are eager to learn.

The development of practical skills and comfort engaging the world outside the boundaries of the family all contribute to a sense of competency. This feeling about oneself is a great asset that contributes to feelings of self-worth, self-esteem, and self-reliance. The image of oneself as competent will help one recover quickly from feelings of helplessness which are unavoidably experienced at various times in a lifetime. That one basically feels they can be reliant on one's own inner resources will help, not hinder, asking for help when needed.

Speech and language are utilized a great deal by latency age children. Sometimes speech is used more to hide and shield than to communicate, e.g., outright lying, or the use of "pig Latin" with initiated friends to exclude others, and the use of text messaging with its encryption among modern preteens and teenagers. But speech is mainly used to communicate to others one's feelings, inner thoughts, knowledge, organizational plans, etc. There is less use of the body to express feelings and a greater reliance on words to label and articulate feelings. There continues to be less use of action to communicate. Fantasy, an organized narrative, is distinguished from rational thought during these years. Nevertheless, belief in magic, the power of thoughts, can still be strong. For example, a latency age child will chant the admonishment "step on a crack, break your mother's back," although in jest, nevertheless conveying its power. Fantasy is most often unconscious, distinguishing it from daydreams.

We encourage our children to use their words, but sometimes beginning with latency, children use curse words and adults become upset about this. They are discovering that some words have a power that can upset adults. Of course, if parents use these words, it should not surprise them that their children will imitate them. I think if a parent reacts in a calm way these words can be demystified and reduce the shock value of them for the child. The task is to clarify that the "f word" has been subverted from connoting a private activity involving love, intimacy, and pleasure between two consenting adults to one involving coercion and violence, thereby becoming insulting and derogatory. This may seem to be a daunting task (see Chapter 11 for suggestions about sex education) but remember that children can comprehend more than we give them credit for. I think that the child is partly experimenting with the power of words, having observed that such words are provocative. This is a good opportunity for parents to have a meaningful discussion with their child about social awareness and social manners, crudity versus civility, catharsis versus articulate verbal expression, forgivable transgressions versus punishable ones, etc. The discussion by parents with their child need not be complicated. It can include an explanation of the social effects of using these words. In most instances the value of these words to get adults upset will dwindle away. We should encourage our children to express their angry feelings without being disrespectful.

The achievement of rational thinking does not come easy. The latency age child can still believe in magic and accept correlation as causation, especially when anxious or fearful. I am reminded of a joke about two nine-year old boys who are sharing a hospital room. They ask each other what operation each is undergoing the next day. One says a tonsillectomy and the other recalls how great it was after he had that procedure at age four to be able to eat all the ice cream he desired post-operatively. The other indicates he is having a circumcision. The other boy says that is not so great. After his at 8 days old he could not walk for a year!

In creative activities, like in the arts and drama, regression when controlled by the ego can be very useful. It can allow the artist, playwright, or actor to be creative. Latency age children can become very interested in creative expression. There is a suspension of reality testing during fantasying. Both regression in the service of the ego and fantasying allow for the magic of the unconscious to imbue the rationality of the ego with a sense of wonder that vitalizes our experiences. But, during creating art or witnessing an artistic event and engaging in fantasy the mind (ego) does not abandon its allegiance to reality.

The use of mental processes to control drive expressions through suppressing, inhibiting, and modifying is relied upon during the latency years. The armamentarium of these mental processes, called defenses, is expanded. Some of the more prominent ones are repression, isolation of affect, displacement, projection, externalization, and reaction formation. In repression the mental representation of a forbidden idea or feeling is kept securely out of conscious awareness. In isolation of affect only the idea can enter conscious awareness, not the connected feeling. In displacement, a recipient is chosen who is different but linked to the intended recipient of a conflicted drive expression. In projection one unconsciously attributes a conflicted wish to someone else and then consciously claims the recipient is directing the wish at him or her. In externalization one attributes an unwanted aspect of one's own self-image to another person. In reaction formation one is aware only of a feeling opposite to one unconsciously felt towards another, e.g., awareness of loving feelings and not hating feelings. There are numerous other defenses. While named defenses are frequently used, **any** mental process can be utilized by the mind (supported by its conscience) as a defense against an unacceptable thought and/or feeling.

Some learning difficulties in children are due to the secondary interference of defenses. For example, if a child needs to squelch their sexual curiosity, for whatever reason, curiosity in general may suffer and this would affect learning. Or if a child needs to deny a painful reality, links between aspects of the denied reality to other components of reality will be disconnected and this could affect learning. When a topic is repressed from consciousness, associative links may not be readily available to memory and affect learning. Such learning disorders have a neurotic etiology.

Latency is a time period when sexual (libidinal) or aggressive drives can have their respective, erotic and destructive, aims modified to more socially acceptable ones. Exhibitionistic display in contemporary fashion is an acceptable erotic expression, as long as it does not go over an acceptable line. Athletics is an activity where aggression can be expressed in forms that society does not punish nor try to induce guilt about. In football, for example, a fearsome tackle is applauded, not condemned. Through various hobbies, collections, and interests, derivative drive expressions can be invested in without social disapprobation. The psychoanalysis of people of all ages indicates that such endeavors owe their origin to erotic or aggressive drives where the aims were successfully transformed (sublimated or de-aggressivized) beginning in latency. Hobbies of all kinds engage children during these years and often are sustained during the whole life span. Musical and dance skills often begin and success seems to be based on inborn talent, an asset that not all children possess. If a child has a passion for music or dance he or she will not need to be pressured to practice. Athletic success also seems to be based on inborn talent.

I do not advocate coercing children to practice. I do suggest encouragement. The latency age child can be engaged in a discussion of the level of skill he or she wants to attain. A discussion can then follow as to how much practice will be necessary to attain the particular ambition held by the child. In this manner a child can feel they participated in a decision about how much to practice.

During latency allowances are probably introduced for the first time. My own sense is that it need not be more than a token sum during these years. The child should be permitted to spend it on whatever they want, assuming it is healthy and safe, although saving the allowance can be encouraged. I suggest that the allowance be connected up with the child being responsible for some token family chore at this age, for example, making their bed.

Parents often ask children to be responsible for a pet at this age. For example, they may be asked to walk a dog. My own belief is that this sort of responsibility, in some instances, may need to be postponed till they are pre-adolescents when they become more reliable. Pets can be very important in the life of a child. I am thinking of the companionship that a pet like a dog or cat can provide. For lonely children this can be invaluable. A child will have the opportunity to show affection and consideration towards another living creature and receive back affection and loyalty. In some instances they will need to be responsible for providing food, water, and exercise for their pet. If done well, I think it can only enhance a sense of competency. Of course, if the child seems to not have an inclination for a pet, the added responsibilities that parents may put on their child's shoulders will only feel like a burden and any positive outcome for the child will be diminished.

The attitudes of each gender towards one another differ during the latency years. Boys demean girls and exclude them. Some girls long to be included and comprise a group of girls we call "tomboys." These girls wish to participate in the more physical activities of boys and in play involving "masculine" themes, e.g., pretend warfare. Such girls often decry girlish clothes and play with dolls, but some tomboys do not and engage in both boyish and girlish activities. Also, even staunch tomboys often become feminine in late adolescence or early adulthood. Boys and girls that like each other will chase each other during school recess. If confronted by the other or someone else about whether or not they like the child they are chasing, the answer will be 'No." Sometimes they will go a step further and say they "hate" the child they are chasing. If the truth is known the child is convinced teasing will result.

Boys often have fewer friends than girls. Boys can have a chum with whom they are very close. When boys enter latency, they often have a foray back into the pre-oedipal days, so that oral and anal themes are never far away. How brief the foray is depends on the strength of pre-latency fixations. Recall, fixations are vulnerable earlier points in a person's developmental history. Boys may identify with mother to fend off her enveloping embrace that they regressively long for but are scared of, causing them to become anxious. The defense of identification backfires and the bisexual implications scare them. Closeness with boys can follow and is partly an evasive "homosexual" defense. This defense allows them not to invest in a wish for a baby or for breasts but instead to focus on masculine activities with a male friend. At times of transitions, when there is a tendency for regression to pre-oedipal closeness with mother, boys will defend against giving in to these wishes by reaching out to their own gender. It is "homosexual" **descriptively** only because of the sameness of gender. We will see it again during the transitions from latency to preadolescence, and from preadolescence to early adolescence. Girls generally have more successfully left behind the pre-oedipal connections to mother when they enter Latency. For some girls this may be because of their disappointment with her or their Oedipal rivalry with her. It is also more acceptable for girls to identify with mother than it is for boys to do so. Boys, on the other hand, have never really "let go" of mother. She is the primordial model for the future woman they will choose to have as a partner.

Presumably, in earliest infancy there existed a "unity" between mother and child. We theorize that this unity was a "blissful" union between infant and mother. This is speculative insofar as we cannot ask the infant to articulate their feelings. Mothers, however, will confirm how they felt as "one" with their fetus during pregnancy. We observe at various times in development during transitions, especially, regressive tendencies to re-establish pre-oedipal ties to mother. At the same time, there are signs of fear in the child of engulfment by the mother. Some have speculated there is an unconscious wish in the minds of children and mothers to re-establish the "unity" that once existed, to regain an undifferentiated state. If this is so, it is an ambivalent wish insofar as children also seem to have an inborn inclination to separate and be autonomous individuals, which mothers also support. Perhaps, the wish is gratified symbolically in the creative arts?

Girls form cliques and they are very exclusive. A lot of mean spiritedness towards outsiders can be expressed. If you are an outsider and it is important to be part of the group, this exclusion can be very painful. While boys are more outwardly aggressive and destructive, such backbiting by girls can be very hurtful. Some girls may feign illness in order to miss school when they are in the midst of these ostracisms. Identifications are endemic and are based on envy rather than on emulation. Despite the interpersonal drama, lifelong friendships among girls are capable. For some adult women, small groups of women can revive the schoolyard dynamics of their childhood. For both genders, heroes come to be important. For girls it is often media celebrities such as rock musical stars. While for boys this is also true, sport celebrities can be heroes. Parents can have a difficult time with their child's selection of a hero insofar as they often cannot see anything redeeming in the choice. As kids get older, choices will be based more on emulation than on envy.

Mid-latency would be the earliest I would consider sending a child off to sleep-away camp, perhaps for a week's duration, during the summer. I think pre-adolescents can handle such separations with greater ease and for longer durations. The experience can be very worthwhile in several ways. Lifetime recreational skills can be mastered, lifetime friendships can be fostered, and an increased sense of competency is possible. I would not, however, insist that children go to camp if they were strongly opposed to it. They must be ready for the experience.

In these contemporary times, mention should be paid to computers and other technology that will start to grab the focus of children beginning in late Latency. It once was not acceptable to be known as a "geek." This label once was an exclusive insult directed at technology-interested boys. Now to be called a "geek" or a "techie" is an honorarium directed at both sexes. Computers, cell phones, handheld Internet gadgets, i-pods, etc., are all part of the scene of children, particularly pre-adolescents and adolescents, but also among many latency age children. I am not sure what impact this has on intimacy. If you always are in touch with friends via cell phone, either talking or texting, does this increase intimacy or is it superficial? Does texting diminish face-to-face communication? Some older children stay up late on a school night in order to text and are tired the next morning. If you are listening to music on your i-pod and never make eye contact with passing people do you feel isolated or involved?

I do not think use of this technology has been around long enough to understand if it has an impact on the mind and on social relationships and what the quality of the impact is. I am concerned about children being allowed to play mindless interactive violent games on a handheld device, despite the fact that ratings should alert parents to the content. Some children spend an inordinate amount of time gaming. While there is not strong evidence that such violent games cause violent behavior, my concern is that children who are "gamers" live in a virtual reality rather than engage in the real world. Will this affect their awareness of social reality? Do adolescents lose sight of their physical limitations when in a cyberspace game they may take on new virtual identities (avatars) wherein they are omnipotent and where their virtual bodies have no physical limitations? Does this delay coming to terms with their changing pubertal physical bodies?

You can see we have more questions than answers at this point. The only thing of value I can intuit is that engaging such video games results in good eye-thumb coordination, and I would discourage use of such programs.

In this age of the Internet, parents can help their older latency age children understand about responsible and safe use of emailing, instant messaging, downloading cell phone digital photos (e.g., "sexting," wherein one sends provocative photos of oneself), engaging in Internet chat rooms, and web sites like My Space, Facebook, and YouTube. They need to understand the responsible use of free speech and to be wary of predators.

Parenting latency age children can be very fulfilling for both parent and child. It is a time when a child will still want to spend time with a parent doing activities. The activities chosen can include interests of the parent. Younger children may insist on fantasy play, an activity some adults may not be interested in. But the latency child is more interested in the world and learning about it. Parents can have their child accompany them to a sporting event, or coach a team that a child plays on. A child can sit through a concert or join in a trip to a museum for an extended time period, unlike a younger child whose interest likely will soon wane. Card games and board games will hold interest for a latency child. More complicated games like chess can be introduced. Family vacation options will broaden beyond Disneyland type venues.

Some fathers of latency age boys will have to come to terms with the fact that their son is not athletically inclined. Worse yet, the boy may be physically awkward and uncoordinated. For some fathers this will be difficult, especially for those who value athletics. More than whether or not you can throw and catch a football can define masculinity. I am sure there are parallels with mothers and daughters. The important thing is that our children fulfill their own unique potentialities and derive pleasure, satisfaction, and competence doing so.

Latency age children will be paying close attention to how their parents deal with other people. Are they polite or impolite, generous or stingy, respectful or disrespectful, civil or bossy, etc? They will notice if parents "walk the talk." Does their parent demand that they say "Please," but rarely does so him or herself when asking something of another person? Insofar as a child's conscience is a force to be reckoned with, they will use it against their parents as well. It is also an opportunity to further help them establish a conscience that has a sizeable reasonable component. If a parent acts reasonably with their children, they will likely be so with themselves and others too. The ability of a parent to apologize will go a long ways and helps their child to do similarly too. Parents best model thinking that is rational, reasonable, inquisitive, creative, and decisive. Parents likely have encouraged their children to "use" their "words" and parents need to as well to model that you can express feelings in a regulated and controlled manner.

A latency age child may be interested in what a parent does at their "work." A parent can talk about it and, if practical, even show their workplace to a son or daughter. It is beneficial for them see a parent who is competent and respected by others.

Interest in a child's schooling will strengthen their interest. If parents take the time to meet with a child's teachers and, if practical, become a room parent or volunteer for school trips, this can be very supportive to their child. Assistance given for school projects like a science fair can provide them with a model of thoughtfulness and perseverance. A parent best try not to be a model for procrastination. This trait if adopted by a child is difficult to be rid of and will be very burdensome throughout life. Being a "workaholic" also is not a trait to be admired. Parents can hope that their child will emulate a reasonable work ethic, as well as a capacity to have fun.

Chapter 10
Divorce: Helping Children Cope

Divorce is a very difficult time for all family members. This is an understatement. It's often an upheaval because of a change in living arrangements and often it involves changes in life style because of economic considerations. As we have said earlier, children thrive on routine and divorce involves multiple changes. As much as sensitive parents try to insulate their child from witnessing spousal arguments, when parents are feeling estranged from each other, children also will not witness demonstrations of affection and cooperative behavior between these parents.

Should parents remain in an unhappy marriage because of children? The child will still witness the lack of love and intimacy between parents that remain married so the possible benefits of avoiding disruption may be cancelled out. Assuming the couple has made a genuine attempt to improve the marriage but failed, it seems to me divorce allows for the possibility of each parent eventually finding a better life and becoming a more happy and involved parent. Of course, a parent will need to deal empathically with the repercussions of the divorce on a child. In families with multiple children, each child's different reaction to the divorce needs to be attended to. Parents involved in a divorce often are preoccupied with their own unhappiness, or if they have been divorced for a while, parents may feel lonely and preoccupied with changing this for him or her. As a consequence, children can be neglected, especially if a downward economic situation causes a mother to return to work outside the home.

Children, especially young ones, are very egocentric or self-centered in their thinking. There is also the magical thinking that colors their immature cognitive processing. The consequence of this is to blame oneself for the divorce. If the parents have bickered because of differences in child rearing beliefs, children will feel responsible for parental arguments. They will deduce that their birth was the beginning of such arguments and caused their parents not to love each other anymore. Or a child will think that if he or she were a more satisfying child the parent would have decided not to leave the marriage. If children harbor a wish, albeit maybe not even a conscious one, for parents to separate, the boy or girl may feel responsible. Struggling with such a wish is a common dynamic during the Oedipal years. It may be buried deep within the recesses of the mind, but, nevertheless, if the wish comes true the child likely will experience guilt. Some children will take on a mediator role. They may enact this more openly with friends who are in dispute, and more subtly with parents who argue. This sense of needing to mediate or to protect a parent perceived to be the weaker of the two parents is very burdensome to a child. After all, a child needs to feel that the adults in their life are protecting he or she and not vice versa. After a divorce of their parents, a child may become very watchful of the mood of a parent and may feel that it is their responsibility to cheer them up if they appear depressed lest they may leave and abandon the child.

Parents can help mitigate but not eradicate such self-blame by talking to their children about the reasons for the divorce, emphasizing that the child is not to blame. Some reasons for a decision to separate might have to be omitted until the child is older and asks for more details and can understand better. I am thinking here of a reason such as infidelity. It is important that parents do not blame the spouse for the divorce, or "bad-mouth" the spouse in front of the child. Remember that the child has deep ties to each parent and blame can lead to hatred and estrangement. When divorced spouses are very angry with each other this may be difficult not to do, but it is worth it for the child's sake. Sometimes ex-spouses take out their anger for the other in ways that directly or indirectly hurt the child. For example, holding out on financial obligations until the last minute, not arriving for visitation on schedule so the ex-spouse is inconvenienced, etc., will hurt the child too. Children hope that their divorced parents will reconcile. They may also feel responsible for reconciling their parents. An unconscious belief in their own omnipotence stimulates such efforts.

Custody decisions need to be made with the best interests of the child given priority. Remember that young children like stability, and the living arrangements should accommodate this. If so, children should not be shuttled back and forth between the divorced parents so that each has "equal time" with the children. It is thoughtful if living arrangements are concentrated in one household and visitation occurs within the other. An ideal arrangement is for the family house or apartment to be maintained and the parents shuttle in and out. This way the family space is not disrupted and children, especially young ones, are least unsettled. Of course, for such an arrangement, spouses must feel amiable towards each other and also practical considerations likely will make such an ideal arrangement impractical. When choosing separate domiciles, preferably they are within close proximity to one another. For the latency age and older child, this will allow a walk or bicycle ride over to the other parent in a spontaneous way if there is a special need.

If a divorced parent is dating, this best occurs in a discreet way. What I mean is that it does not benefit the child to be introduced to and be involved with every person a parent is engaged with in a relationship. This is to be avoided because of the feelings of loss that could be engendered if a connection is established and the relationship ends. If there is a serious relationship that will endure and maybe become permanent then introductions and involvements will inevitably happen. Here a divorced parent benefits their child if they establish a working relationship with their ex-spouse's new partner. A divorced parent can indicate to their child that it is all right to establish a good relationship with father's or mother's new partner. A parent needs to let their child know this will not hurt the parent's feelings. If there is ill will the child will sense it and loyalty issues will ensue.

Perhaps a divorced parent remarries. The new partner may have children and may even be a primary custodial parent. These arrangements are known as blended families. Stepparents now enter the picture. This can be a difficult relationship for former spouses and the new spouse. This also can be difficult for the stepparent and stepchild. Each knows they are not the biological parent or child. Recall the brothers Grimm's mythic tale of Snow White illustrating the fury of an envious stepmother towards her beautiful stepdaughter. How much authority does the stepparent have and what compliance does the stepchild need to have with them? Each blended family will need to work on this and establish sensible and practical guidelines. I think it is sensible for the adults to acknowledge the difficulties and confusion that may beset their children and affirm the tie to the biological parent. With time and multiple empathic interchanges between stepparent and stepchild, a good relationship can develop, loving and growth promoting for each participant.

Likely, there is an inborn incest barrier between biological parent and child. In the case of a stepparent and stepchild this will be absent. The presence of such a barrier, regrettably, does not prevent incest or sexual abuse, nor will its absence necessarily cause sexual abuse. Even in intact families, issues of modesty and over stimulation remain and need to be on the radar screen, too, of blended families.

What if the blended family brings together children from each partner? They may be of similar ages and the same or different gender. Step-sibs need to be dealt with. In many instances this can be a fulfilling relationship for a lifetime. But for others it can be strained. There can be issues of favoritism of a stepparent towards their biological child, or perception of such on the part of a child about the stepparent. A stepparent needs to be aware of this and fairness be accepted as a goal. Strain can enter if a blended family has two adolescents of similar age but opposite gender. Sexual attraction can be an underlying determinant of a tense relationship between the two. Friction and bickering may be defensively employed as a way of keeping distance between each other. Presumably, once each establishes a heterosexual relationship outside the family, the tension will remit. But until it does remit, the biological parent and stepparent can offer to be mediators. In serious cases, one adolescent can temporarily live with the other biological parent, or if this is not possible or practical, professional help may need to be obtained.

Chapter 11
Sex Education, Media Exposure, and After-School Enrichment

Sex Education

From the above you have learned that young children are sexual to begin with, not in the usual adult sense, but that sexual (libidinal) pleasure is a feeling that they experience. Perhaps, you have come to this observation independently. The question probably has arisen in your mind as to what is the best age to provide sex education to a child and who should dispense it. Earlier, I pointed out that children create theories of their own about conception and birth based on limited personal experiences and bits of information they have gathered from different sources. For example, that conception is oral and based on eating, and birth is anal and based on elimination.

My own belief is that parents, preferably the parent of the same gender as the child, should provide sex education. I want to distinguish between answering a child's questions about sex which can occur at different ages and parents taking the initiative, raising the topic, and providing information if their child avoids it. I suggest that the mother talk with her daughter and the father with his son because this likely will be experienced by the child as less seductive. I am thinking of a parent taking the initiative when the child is preadolescent. The facts of procreation and reassurance about masturbation can be imparted and comprehended.

At an earlier age, children will ask questions indicating curiosity about conception and birth. Most likely, both a boy and girl will ask their mother but fathers get asked too. The question may not be direct, such as, "How do babies get made?" Instead, you might have to infer it from observations the child makes about a pregnant woman or queries about storks bringing babies and dropping them off at homes. Some children know of pets that have had babies and they ask questions about this. Some latency children might start using the "f word" as an indirect way of expressing sexual curiosity. Many parents have qualms about explaining how a sperm gets into a mommy to fertilize an egg. I advise to answer a question first by asking a child to tell you what they believe. If the child has a misconception then it should be corrected with the facts. Information should not be provided beyond the answer called for by the child's question. In other words, let the child process or digest what they have been told. To give more information will only over load the child's mind. It may take months before the child asks another question. Children need to be allowed to go at their own pace.

This is why I do not think sex education should be taught to young children in schools where individual differences cannot be accommodated as they can in a family. However, human reproduction should be in the curriculum for adolescents along with information about birth control, including abstinence, in my view. If there is an objection to this on religious grounds, then these children can be absent and instead abstinence can be discussed by the parents or by a religious institution. Many parents prefer euphemisms to the correct scientific terms for anatomical parts. This is because of the adult's own discomfort talking openly about sex. I discourage this because it contributes a quality of shame to the topic. A penis is a "penis" and not a "wee wee." A vagina is a "vagina" and not a "hole" or "private."

I do believe young children need to be educated, without alarming them, to be wary of strangers who invite them to accompany them with bribes of candy or other enticements. Also young children can be told that their bodies are private and unless they have the permission of a parent or parent surrogate, or one of these people are present, they should refuse to allow an adult or older child to touch parts of their body covered by underwear.

Media Exposure

Media exposure has become an issue particularly since 9/11. Many children were exposed to the news as countless parents listened to it in cars and on television, too shocked to turn it off when their children were within earshot or watching the television along with them. They heard things or saw images that were scary and watched as their parents were horrified, conveying shock, fear, and helplessness, all of which exacerbated their own fright. If adults cannot comprehend terror they cannot expect that a three, five, or eight year old can do so. This is an instance where censorship is meaningful. Young children of fearful and anxious mothers are more fearful and anxious than children whose mothers are not so.

Parents need to be prepared, however, to help young children process thoughts and feelings so they can begin to comprehend events such as terrorism or naturally occurring disasters like earthquakes. Even if a parent exercises caution in one's own home as to what children are exposed to by the media or conversation, other households may not and likely a child will hear about or see some images pertaining to a terrorist act or natural disaster. Words can be used that children can understand and can be reassured it is unlikely that where you live a natural disaster will occur, or if it might, tell them of the precautions being taken. Some children, even after processing the facts of a natural disaster, may continue to be preoccupied by such events or even show a fascination with them. In my experience natural disasters such as tornados are used, like a metaphor, for some children to communicate their worries, without conscious awareness, about losing control over some intense inner feelings, such as anger. This is their mind's way of trying to master (regulate) these feelings. By learning the facts about tornadoes and safety precautions regarding them, children process, albeit in a displaced way, thoughts accompanied with anxiety about imagined consequences of expressing uncontrollable impulses.

In general, it is a good idea not to use television as a baby-sitter, especially with young children. An adult alongside them can help them comprehend what they are viewing. Also, parents can take every opportunity to enjoy and have their child enjoy the interactive pleasures of a common experience. Of course, there will be many instances when a parent will need to be busy with a task, such as preparing the family dinner, and cannot be attentive to child-care. On such occasions, television can serve as a safe activity for a child. However, in some instances, a pre-selected DVD might be a better choice than a television show whose content a parent has no control over.

A related issue, is a child hearing about illnesses that parents of friends or relatives have been stricken by, or even peers. Concerns about dying and death may follow. The reality is that people get ill, sometimes fatally, and the older you are the greater the risk. This fact can be conveyed to concerned children. My own belief is that parents should not overwhelm children about the harsh aspects of reality but if they are exposed to them nor should a parent lie. Parents should always be allied with reality and not fantasy. This will help their child do the same and not feel betrayed by a parent. It also will encourage them to use parents as a resource about reality.

After-School Enrichment

Parents these days are very concerned about helping their children have a "step up" on their peers, rivals for a place at a prestigious college in the future. In the past twenty years, there has been a growth of after-school enrichment programs. Many of these are involving athletic skills such as soccer or hockey (which may even take place before school to insure ice rink availability), or talents in areas such as music, drama, or art. My belief is that when used judiciously, such activities make sense. They cater to a child's interests and strengths. The enhancement of skills and development of talent increases a child's self-esteem. I do not, however, think it increases a child's chances for acceptance at Harvard if enrollment in such activities is included on a resume. Thus, whether it is sensible or not to have a child participate has to do with the purpose of such involvement. Is it initiated by the child, agreed to, or coerced upon the child? There is value for a child to have leisure time to do whatever it is that he or she likes to do, even if its to daydream, climb a tree, play with the dog, etc. It may appear to some parents that there is little redeeming in these activities, but the child may disagree. Having fun is part of childhood, too.

Some older children want to use the computer or watch television after school. My own belief is that children need some kind of physical activity to inculcate a positive attitude about physical exercise. If a child dislikes team sports then there are non-competitive and/or solitary physical activities like bicycling, swimming, gymnastics, skate boarding, etc. I think there needs to be a limit on how many hours a day television is watched. Also, selection of programs may need parental oversight. The same goes for video games. I do not recommend that I-phones and other such devices be used as toys for toddlers. Children at this age learn best by physically engaging their environments. Parents engaging verbally promote language skills with their children. The use of a computer by older children is more complicated. Assuming the use is more than to play games or to go to inappropriate Internet sites, becoming skillful with a computer has redeeming value given its central role in our modern world. This, however, does not require endless hours looking at a computer screen.

Reading good children's literature is a very worthwhile activity for after-school. It will increase children's vocabularies, stimulate their imaginations, contribute positively to their narrative skills, both spoken and written, and increase their knowledge of the world. A child might gravitate towards comic books. Some of these are of a high caliber, being well drawn and having a worthwhile message. More importantly, the child will be reading.

Chapter 12
Sexual Abuse

There seems to be an "epidemic" of sexual abuse reports in the media. I do not think we really know if the incidence is greater than years ago. In any case, it is always alarming to hear reports about this. My definition of sexual abuse is probably narrower in some respects and broader in others, than what is commonly talked about. Sexual abuse to me is when an adult or older child knowingly exploits a younger child for purposes of gaining their own sexual pleasure. To satisfy this definition, it does not require physical contact, like penetration, fellatio, cunnilingus, or touching of genitals. Such actions are clearly sexually abusive. It could, however, be repeated immodesty about nakedness or exposure to pornography. Or it could be parents never taking precautions, keeping the bedroom door open or unlocked, so the child is repeatedly exposed to parents engaged in sexual acts. Some parents allow the child to be present in the bathroom as they bathe or in the dressing room as they get dressed to go out. This is unnecessary and too stimulating. All of the above are seductive, sometimes intentionally. It is misguided to think that exposing children to nakedness and immodesty will allow them to be less "neurotic" about their bodies. What is the child to do with the excitement? Often they "act up."

I include in my definition of sexual abuse a disparity in ages between the doer and recipient. This is important because young children under the age of six express sexual curiosity by exposing their bodies to one another or by playing "doctor." Usually, they are of similar age. This is voluntary and does not have deleterious effects. It might if the instigator was an older cousin, like an adolescent, or a baby sitter. The differences in the size and appearance of the genital will likely be frightening to the much younger observer.

Children who are sexually abused often repeat the abuse with other children. Parents may not know directly that their child has been abused. Children tend to be ashamed or guilty and are scared of punishment and keep the experience(s) secret. Sometimes they may feel guilty because at some level they may be aware of their own sexual wishes, or, possibly, of pleasure they experienced. I state this not to blame the victim but to underscore the self-blame of victims. This is especially so if incest is involved. The guilt is exacerbated because of continual contact with the abuser, someone whom they love.

If a child becomes acutely anxious, a gentle inquiry about whether he or she have been frightened recently by something might encourage them to volunteer events they are ashamed of or frightened about. I am not encouraging asking direct or leading questions. There have been reports of claims of sexual abuse that are really reports of sexual fantasies. Sometimes, adults, mainly fathers, have been falsely accused of abusing their own children. Professional help may be required for a child to disclose the abuse and later to process the sequela. When the abuse has not been a single event (shock trauma) but rather a cumulative trauma, the etiological significance of the incidents in the total dynamic picture of the child may be harder to specify.

Chapter 13
Pre-adolescence

The hormonal changes associated with puberty begin to express themselves usually around age ten or eleven for girls and usually a year later for boys. Girls may start to have some acne, have some underarm odor, sprout buds on their chests, and get a little taller. Menses usually is a couple of years away. Girls seem to be menstruating earlier these days, perhaps as a result of nutritional factors or additives put into foods. Boys follow in maturing. They may have an initial lowering of their voices. Facial hair will usually not appear until further into puberty. Penile emissions are usually a couple of years in the future. We call this the pre-adolescent phase of development.

This can be a difficult time for children. Girls may be proud of their beginning breast development. They may anticipate its arrival by purchasing bras before they really need them. Many, however, try to hide it by slouching when they stand. It is not uncommon to see girls with rounded shoulders during these years and into early adolescence. Some find it difficult to be the only one in their group of friends who has begun breast development. Boys can be embarrassed by voice changes that are erratic.

For both genders, but especially for boys, the beginning of pre-adolescence can be stressful enough that a regression in drives may appear. Recall, the focus on their bodies just before entering the latency years was on the genitals. During these pre-adolescent years there can be a re-awakening of even earlier types of drives. There is an indiscriminant arousal of excitement. Boys can become very crude in an anal way. Anal sounds are joked about, and a fart can reduce a group of boys to laugh uncontrollably. Orality may demonstrate itself in excessive drinking of soda pop or eating of sweets, a feature for either gender.

Girls seem more resistant to this regression around the onset of the pre-adolescent years. This seems so, as mentioned earlier, because they appear to have more completely repressed earlier types of wishes prior to entering the Oedipal drama. They shifted their attention to father from their mothers. Hence, early type wishes that center on mother may be less available to girls when pre-adolescence begins. When I speak of the diminished ties girls have for mothers I am not referring to overt behavior. Rather, being **like** mother (identification) predominates over a focus on mother for pleasure seeking (object desire). Boys, on the other hand, as mentioned earlier, have not reduced ties to their mothers but have only changed their aims. Within their minds, or intrapsychically, investing mother as an object of desire, especially genital desire, diminishes for girls. For a minority of girls the closeness stemming from identification makes it difficult to separate from mother. Most girls as women, however, are able to satisfy residual feelings for closeness originating in their tie to mother via mature relationships with female friends. They can be close and sharing while maintaining separateness and autonomy.

Girls and boys differ as to how they regard each other. Boys seem scared of girls, who are usually more mature, both physically and psychically. They defend against this fear by demeaning girls. This fear of girls includes mother. Boys are drawn to mother because of the reawakening of passive longings. These longings, however, also scare them. Boys can become afraid of being enveloped by their mothers. There may be a re-emergence of the unconscious wish for a baby. Bi-sexual conflict intensifies castration anxiety. They identify with the active mother, the doer, (in their minds, the so-called "phallic woman"), as a defense against their own passive wishes. To deal with all of these dynamics, boys immerse themselves with a male peer. This is a sort of evasive homosexual period that is transitory. This dynamic for the pre-adolescent boys is reminiscent of the same unconscious dynamic experienced during the transition from the Oedipal phase into Latency. (As mentioned earlier, the use of the term "homosexual" if used **prior** to puberty is used descriptively only. It is only after puberty that sexual orientation is decided upon.)

Girls, on the other hand, run in packs and boys view them like Amazons. The girls are full of secrets and shifting alliances. One day a particular girl may be part of the group but the next day she is excluded. For a few girls there can be a pseudo-heterosexuality that might appear on the surface to be the real thing, but underneath the aim is to overcome fear of and resist a resurgence of earlier modes of drive expression involving mother. Girls can be interested in smutty topics but too direct sexual interests are not yet part of the culture of this age group. They become ardent fans of female pop singers and some may profess crushes on these pop stars or even on a male teenage pop singer. Girls particularly want to be like every one else in their group. The pre-adolescent girl who does not wear braces on her teeth may feel like an "outsider."

Some boys may become bullies to other boys. It may become physical. The motives vary but what may be in common for bullies of either gender is attributing their own hated personality or physical features to their intended victims. Bullying behavior discloses unconscious feelings of inferiority. Perhaps, too, it may be an externalization of unconscious sado-masochistic wishes upon the chosen victim? Girls can be particularly mean to other girls during this stage. Bullying from girls takes the form of excluding and verbally denigrating another girl. Intervention needs to help the injured party not to feel victimized and the perpetrator to feel more empathy for the intended victim. Peer confrontation of bullies under adult guidance has proven to be useful.

Parents can find this a particularly trying time. The beginning defiance of the pre-adolescent can be disturbing. What happened to the cherubic little boy or girl? The child's interest in a popular pop star whose lyrics are suggestive becomes an issue. A change in tastes regarding clothes based on older adolescent trends is unsettling to parents. For girls, an initial interest in the opposite sex can cause parents to become nervous. The pubertal bodily changes, not yet in noticeable bloom, can begin to be very disturbing to some parents. Fathers begin to feel uncomfortable having their daughters squirming on their laps. The immodesty of children can be difficult, especially when they are beginning to show pubertal changes. More about that when we discuss adolescence proper.

This is a good opportunity for fathers to do more things with their sons and mothers with their daughters. Of course, doing things with a child of the opposite sex is not so easy at this age because of gender-specific interests of some. Children of this age seem to feel embarrassment to be seen in the company of a parent by their peers. Parents can participate with their children in interests that the child enjoys in non-public venues.

Pre-adolescence is a good time for parents to consider the introduction of serious responsibilities to be assigned to their child. What I have in mine are such household chores as expecting your child to do his or her own laundry, to be responsible for tasks such as help in preparing family meals by setting the table, or cleaning up, or in some cooking, or in maintenance tasks such as cutting the grass, taking out the garbage, shoveling snow, etc. If there is a family pet, tasks such as feeding them and walking the dog or changing the cat's litter box are all reasonable requests. The pre-adolescent is old enough to be reliable and competent in carrying out these tasks. Additionally, lifelong skills will be learned and self-esteem in feeling competent and responsible will be enhanced. Allowance can be connected to such family services. Learning about saving money and budgeting it is also a skill that can be inculcated. When children get older they can be given a lump sum of money and be asked to budget it for the purchase of clothes.

Chapter 14
Early Adolescence

Do you recall your entry into adolescence? It is not as if one day you were pre-adolescent and the next day you were a full-fledged adolescent. Unless we substitute pre-teen and teenage as the criteria for the division, then, you became a teenager on your thirteen birthday. Of course, there are the pubertal changes that herald entry into adolescence. Recall that during pre-adolescence puberty begins in a less noticeable manner. The onset of puberty proper or sexual maturity that is more noticeable varies from individual to individual. For girls sexual maturity usually begins earlier than for boys. For many girls maturation could be achieved by age twelve or thirteen, and for boys at age thirteen or fourteen. There are many healthy adolescents who mature later. There are rare instances of precocious sexual maturity, mostly in girls, as early as mid-latency. Precocious puberty of this sort is a medical glandular abnormality. But adolescence, mainly, is a psychological concept. It kind of coincides with entry into high school. Some cultures provide initiation rites of one sort or another to mark the entry into adolescence. Adolescence predominantly has to do with a change in the way you see yourself and others and how you relate to them. For girls physical changes with maturation are more noticeable. Such changes can be a source of shame or pride.

Let us imagine what an early adolescent boy or girl might be thinking (expurgated). Our imaginary girl may be thinking the following: "I'm starting to menstruate and need to be concerned about personal hygiene because of these 'periods.' Sometimes I want to scream! I don't want dad to know I have got my first period but I know mom will tell him and I'll feel embarrassed in his company. How do I master putting in a tampon? 'Bad hair days' can ruin my day. Why am I so vain? Thank heaven for jeans. I can always wear them. The more faded the better. Why was it stylish for them to be torn last year but not this year? And they are so expensive. I need to have the designer jeans like the other girls. They are so tight, I can hardly get into them, but it's worth the struggle to get the boys to notice. My first high heels! How do you walk in these? The boys seem to like them so I'll suffer. Ugh! This bra is so uncomfortable but it makes me look bigger than I am and I see the boys noticing me more, so I'll put up with it. Will my breasts get bigger this year?"

Our imaginary boy is thinking: "I worry about nocturnal emissions that will need to be hidden from my mom. Even worse are the spontaneous erections when I'm in class. What will I do if the teacher asks me to go up to the black board? I really want to become "buff" and feel strong so that both girls and guys will notice. I don't know why I wear my pants so low that it looks as if they are ready to fall off, but I want to look cool. Which way are baseball hats to be turned this year? Shoes are a whole other matter. My parents tell me that I need to wear leather shoes if I get dressed up and wear a suit but I don't have any."

Both genders also likely are having thoughts about the other gender's body. A girl may notice a cute boy and embarrassedly imagine him as a boyfriend but notice, with dismay, he is a head shorter than she. A boy, with titillation, may notice the same girl looking furtively at him but lament privately that the other kids will tease him that he only comes up to her chin.

Both genders share some common thoughts: " 'Zits' or acne makes me not want to be seen. Mom tells me repetitively to wash my face and to exercise self-control about not squeezing pimples. My appetite can be ravenous, especially after I get home from school. I can eat a whole box of doughnuts or a whole loaf of bread. I worry constantly about gaining weight. I can sleep to noon on a weekend morning. I am always tired from going to sleep too late to get up before the sun does in order to get to school on time before the first bell in the morning. I need to take showers daily because if I don't the other kids might tease me about body odor. Before I could get away with not taking them unless my parents made a big deal about it. Will I get taller this year?"

Let us look for the "silver lining" for a moment. It is with the beginning of adolescence that the process of taking "ownership" of one's own body really begins. Adolescents will become increasingly responsible for personal hygiene, for dressing appropriately for the weather, for taking medicines, and even for eating properly. But do not expect this to happen abruptly. An adolescent still may go out on a cold winter's day wearing a tee shirt and shorts.

I know I am presenting a picture of a superficial person and adolescents are much more than that. There are many who are fervent about humanistic causes. I will speak more about that later. But concerns about appearance suddenly reach ascendancy. "I'm overweight and no boy will ever ask me on a date. I cannot stop eating." "I'm shorter than almost every girl in my class."

Regretfully, the adolescent girl who laments about her weight is not in touch with the underlying feelings about how food is a symbolic substitute for other things. She can be so self-conscious about being overweight she will be inconsolable. Another boy or girl is so shy, they feel so awkward around the opposite sex. In the privacy of their bedroom they can rhythmically and gracefully move their body to the music on their i-pod but it's impossible to do this in public. They rather not go to the party. To be popular is an ideal. The popular girls and boys are envied. Let me continue with my portrayal of the imagined private thoughts of my composite early adolescent girl or boy.

"School is so stressful. The adults all tell me that grades now count. I practically have to be a straight-A student to be able to get into the state university. Some how, I need to stand out from all the other students with straight-As to be noticed by any prestigious school. What 'good cause' should I volunteer for so I can put this on my college application? I cannot think that far ahead. I'm worried about the exam tomorrow or how to get up enough guts to talk to the girl (boy) sitting alongside me. I feel such intense feelings I sometimes even feel suicidal. Whom can I confide in? My parents won't understand, they're too old. I need a best friend more than anything else in the world. Maybe my dog will do in the meantime. I know, I'll eat a doughnut or get high and it won't matter."

Of course, the above reveries are not those of all early adolescents, but regretfully, of too many to dismiss them as of little concern. It is a tough time and we do not pay enough attention to this age period. Educators in the USA have tried to come up with the most suitable arrangement for learning. There used to be "junior high schools" which 7th, 8th, and 9th graders attended. It was believed the 9th graders were too immature to be with older high school students. Now, instead there are "middle schools" where 6th, 7th and 8th graders attend. It was felt that the 9th graders were too mature for the 7th and 8th graders so they were grouped once again with older students. You can see there is not a simple solution!

Unlike the above composite adolescent, there are many early adolescents who are enthusiastic about the changes they are ongoing. They are engaged in school and extra-curricular activities like sports and with family. They are pleased with their growth spurt and proud of their maturing bodies. A mother has told the girl who is menstruating for the first time that it is a sign of health and progress and a symbol of her femininity and generative powers. A boy who has a mother that admires his newfound strength and stature without being seductive and a father who welcomes his son almost beating him at tennis allows a boy to feel comfortable with his burgeoning masculinity. It helps a pubescent girl if her mother is comfortable with her own mature body and her femininity. After all, her mother is a model to emulate.

Some women have problems with menstrual cycles, whether the problems are caused by psychological or biological factors. If they get pre-menstrual symptoms and are temporarily "put out of commission," their daughters may take this as a model. There is a saying, "The acorn doesn't fall far from the oak tree," which, regrettably, is true about children and parents. The former identify with the latter, which is a good thing if we're speaking of desirable traits, but an unfortunate thing if it involves traits that the child swore never to adopt. If a father compensates for a strong identification with his own mother by being demeaning of passive men and acts excessively macho, pity his early adolescent son who is not interested in "manly" activities. What if this son has to "do" the father "one better" and becomes a schoolyard bully and misogynous?

What is the most important psychological task of the adolescence phase of development? I would say that it is to find a non-incestuous person to love. The primary love interests of children are their parents. They have to accept the premise, intrapsychically, that they eventually will need to find a person to love sexually that minimally links up with a parent. I do not mean to imply that this is accomplished as a decision via conscious problem solving. Instead, an unconscious struggle goes on within the psyche (mind) that can cause much internal and external conflict. If this is not accomplished, more than less, by the end of adolescence, the adolescent likely will experience conflict with their future partner. We call this achievement object removal. We are wrong to think that the Oedipal Complex is ever fully eradicated. It's effects wax and wane throughout our lives.

A correlated task of adolescence is what is called the second separation-individuation. In early childhood, it was an accomplishment to be able to separate from the physical mother (first separation-individuation). Once accomplished, the child is able to begin to function autonomously with peers and other adults. This was achieved by means of consolidating the image internally of mother (object constancy), as discussed earlier. Now, the adolescent must be able to disengage from the internal representation of the childhood parent(s). Actually, transformation is more accurate than disengagement. This achievement and object removal are interwoven processes.

Another important task of adolescence is for the adolescent to come to terms with his or her maturing sexual body. The adolescent is now capable of conceiving a baby in reality, not just in fantasy. Accompanying their mature bodies are sexual urges towards other persons, usually of the opposite gender, but sometimes directed at someone of the same gender. Thus, the issue of sexual orientation is a correlated task of coming to terms with one's maturing body. I will speak more about sexual orientation in the chapter below dealing with homosexuality.

Corresponding to their child's separation-individuation efforts, parents, too, are undergoing developmental changes in parenthood. They, too, need to psychically allow their child to emancipate. The beginning of this process occurred earlier when their child was physically separating from them during their third year of life, and then again as the child moved into the latency years, weakening their Oedipal ties to them. Some parents find this change in the nature of their parenting to be difficult while some welcome the opportunities to have more leisure time to pursue interests. For those where the change is difficult they have trouble modifying their self-image as a parent defined mainly as attentive to a dependent child to that of being a parent to an independent and more self-reliant child.

A consequence of beginning the processes of object removal and the second separation-individuation is for the early adolescent to start to feel an inner emptiness or internal void, as well as feelings of loneliness. The adolescent is not consciously aware that this intrapsychic process is ongoing. Insofar as the internalized parental objects are the foundation for the conscience (the mental agency comprised of prohibitions and ideals), disengagement from parents weakens the adolescent's ability to exercise self-control over feelings and urges. Hence, a regulatory agency of the mind is put sufficiently out of commission. The ego, the executive part of the mind, loses an ally, or is left with a weakened ally. This, however, allows for the adolescent gradually to revise his or her superego so that it can become more mature in its expectations insofar as it no longer needs to be based solely upon early parental introjects. Hence, early on in the process of secondary separation-individuation and object removal, adolescents have a proclivity to act out, to disregard prohibitions. The peer group's moral code is adopted. Hopefully, the peer group is not a delinquent one. Friends feel very important to adolescents, even more so than parents. Adolescents are very susceptible to peer pressure. Have you had to deal with an adolescent on vacation away from his friend(s)? They always welcome inviting a friend along. With cell phones these days they are always in touch with their friends. Later, we will discuss the means to which some adolescents go to attempt to fill the inner void felt after they disengage from their primary objects (parents).

Acting-out, or engaging in un-regulated behaviors, can be reduced if an early adolescent has a close friend. The friend becomes a confidant. The chum chosen is based on an ideal self-image and the friendship thereby "absorbs" feelings about the self (narcissistic feelings) and is a homosexual choice insofar as one chooses someone like oneself. Hence, it is not based on libidinal desire but on narcissism. The earlier homosexual stance of preadolescence was a defensive one to ward off passive identificatory wishes directed at mother. During early adolescence, it is based on an idealized view of oneself, the person the adolescent wishes to be like. This, too, is usually temporary for the boy who usually is ashamed and uncomfortable with his femininity and bisexuality.

Friendships are also important for the early adolescent girl. Without one she can become depressed. The "crush," beginning in pre-adolescence, comes more into play, either towards another girl or a boy. This eroticized relationship also is based, like the boy, on an ideal self-image. Girls find it more acceptable to claim their masculinity than do boys to claim their femininity. In the "crush" she can play the male role if the friend is a girl, or insist on equality if the friend is a boy. For most girls, this bisexual position will be abandoned during later adolescence for a heterosexual one. There will be proud acceptance of her femaleness and her whole body's femininity. For a minority of girls there will occur sexual acting out, sometimes in a promiscuous way. This is defensive against puberty's re-awakening of early needs involving mother. The girl will mal-adaptively, without conscious awareness, seek to satisfy such needs through sex. It is the unconscious wish to be held, as the girl once was by mother, and not to be penetrated sexually, which is sought.

An interest that is very important to many early adolescents is music. Some adolescents are almost preoccupied with music. You can see them always listening to their i-pods. A few may have an interest in learning how to play a musical instrument such as a guitar. The music allegiance of each generation differs as to genre or to group or individual pop stars. One generation may feel unable to relate to the next generation's musical interest. It may be that this gulf of musical appreciation, and popular culture in general, helps to facilitate the separation of the adolescent from the older generation and gives them solidarity with their own generation at a time when they feel a reduction of affiliation with parents.

Sports are another activity that many adolescents gravitate towards. Parents can be supportive of their adolescent's interests. Since the passage of Title IX more girls in the States are also participating in sports. Many adolescents are aware of their bodies' new strength and agility. Young adolescents enjoy the competitiveness and exhibitionism of being a talented athlete. Some are too conflicted about both to participate in sports. Some girls may seriously engage in dance during these years. For others, the exhibitionism is too conflicted and cannot be overcome. A few girls may be able to participate in equestrian activities. Athletic or dance talents can be a source of positive self-esteem for many adolescents. Involvement in team sports, allowing for camaraderie and physical contact, is an opportunity for boys and girls to sublimate homoerotic feelings.

Parents during this phase of early adolescence need to make themselves available. As mentioned earlier, when we discussed preadolescence, fathers and mothers can, respectively, help their sons and daughters by participating in enjoyable activities together. With opposite sex children, it might be easier for the child if a friend is invited to join. "Togetherness" might feel impossible for parents because of the defiant attitude of their child. Its worth the effort for parents to overcome their self-protectiveness against rebuffs. A parent should never be seductive. To be so is always destructive but it is particularly so during a child's adolescence. Parents need to remember, it is the behavior that is abhorred, not the child, whom is loved. This needs to be made clear to children.

During this age period, it is important that parents maintain their stance about limits and reasonable consequences when there is disobedience about them. Parents need to try to live up to their own standards that they hold their children to. Otherwise, an adolescent will show up a parent's hypocrisy and it will be very disillusioning for them and encourage further estrangement from adult values. Parents best try to remain the adult in the family. If a parent tries to act like an adolescent with the aim of bonding this is misguided. Adolescents need adult parents, as much as they say they disregard them. At some level, if a parent objects to their outlandish behavior, he or she will notice that you care and it will pay dividends later on. So, parents are advised, for example, not to smoke pot with their children or accompany them to movies that are aimed for the adolescent market. At least, do not sit with your adolescent and his or her friends.

An issue that invariably arises during a child's early adolescence in connection with entry into high school is whether or not parents should remind their child to study and/or do homework. Parents are very aware of how competitive it is to gain entry into good colleges. I think that by this age most children also are aware of the need to study and to do one's homework. They are at an age when self-motivation and self-responsibility ordinarily is internalized. There are some children who may have serious impairments in concentration and organization that may need more parental supervision. Parents can make clear their expectations regarding priorities but children need to establish their own priorities. Inherent in making poor choices will be natural consequences, e.g., an inferior grade. The last thing a parent needs to do is to get embroiled in a power struggle with their early adolescent. The switch from middle school to high school will take some period of adjustment. Parents can enter a dialogue with their youngster as to how they can be of assistance. If rejected they can let their child know the invitation is still there. They can agree with the child that they will not micromanage, as it seems to have negative effects. I would encourage parents to help their child organize a plan to balance schoolwork and leisure activities. Parents and children can agree to revisit the issue if expected results are not met.

Chapter 15
Middle Adolescence

What was begun in early adolescence progresses further during middle adolescence. By its completion most adolescents have successfully transformed the ties to their parents and they have made the switch to a heterosexual choice that is not intimately linked to the parent of the opposite sex, a non-incestuous choice. As a result of this internal process, many adolescents are feeling a sense of loss, and, simultaneously, for those who are in a relationship, a feeling of "being in love." Sexual orientation is settled for most adolescents. By sexual orientation we mean adoption of homosexuality or heterosexuality as the preferred choice of a partner. This is different from gender identity by which we mean acceptance of being male or female. This is firmly **established by age three.*** Gender role involves behavior that is **masculine or feminine.**

As mentioned above, the process of disattachment to the "infantile" objects (parents) results in feeling lonely and an inner feeling of emptiness that the adolescent tries to fill in different ways. We call such attempts restitutive. The adolescent cannot simply undo the ties without painful feelings akin to mourning. At an unconscious level, there are wishes to re-establish the infantile ties, but there is also resistance to this. Adolescents really need to transform the nature of their tie to infantile objects. Severing ties is not in any one's best interests, in most instances. Exceptions might be if a parent has been abusive or criminal. A new object must be acceptable to all of the mental agencies involved in the adolescent's mind. Adolescents seek to substitute the relationship with parents with identification, particularly to the parent of the same sex. Until this is successful, they will make transitory identifications with all sorts of people, some "good" and some "bad." The bad ones are troublesome because of the weakened

---
*Gender identity is less fixed, however, than psychoanalysis has believed given the current clinical incidence of transgender clinical issues.

status of their conscience. Identifications with unethical figures could encourage delinquency.

One way that restitution is attempted is to shift the emotional investment withdrawn from the parents and re-distribute it upon oneself. This often is temporary until a new object has been invested in. We call this self-investment narcissistic. A result is that many adolescents exhibit self-aggrandizement and arrogance. The increased self-investment also can result in an increased bodily concern, a hypochondriacal worry about their bodily functioning. That is, a preoccupation with early signs of imagined serious illness.

A particularly self-defeating way resorted to fill the void and not feel lonely might be to become gluttonous regarding food. An even more self-defeating enterprise is resorting to drugs. Adolescents often have keen sensitivity to their environment. Many adolescents become keenly aware of the beauty of (Mother) nature. Perhaps resort to hallucinogenic drugs is to make sensory processes, such as vision and hearing, even more sensitive. Is this an attempt at restitution to hold onto the external world populated by parents? Only a few adolescents will experiment with hallucinogenics. Drugs like marijuana, however, are very present in high schools. When used recreationally, and rarely, there seems to be no lasting psychological danger. Used rarely, it seems to not harm the brain or lungs. There is, however, a potential legal consequence. A concern is when the adolescent uses it daily, maybe multiple times. The danger then is it drains initiative in all areas of life. Whether there are permanent neurological or pulmonary consequences is unclear.

Parents can be a resource for their children to talk about drug and alcohol use. Adolescents probably already know the basic facts from school presentations. They will ask parents if at their age they drank and/or used drugs of any kind. As always, I think the truth is called for. Parents can acknowledge that when they were once their child's age they, too, were curious about drugs and subject to peer pressure. Parents need to recognize they are not a witness in a courtroom being cross-examined by their child. Parents have the benefits of experience and a perspective different from their child's peers. If a parent did experiment with a drug I believe that this can be acknowledged as well as how, with hindsight, that an altered consciousness was not all that it was held up to be. Children can be told that pleasure can be experienced while sober and not influenced by drugs. The potential slippery slope of recreational drugs like marijuana and dangers associated with contaminant-laced drugs can be pointed out to them. The health risks of alcohol abuse and the benefits of sobriety can be underscored. The occasional use of moderate amounts of alcohol and wine with food can be distinguished from abuse.

Parents can also be a resource for their children about safety issues with regard to driving a car. Most adolescents have better reflexes than adults. The danger lies in the inclination for the adolescent to take risks. Peer pressure can also play a role. Distractions and lapses in judgment are more likely when there are many adolescents in the car. Parents can set limits and educate an adolescent about the dangers of driving while under the influence of alcohol or drugs. They can be examples of safe driving.

In some instances, an adolescent can become so distraught they make a suicidal gesture or even an attempt. Adolescents may still be operating in an omnipotent way and thinking of themselves as immortal when suicide is considered. Often the depression covers over rage at significant people in their lives, e.g., jealous rage towards a girl or boy who has chosen someone else. If suicidal thoughts are acted out the adolescent and family will need professional help. Often a suicidal gesture is a "call for help."

Many adolescents become defiant and rebellious. Some do not accept compromise. It makes them feel weak and dependent. This is in the context of underlying pulls on them to regress and give into the resurgence of early forms of urges connected to their earlier relationship to mother. They employ defenses that will keep the mother at a distance, e.g., feeling hate in place of love, and directing feelings meant for mother onto other people. A few adolescents resort to asceticism, as a way of controlling all urges. This was more prevalent in previous generations. Some adolescents may use intellectualization, a passionate conviction about the rightness of their position about a social cause or the wrongness of a social injustice, where the personal meaning of it to their life is obscure. In our culture, there is an emphasis on action and materialism. This means that the creative and safe restitution forms open to earlier generations of adolescents, are not "in the radar" of contemporary adolescents, such as keeping a diary or journal. Modern adolescents are members of groups. Group affiliation lends itself to filling some of the inner void. Modern gadgets, allowing for emailing or texting, and the Internet with web sites that allow social networking, such as My Space or Facebook, contributes to satisfying the object hunger of adolescents. While this may be a positive consequence for some adolescents, earlier, in the chapter on Latency, I presented some concerns about virtual or cyberspace reality on children, particularly on adolescents.

Once the adolescent has successfully traversed the rocky terrain of finding a heterosexual love object, the sense of mourning and loneliness is reduced or goes away and the need to seek restitution is diminished. The adolescent is in the throes of "first love." The defusion of loving and hating feelings during the internal detachment from the infantile love objects (parents) can be refused in the attachment to the new love interest. Fusion of erotic and aggressive urges results in a dilution of the aggressiveness. The rebelliousness and defiance of the adolescent often diminishes at this point. The male and female adolescent, may express tender love, respectively, towards a girlfriend or boyfriend. This underscores the lasting value of expressions of tender love by parents towards their young children. The defiant adolescent presumably can express tender love insofar as he or she once felt it.

Adolescents are capable of more complicated forms of thinking compared to their younger counterparts. They are now capable of formal operations, a level of thinking enabling them to be less self-centered and to be more objective. Theorizing is advanced, much different from the theorizing of the four year-old trying to make sense of conception and birth. Abstract thinking is advanced. Thinking now serves trial action. Consequences of actions are thought through in the mind. Hence, overt action tendencies are under better control. Risk-taking diminishes and impulse control increases as the brain matures. Problem solving reaches new heights. Interests and skills insure self-esteem. Thinking is not restricted to the present. The future can now be contemplated, at least sometimes.

Sublimation (and de-aggressivization) is increasingly possible. As described above, this is a process whereby drives have been altered sufficiently from their original sexual or aggressive aims so that the mind need not be on continual defense against their entry into consciousness and/or expression into action. Sublimation is involved in creativity. Adolescents can be very creative. The ability to fantasize and suspend reality testing and to engage in controlled regression is increased so as to enliven the reason of the ego with the magic of the unconscious. Adolescents are more capable to regulate these mental processes. Creativity will express itself in performing arts like dance, music, and theater, as well as in writing. If you have ever gone to a high school theater production, either of a drama or a musical, you know what I mean. Adolescents are some of the most energetic and devoted fighters to correct social injustices. They volunteer at homeless shelters, they assist at animal protection centers, they protest against bigotry and against international violence, etc. This generation of adolescents are much more accepting of divergent life styles and cultures than previous generations.

Sexual intimacy among contemporary adolescents is common. It may involve everything but actual sexual intercourse. Indications are that many young adolescents "hook up," i.e., engage in sex short of intercourse. I doubt that prevalence is greater now than in previous generations. It seems, rather, that it is less hidden. I am not confident as to what most accounts for this observation. Perhaps it is the diminished social taboos in society about sexual expression, adults as models who are less inhibited in dress and behavior, in the diminished importance of the church or synagogue in family life, the risqué display of sex on television and in movies, the increased prevalence of divorce undermining parental authority, the increased awareness and availability of birth control measures, etc.

For many adolescents, sexuality is a scary enterprise. Girls, especially, may attempt to shield themselves from boys noticing them. They may wear baggy sweatshirts. They even may resort to extreme dieting and exercising. This is called anorexia. Binge eating and purging is known as bulimia. Anorexia often is an unconscious attempt to rid the body of feminine contours so a girl will be less physically attractive to boys. An additional meaning is to get out from under the perceived control of mother whom is associated with food. This behavior is provocative insofar as it jeopardizes health, and, if anything, a mother will get concerned and become even more involved in a daughter's life. This belies the overt protest of an adolescent that he or she wants more independence. Unconsciously, the adolescent is conflicted about wishing to be dependent. If a child becomes anorexic, it is prudent to seek professional help. It makes no sense to wait till hospitalization is required to feed an adolescent intravenously. Close contact with a pediatrician or adolescent medicine specialist is a good idea insofar as the health of an anorexic or bulimic child is compromised.

But what is the consequence of sexual experiences for adolescents? It probably depends on the age and maturity of the adolescent, on if the sex was forced or voluntary for both parties, on the frequency, etc. I think males are more inherently promiscuous than females, in general. An adolescent girl more than the boy will likely feel an emotional attachment to her partner. There is a gender difference here, insofar as males are more governed by their libido and females take into account feelings too. This puts a girl in a vulnerable position to experience hurt feelings if it is not mutual. For some adolescents, parental disapproval of adolescent mores will not act as a strong deterrent. Self-regulation is lacking in many adolescents who are sexually active. Some of this group may not have experienced limits as younger children. I believe that lecturing will not constrain adolescents. Hopefully, there will be opportunities for a meaningful conversation.

We need to be clear that when we speak of "sex" what is it that we mean? Does "sex" refer only to intercourse or could it refer to kissing? Parents must decide what they consider acceptable and non-acceptable. I think, more importantly, is the communication that sexual intimacy will cause intense emotional feelings. I think it is a mistake to be untruthful about the pleasure that is part of a sexual experience. Most adolescents, having experienced masturbatory pleasure, will know you are being duplicitous. I suggest letting an adolescent consider that when sexual intimacy is experienced casually, and not in the context of a sustained emotional connection, intense hurtful feelings may result. I encourage linking up sexual intimacy, particularly intercourse, with emotional maturity. It elevates sexual intimacy to something special, an emotional experience in the context of a mutually respectful relationship that can be looked forward to and can prudently be put off to the future. The risk of unwanted pregnancy can be part of this discussion. Also on another occasion, without scaring them, adolescents need to be educated about STDs and HIV. Presumably, these heath issues have already been taught in high school as part of the curriculum on personal hygiene and health. For religiously observant parents, sexual involvement will be linked to marriage and abstinence will be valued.

    Masturbation in adolescence is engaged in by both sexes. Actually it starts years earlier but during the adolescent years it is essentially universal. We know there is no physical or psychic harm resulting from this activity. Masturbation helps to integrate the mind and the body; erotic thoughts connect with bodily feelings of desire. Children should not be made to feel ashamed or guilty about the activity. Often they are more ashamed by the accompanying fantasies than by the actual act of masturbation. Here again one should not imply fantasying as shameful. The content of such fantasies change although a central one may be held onto forever. This particular fantasy is valued because it expresses the ultimate imagined pleasure to the person. It is like an erotic signature. Some older adolescent boys masturbate daily. For excessively shy boys there is some concern. This concern is not because of the activity or fantasy *per se*, but because the daily activity may result in a side effect of elevating fantasy to a position superior to the real thing and diminishing interpersonal initiative even more. When masturbation has not attained addictive status, it can beneficially contribute to comfort with aloneness.

    Adolescents are now capable of taking over full ownership of their bodies, although by some of their actions, as a parent you might disagree. They still might wear only a tee shirt in cold weather! They need to be given the responsibility of managing their own bodily needs. I'm particularly thinking here of bedtime. If they are tired in the morning because they stayed up late doing homework because they were on the phone too long, then they will learn there are consequences for actions. Adolescents will learn to manage time better because they will understand they need more sleep. It need not be a catastrophic event.

Being a parent of an adolescent can be very trying for reasons already mentioned. I'm thinking particularly of the arrogance, defiance, and uncompromising attitudes of some adolescents. Also, the exclusion of parents from their child's life is difficult. Rejection of parental values or mocking of them in an attempt to humiliate can be hard for a parent. Failures in school are especially difficult for high achieving parents. The most sanguine advice I can give is "stay the course." Parental aims, ultimately, is for their adolescent to self-regulate. Parents can try to process events with their adolescent. Parents are advised to maintain conviction about family values, set limits when the concern is about safety and mete out consequences where warranted, not in an authoritarian manner but in an authoritative one. An adolescent will argue with his parent and try to test their resolve, especially about curfew. Parents best not take the expedient way out. Parents can consider a professional consultation to discuss concerns before a crisis occurs.

Parents can let their adolescent child know they are available if the child wants a perspective different from that of their peers. Parents can show interest in their adolescent's interests. The "silver lining" is that even very difficult adolescents mature. Parents need to listen to their children's gripes and not dismiss them outright. Children may have legitimate complaints and they will value an apology. By doing so a parent sets an example. In the long run, it is better for children to idealize a parent less and value a parent more, including a parent's warts.

Adolescents are in that stage of life when their sexuality and vitality are waxing, while that of their parents is starting to wane. I think parents mostly admire this new maturity in their children, especially if its expression is controlled and thoughtful. But some parents, perhaps unbeknown to themselves, envy and resent their attractive, sensual, vigorous children. This dynamic could intensify as the child progresses through adolescence into young adulthood. This could lead some parents to act competitively in a variety of ways, for example, by dressing in an adolescent fashion or acting "cool" in an adolescent way. In short, in a misguided way they can act more like a peer than a parent. As commented upon earlier, what adolescents need are adults in their lives who can give them a different perspective on the world from that provided by peers.

Chapter 16
Late Adolescence

Adolescence ends with entry into the third decade of life. We consider the period between roughly seventeen or eighteen and twenty to be the late adolescent phase of development. It corresponds with the last year(s) of high school and the first year of college. It is a time of consolidation, or firming up, of the many achievements of adolescence proper.

For most adolescents, a stable and irreversible sexual orientation has been achieved, they are comfortable with their masculinity or femininity and their gender identity as a man or a woman is part of their self-identity. Repudiation of one's bisexuality is not advocated, but rather an acceptance of its presence. A male can recognize traits in himself that may be conventionally assigned to females, e.g., sensitivity, access to feelings, etc., without feeling this is wrong or pathological. A female might like athletics, be assertive, etc., traits conventionally assigned to her male counterparts, without feeling she is disturbed. It used to be accepted that bisexuality had to be expunged if a late adolescent or young adult was to have a normal adult gender identity.

In psychoanalysis we speak of genital primacy. What this means is that all of the early phases of sexual development and their aims have been subordinated to the primary aim of pleasurable sexual intercourse, even if they have not yet experienced it. The earlier aims serve to arouse, as in foreplay, but not to supersede the genital aim. While this is usually the case, if not, the future sexual life of the adolescent may be at risk. In extreme instances a sexual perversion can result.

During this age period, relationships are stable. Friendships and relations with parents are enduring and, hopefully, fulfilling. The internal representations of these significant people are stable. The senior in high school may already have experienced a long-term relationship, or instead dated several different partners. The late adolescent as recently as two generations ago may have found his life's mate. Now this is commonly delayed into the third decade. As a college student the exposure to lots of peers allows for the establishment of friendships that often endure for a lifetime. Women tend to be more inclined than young men to talk about personal things with girlfriends while guys are more inclined to "hang out," do things together with male friends.

Some interests of young children originate in conflict. For example, sexual curiosity could have been a locus of conflict and resolved by displacement into interest in breeding tropical fish and later into an interest in evolutionary biology. When an interest has become free of its origins in conflict, it becomes part of the secondary autonomous sphere of the mind. In late adolescence there is an extension of this sphere of interests that are stable, seemingly resistant to being drawn back into conflict. Some of these interests may be peculiar (idiosyncratic) to the individual. The functions of the ego that are autonomous congenitally (primary autonomous sphere) or from very early on remain so. Characteristic ways of dealing with stress and anxiety are employed to safeguard the integrity of the self (mind). We refer to this typical response to internal and external stressors as the character of the individual. It is meant to be like a "firewall," although it can be breeched. By late adolescence, the idiosyncratic character should be in place in the personality. More or less, the integration of ego ideals or ideal selves will be integrated. For some, this will be delayed until young adulthood.

It is during late adolescence that voting in local, state and national elections becomes legally possible. This is of significance because it coincides with a rise in awareness of the late adolescent to the larger community outside of the nuclear family, circle of friends, high school, church, athletic team, etc. It is important that this awareness begins for the late adolescent insofar as the larger community is a potential resource for re-evaluating his or her values and ideals. The greater acceptance of parents as representatives of the greater community begins this process. In some instances a modification of values could occur, or broadening, or even replacing of them, with such exposure. It is through such experiences and the exposure to new models that the superego and ego ideal can add additional mature figures to emulate. The conscience can become more compassionate.

Parenting issues are a continuation of earlier adolescent ones. What are unique are the preparation for many parents and their children for the separation that will follow when their child goes off to college. This separation is different from others insofar as parents cannot be reassured that parental surrogates like camp counselors will be looking over the shoulders of their child to make sure safety is not an issue. One only hopes that all the prior years of parenting will have helped to inculcate good sound judgment in their child so correct choices are made.

If a child goes to college out of town, which in the States seems to be taken as an inalienable right of youngsters, then there will be the visits to colleges that parent(s) and child can do together. These visits have the potential for good bonding experiences. My own feeling is that some adolescents may not be ready to leave the nest the first year they graduate from high school. If this is so they should not be forced. One may be able to tell if the adolescent procrastinates sending off the applications. A good heart-to-heart conversation might clarify things. If an adolescent stays around home and attends a local college or community college the first year, the adolescent can always transfer. The child can live at home or in a dorm or apartment with other students in the vicinity. Parents often forget that a "late bloomer" can transfer. If a child goes to college out of town, a parent probably can expect home visits every opportunity. This will diminish more each successive year. Many students adjust easily to being away. Some gain weight, partly because of the high carbohydrates served at school, and partly because of feeling homesick and using food symbolically. It is mother who is associated with food. Parents can be available but best not be intrusive. This is a time for a child to be independent and autonomous and responsible for him or herself. Hence, budgeting money may be a new experience. Setting up a child with a checking account or debit card account makes sense.

Many freshmen entering college already know what career they wish to pursue. Many, however, are uncertain. With the array of different academic courses they will be exposed to, and exposure to peers having diverse interests, hopefully, they will emerge by the end of the second year of college with a direction that they would like to pursue. I believe this will contribute to an inner sense of calmness.

In some communities the majority of high school graduates will not be going onto college. This will be a stressful time for them, given the current economic downturn. Jobs will not be plentiful. Some will become apprentice tradesmen; others might be employed on the family farm, while others will be uncertain as to employment. A small minority may look forward to volunteering in the military services.

PART 2

Chapter 17
Young Adulthood

Young adult years begin roughly with the ending of the second decade of life and conclude with the beginning of the third decade. Many late adolescents will graduate from college at approximately this age and enter their young adult years. In some respects, going to college was a moratorium in life regarding many of the life choices that will need to be made upon graduation. For some youngsters who do not go to college many of these decisions may have already been made. Some life choices will be put off, in these contemporary times, until the fourth decade of life, e.g., marriage and parenting. For some, it may be the time for their first job in their chosen occupational interest. For another group it could be a decision to enlist in military service. Often the choice of military service is based on economic necessity such as planning to use veterans' benefits to get further education.

A practical decision is where to live. In the same town you grew up in or a different region of the country? It used to be, several generations earlier, for children to join parents in the same trade, business, or profession. While this still occurs, it seems there are so many more occupational choices that have opened up with modern advances in technology. Young adults nowadays may choose an occupation that did not even exist when their parents were their age.

Some will choose not to go to college, and instead elect to learn technical skills in one of the trades. They will enter apprenticeships upon graduating high school. Others will go to a community college for such training. Not every high school graduate wants or needs to go to college. Our culture, however, at least in urban areas, seems to value going to college while devaluing "blue collar" employment. There often is a dearth of skilled plumbers, carpenters, electricians, etc. These occupations can provide a good and steady income for those who are less interested in academics and more in craftsmanship.

Unfortunately, such work has less status for most people. Nowadays, choosing a serious job my be jeopardized because of a prospective employer's rejection of an applicant because of their earlier adolescent exuberant exhibitionism on social networking Internet sites such as MySpace and Facebook.

For a minority of graduating seniors from college, graduate or professional school will present another challenge and a further postponement of the "real world." As educational opportunities and economic conditions change, a baccalaureate degree today is almost like a high school degree was for my generation. This means that there is a lot of competition to be admitted to such schools. This adds much stress to young adults, as they go about choosing a career.

Assuming sexual orientation has been decided upon and is stable, which is the case among most young adults, dating that began during late adolescence usually now takes place in earnest. The young adult often is ready for an intimate relationship. Object removal, i.e., finding a partner that is non-incestuous, an unconscious process that begins in adolescence, is usually consolidated in young adulthood (see Chapter 14). Replacements for parents are minimally sought after as love-objects. The circumstances under which young men and women now meet have changed. Dating services, Internet's chat rooms and social networking websites like MySpace and Facebook are important features of the culture of contemporary young adults. Having never experienced the Internet as a young adult I cannot speak from direct experience, but I hear from young people about its popularity. Some people actually meet for the first time, while others keep in touch. It is interesting to me that on Facebook people list many details about themselves, their likes and dislikes, so that there is no longer such a thing as a "blind date." Perhaps this is a good thing insofar as compatibility can be pre-determined somewhat, but it does seem to eliminate the excitement of discovery.

In the States there is a trend towards young adults cohabitating, having children, and not marrying. Reasons given for cohabitating are often to test out compatibility, yet such couples seem to be breaking up more than do married couples get divorced. It is not clear why this is happening.

Changes in what is considered masculine and feminine, and in expectations regarding gender roles, effects young adults. Contemporary young adults seem much more comfortable with divergent life styles than was my generation. Gender identity is not as rigid as it was for earlier generations. Young adults also are more accepting of racial differences than previous generations. These changes have been present for a while now, so that most late adolescents entering young adulthood know what to expect. But for some who grew up in more traditional families, there may be some adjustments to be made. For those where this is not something they can accommodate to, it is likely they will search for a more traditional partner. In some religious groups, arrangements approximating arranged marriages exist.

The sexual revolution of the sixties, of course, has reduced inhibitions so that premarital sex is more commonplace these days. For those without religious objections, birth control methods are readily available. But with increased liberties regarding sexual experiences, also come increased exposure to sexually transmitted diseases. Young adults are aware of this and most take precautions, but some take risks. If an unwanted pregnancy occurs abortion is a possibility, assuming a woman has no religious objection to undergoing the procedure. Some women feel very comfortable with a pro-choice viewpoint regarding abortion. For some other women, there may be mixed feelings that can be conscious or denied.

Young adulthood is a time for further consolidation of personality trends that have taken on stability during the late adolescent years. I am thinking here of such internal psychic achievements such as a synthesis of different aspects or components of the personality. When this is very stable there is likely to be less conflict and feelings of self-worth and self-esteem are sustained. Reconciliation with, or better, an affirmation, of parental values takes place via the endorsement of societal institutions.

Parents of young adults are now dealing with adults. Of course, he or she always has the status of being "your child." The nature of the relationship, however, has to be transformed. They must be treated as adults with recognition of their knowledge, strength, reproductive powers, possibly divergent interests and viewpoints on diverse topics, e.g., politics, religion, etc. They may already be more knowledgeable than their parents about various topics. Most parents wish their children to "outdo" them, but this may threaten some parents. For most, it is not so much competition with their child, as much as it is the realization that some of their own goals and aspirations in life have not been achieved and likely will never be reached because of advanced age and circumstances.

It is a mistake for parents to get too much vicarious pleasure from a child's success. What is "too much?" It is too much if a parent's own self esteem hinges on their child's additional successes and drops with failures. A parent should not own a child's success. If a parent take proprietorship of it, a child will sense it and it will feel very hurtful. If a parent gets depressed if a child fails, it can result in planting the seeds of guilt in the child. A child may recognize and appreciate a parent's life experience and ask for advice regarding job or career decisions. A parent best remember it is advice being sought, not a decision.

There may be a minority of young adults who are not sufficiently prepared yet for the "real world." They may move back into the parental home until they "find" himself or herself. Usually, this is temporary. Parents need to remember, they are adults not children even if they are living "under your roof." If a parent treats them like children or failed adults, a parent is looking for trouble. If the stay in the parental home is not temporary, these young adults may need to be encouraged to get professional help. They may be undergoing a prolonged adolescence.

Chapter 18
Homosexuality

Societal attitudes about homosexuality have drastically changed the past twenty years. Same-sex commitments guaranteed to have the same legal rights as marriages between opposite sex partners are accepted by many legal jurisdictions in the United States. It is a current political issue whether or not to allow same-sex marriages. Several states already have such laws. Twenty years ago this would have been unthinkable. Youngsters have been exposed to all sorts of non-traditional families among their school peers. The younger generation appears relatively nonchalant about homosexuality, accepting of it as a divergent choice among some peers and adults. This is not to say that for any individual adolescent who is dealing with bisexual issues that he or she will be immune to conflict. While contemporary society is more tolerant it likely is not much more accepting of homosexuality. It's analogous to being in support of homeless shelters, as long as they are not in your backyard. Bisexuality, while psychologically present in all people, creates conflict universally. It is one of those inner conflicts, like active vs. passive, or love vs. hate. These kinds of conflicts are unavoidable and result from incompatible inborn aims. This does not mean that an individual cannot find a comfortable solution to an inner conflict.

The view of psychoanalysts about homosexuality has also changed over the years. It used to be that homosexuality always was considered pathological and we were zealous in analyzing it. Now we are more accepting that if a patient is not conflicted about this choice there is no need to pursue it. Some would say, rather, the choice needs to be affirmed when there is a strong inclination held back by concern about social ostracism. Furthermore, many analysts now accept that for some homosexuals it is a normal variation of sexual orientation that is predominantly biologically determined. Transgender attitudes and behavior in both males and females is not immediately pathologized. We know that identifications with both parents are not the exception but the rule. It is also accepted that heterosexuality does not correspond to "normal." There are variations of heterosexuality insofar as it is a compromise formation, too, and some heterosexual orientations include perverse attitudes and behavior.

Commonly younger boys, and girls less so, gravitate predominantly towards peers of the same gender. Many gay men and lesbians will tell you that as very young children they remember feeling different from same sexed peers, instead feeling a greater affinity for opposite sex friends. Boys may have secretly preferred to play with dolls and play "dress up," while girls may have preferred to play with toy guns or throw around a football. As mentioned in Chapter 9, some girls grow up during their latency and adolescent years thinking of themselves as "tomboys." Most of these girls, however, go on to choose a heterosexual orientation after puberty.

Homosexuality as a preferred sexual orientation does not get determined until after puberty. Prior to that, things are in flux and with puberty choices can change. It is much more difficult to be homosexual in our society so one does not make this choice because of life style affinity but, rather, because of compelling sexual attraction. When a young adult who is inclined to become homosexual but has struggled with this decision for years, "coming out" openly can feel very liberating, especially if there is a supportive community of like-minded young adults.

Clearly, there are some homosexual men and lesbian women who have made their sexual orientation choice based on neurotic conflict. Choosing to abandon heterosexuality for homosexuality may be based upon many different reasons. An individual may feel very uncomfortable and seek help. Males may be scared of women's genitals and want to avoid penetration because of castration anxiety. Other males may have had an absent father and an emotionally unavailable mother and in an attempt to get closer with mother totally identify with her, preferring a male as a love object (partner). For others, they retreat from a positive Oedipal position (where father is the rival) and adopt, instead, a negative Oedipal position (where mother is the rival).

In such instances, competitive wishes regarding father create intense castration anxiety and these young men retreat from such impulses. Girls who become lesbians may have had an absent, or cold father, and a very warm embracing mother whom they remain very attached to. Or they may have had a critical and cold mother so they seek to rectify this in a lesbian relationship. Other girls have rejected their femaleness, may envy males and develop defensive contempt for males in general. When the choice is made on the basis of conflict, professional help is warranted.

Some contemporary young adults feel comfortable having sex with both genders. They consider themselves to be bisexual. In some instances they are making a political statement, often one compatible with a militant, radical feminist position on relations between the genders. In others, my hunch is that they are acting out a bisexual conflict. If this is the case, some may find that they feel more comfortable with one gender compared to the other. I doubt that this is a true resolution of the conflict, but more a temporary cessation of it, only to reappear at a future date. I do not believe we have enough clinical experience with this "solution" to know the long-term results of such an early life style decision.

Parents whose children adopt homosexual life styles are most often in conflict about it. This is less so as our society has become more open-minded about it. But it is a divergence from what they grew up with and strange to them. They wonder why is my child rejecting the life style I chose and modeled for them? Are they rejecting me by choosing to become a homosexual? Have I failed them in some way? For some parents, the objection is religion-based. The presence of HIV virus causes contemporary parents also to worry about the future health of a homosexual child.

Once parents can get distance from taking their child's choice as a personal attack on them, I think they can be more supportive of their child. They can help their child by affirming their choice of an orientation that is natural for them, or if it is a conflicted choice they can support their child's seeking professional help to sort out wishes and feelings. In some instances parents may have to mourn a fantasy of having grandchildren from that child. However, nowadays, gay couples are adopting and lesbian couples also are adopting or arrange artificial fertilization for one partner. Becoming a grandparent is still possible. When senior citizens gather, they often talk about their children. Parents with a child who is gay or a lesbian are uncertain about a listener's acceptance of such a life style and may worry that their parenting will be judged. It may be that the more they have accepted it and support their child's choice, and can convey this, the more a listener can be put at ease and be more accepting.

Chapter 19
Middle Age

I'm considering the period of middle age between forty and seventy years old. This period of life could be divided up into the working years and the years approaching retirement. The current world economic crisis of this current decade has underscored how essential it is for middle age people to have a proactive appreciation of saving for retirement and a thoughtful plan about investing these savings so they are not subject to severe downturns in the economy. Also, future retirement plans, even if not well formed, may effect many decisions during the earlier middle age years, e.g., location of residence, educational and job goals, etc. Looking to the future does not mean that the present cannot be experienced "in the moment."

What are the developmental issues for these years? There are many life situational outcomes that have psychological correlates. I am thinking of economic and financial issues, career or job decisions, "empty-nest" adjustments, health issues, grand-parenting experiences, marital relationship changes, friendship losses, etc.

It is during these years that men are actively engaged in their work. There are successes and failures. One may get promoted or fired or laid-off. Being a provider has been the traditional role of men forever. It still is the major role, although other gender roles have been added, such as being a hands-on caregiver. Self-esteem may be based on how much money you earn or the title you hold in the corporation or in the academy. Of course, if one loses one's job there are financial repercussions. For some it might mean relocating the family to another area of the country. This involves loss of close contact with friends, or could mean severing ties with various interest groups that one may have served in or volunteered with. For children, a geographical move means the loss of friends and entry into a new school. These changes can be very trying and, on top of every thing else that parents may be dealing with, their child's feelings will need to be attended to. For non-skilled or skilled blue-collar workers a move might mean a loss in seniority. One's inner sense of security will be jeopardized.

In today's world we are bombarded with media promotions of various material things. We seem to believe we need every innovative technological gadget on the market. We seem to want things to happen quickly, so that we trade up for a new computer because it is "faster." Our automobiles have so much horsepower, much of it is never used. The garment industry is always changing styles and convincing us that unless we buy the latest fashion we will be seen as stodgy or old-fashioned. We can keep purchasing because of the introduction of credit cards, an entity that did not exist for my generation's parents. The point that I am getting to is that people do not save money, or as much as they should according to economists. This has implications for retirement, which will follow at the end of being middle-aged.

Young people do not project themselves into the future. Someone in their forties needs to start a retirement fund. If they do not, as they enter their sixties they will become increasingly insecure about their financial viability after they retire. Of course, the latest world wide financial crisis of 2008 has everyone worried about his or her financial security. Retirement savings have dwindled in amount. This worry affects all social classes. If you are affluent you might worry that you will be unable to maintain the life style you have become accustomed to. If you are a blue-collar worker you may worry about keeping up with mortgage payments or if your employer will drastically reduce health benefits after you retire and before public health benefits are applicable. These concerns all impinge on the sense of wellbeing for the later middle-aged individual.

It is early during the period I am calling "middle age" that a married couple or even a single person thinks of home ownership. To own a home is part of everyone's dream. Why is home ownership so important in the psychology of adults? Perhaps it is connected to a primordial need for a permanent campsite (fireplace) protected from the weather. I think it also may have to do with a latent fantasy of being the "lord of the manor" or that "my home is my castle." Within the boundaries of your property you are like a king or queen. Outside of your home you are an ordinary "citizen," not a "powerful monarch". Of course, owning a home has many practical financial advantages, too, that I am not focusing upon. For those individuals whose ownership is in jeopardy because of finances their sense of wellbeing will be undermined. If mortgage foreclosure is a possibility, where to relocate is a real practical issue.

Job or career changes may be considered during these years. The older one gets the more difficult it will feel and be to "re-invent" oneself. It is a natural tendency to become more risk-aversive as you get older. I think this is because the future feels less open-ended and if you make a mistake it seems as if there will not be enough time to correct it. During these years the issue of being a "workaholic" is always present. Because of inflation, overtime is attractive and career promotion is always an incentive to work harder. If you have lost money in the stock market you may also work more hours, if you can, in the hope of replenishing the money. I mention this because a consequence is always a cutback on time spent with partners and children. This is an opportunity "lost." As you get older your children may have moved out, but that still leaves your spouse or companion at home.

The so-called "empty nest" affects every one, especially women who traditionally have been the caregivers and fulltime homemakers. Women benefit if they are not working in a career or a job to anticipate the idle time that will become available as their last child leaves home. There are many different opportunities to get involved in to fill the idle time. A woman may choose to return to school to restart a career or retool for a new career. Job opportunities, however, may not be plentiful in the current economic climate. If being a homemaker and parent is essential to a woman's identity, there will need to be some modifications made. Otherwise her sense of self-worth could be diminished. Her husband or companion, perhaps the sole provider up till then, needs to recognize that his spouse will need support and encouragement. If he is a workaholic then the marriage could suffer at this transition point.

When someone middle aged feels that there is little importance to what one does, one feels vulnerable. It is a time when middle-aged people seek compensations for these vulnerabilities. Popularly, this has been termed the "midlife crisis." A compensation might be the purchase of a new house or car, or engaging in an extra-marital affair. It is as if the new car or lover will be a panacea and revitalize you and you will feel young again. This sounds like a cliché because it is. It does not solve anything but is turned to as a solution by many middle-aged men and women. It seems to me that this is an opportune time for a husband and wife, unburdened by the responsibilities of hands-on parenting to re-find each other. If finances allow, then weekends away or travel and vacations can allow the couple to reacquaint themselves with romance, if it has been neglected. If this can be achieved, then maybe compensations need not be resorted to. Those who are fortunate to have hobbies or talents can turn to these interests with renewed vigor.

As one ages, of course, health usually deteriorates. The potential for a life threatening illness increases. Middle-aged people in relationships usually are available to support one another during scary times. There is nothing harder than to face a life-threatening illness alone. If you have been fortunate to have children who are now grown, they and a spouse, friends and relatives, are invaluable during such a period. During this period of the lifespan, there may occur non-life threatening losses such as diminished visual acuity and/or hearing, decreased strength and agility, etc. When people are younger, health is taken for granted. This is the usual feeling, of course, until one is afflicted with a serious illness. A satisfying and fulfilling life, while not fully dependent upon health, is achieved with greater ease if present.

As one moves towards the end of middle age, there are important losses to deal with. One's own parents likely die during these years and some friends may have had a tragic young death. We have already mentioned mourning of the role of a hands-on parent as one's children leave the nuclear home to seek their fortune. So many losses will make unavoidable a beginning consideration of one's own death. We will talk more about this later in Chapter 21. Loss and the sadness that is felt is a natural feeling. It is part of the healing process and is healthy. There has been, in my judgment, the medicalization of sadness, so that it is treated like something pathological and in need of medication. In most instances, mourning of different intensities fitting the particular loss, runs its course and the person feels better again. There is a phenomenon called an anniversary reaction whereupon on the anniversary of a loss, a person will experience sadness, sometimes not linking it with the earlier loss. It's likely the mind's way of reworking the loss once again in an attempt to reduce grief further. The experience of becoming a grandparent will likely begin sometime during the span of ages that we are calling the middle-age period. I will devote Chapter 20 to this role.

Whether or not to retire will become a major issue for those at the end of their middle age. A decision sometimes is made for you by an employer, as is the case for many blue-collar workers, but even for some in the corporate world or in academia where mandatory retirement rules may exist. For those who are self-employed as professionals or free-lancers there are some incentives to retire once pension plans are required to begin to disburse funds. Sometimes, health reasons are decisive factors determining the decision. If you are in good health, both mentally and physically, and enjoy your work, you may decide not to retire. Some people at this point, if it is possible, may decide instead to cut back and continue to work at a reduced schedule.

For some people, retirement is an opportunity to do an entirely different type of work at which they can still earn income. For others, it is an opportunity to have leisure time to engage in activities or interests that they could not find sufficient time for when fully employed. Grandparents might spend more time with grandchildren. Those with wanderlust may travel. Still others may decide to resume playing a musical instrument they have neglected for years. Hobbies can be re-engaged and interests deepened by means of retirement education offered by colleges and universities. For some, it might mean meeting with friends over morning coffee. Obviously, the permutations are endless.

It is a cliché that some men at the age of retirement when asked how they will spend their time say they plan to "drive their wives to distraction." If a husband has been a workaholic and has had no hobbies, a lot of idle time becomes available. If their wife has been a homemaker she has lots of routines she has established. Now, a retired husband expects her to be available to spend more time with him. But it is not so easy. Tension can result. If the marriage is strong, undoubtedly, accommodations are made on both sides.

Engaging in mental activities that are challenging is a sensible plan. Gerontologists tell us that there is data to support the idea that keeping the mind challenged slows down the brain's aging. Reading books, magazines, newspapers, going to lectures, searching the Internet, playing bridge or chess, volunteering to teach youngsters in elementary schools, etc., are the types of activities that will keep minds active to sustain memory efficiency and to forestall senility. It seems to me that the fundamental foundation for a good retirement is health. If you are healthy you have many more options than if you do not. Financial security is another basic ingredient.

What about being a parent to a middle-aged child? Not much direct parenting of middle-aged children occurs. Parent's hope that the earlier investment in parenting that was made is now paying dividends in their child's parenting of their own children. A parent cannot take all the credit, only some, if children are great parents, and nor should you take all the blame if they are inadequate, only some. I hope from my earlier exposition the conclusion has been reached that parenting is a very complicated business. There are many variables and many that are uncontrollable. It usually brings bittersweet pleasure to older parents to observe their own child being a good, maybe better, parent than they ever were. It is bittersweet because such observations will cause regret that they did not do better as a parent. With age, hopefully one may attain wisdom from experience. Sometimes middle-aged children consult their parents about things, sometimes even about parenting.

Chapter 20
Grand-parenthood

Being a grandparent has been described as an opportunity to have fun without responsibility. I am sure about the fun but not about the lack of responsibility. Grandchildren are a grandparent's legacy insofar as they share your DNA and your own parenting of their parents has indirectly been transmitted to them. Undoubtedly, some grandparents are imps of fun, over-indulging and over-stimulating, leaving the parents, their children, to clean up the mess. The majority, however, do not make such a mess. Most grandparents have a fantasy of an ideal grandchild and they wish to see it actualized. Grandparents with adoptive grandchildren will need to deal with some of the same issues as their children, the adoptive parents. I am thinking specifically of mourning the fantasy of biological grandchildren having inherited some of their genetic potential and thereby passing on a legacy.

I suppose there are some grandparents who envy their grown child's vitality when their own is waning. Most admire it, however, and get vicarious pleasure from it. There is great pleasure watching one's own children be parents themselves, especially if they do it well. Sometimes grandparents are put in the position of mediating between their grown adult child and a grandchild. It can come in the form of a direct request from either party or it is strongly implied. The grandparent is viewed and experienced as a neutral figure. Sometimes this can be helpful, but I think the grandparent needs to reaffirm the authority of the grandchild's parent to help the parties reconcile. In some extreme circumstances, grandchildren are sent to live with grandparents because the parents are emotionally unable to parent. Of course, most grandparents take on the responsibility if no other arrangements can be made, but it must be both physically and emotionally very draining. On the one hand, they're dealing with the disappointment of their adult child being unable to be a responsible parent. On the other hand, at advanced age, their stamina is pushed to its limits by needing to look after an active young child or rambunctious adolescent. There are lots of adults who grew up in unfavorable circumstances of poverty and substance abusing parents who are successful and give credit to and pay homage to a grandparent for being there during their childhood.

In better circumstances, grandparents lend a sense of personal origin and belonging when they tell narratives of personal history to grandchildren. The real appreciation of this will not be felt until the grandchildren are late adolescents, a time when family history and one's place in it is in the context of one's place in the larger world.

Grandparents attend their grandchildren's sport events, and school graduation ceremonies and take pride in their emerging skills and talents. For artists and scientists, their creation or discovery will remain and be valued after they die. For most people, however, a grandchild is our hold onto immortality. We value them for themselves, but also for ourselves.

It is a good idea for grandparents to be involved with their grandchildren from an early age. This way they will be important persons in their lives. In contemporary time when grown children live distances apart from their parents it may not be practical to visit often. There is always, telephone and nowadays, Skype, as a way to keep in touch. When grandchildren get older a grandparent can email or text. If practical, having grandchildren come out to visit without their parents is a beneficial way to bond. Taking vacations with grandchildren is another way to bond.

Are grandparents necessary for the progressive development of grandchildren? Is there something unique that only a grandparent can provide? Could another adult, like an aunt or uncle, do for the child whatever it is that grandparents' do? I guess this is an empirical question that likely will never be answered. There are too many variables to control for an experiment. In the view of grandchildren, grandparents are unique insofar as they are their parent's parent. My gut feeling, however, is that grandparents are unique in what they potentially can provide to grandchildren because of the special biological link they feel to them regarding legacy. I wonder, too, about the second chance they are given to "do it right," so to speak. Grandparents could do a better job "parenting" this time. This can be a powerful motivator to show affection, empathy, set appropriate limits, admire, etc. Of course, grand-parenting grandchildren is not the same as parenting insofar as you are a surrogate. Grandchildren may not view their grandparents to have parental authority. Nevertheless, a grandparent has learned hopefully from past mistakes and does not need to repeat them.

Chapter 21
Old Age

    I am considering old age to begin at seventy and end at death. I know there are many people out there who fall within this bracket but who do not feel old but are spry, vital and looking forward to the future to realize new goals. This notwithstanding, there can be no denying that the physical body and the mind is in a period of decline for most all people. The rate of decline may vary but it is inevitable. People younger than seventy think of themselves as "getting older" and not as "old." While society's views during the past decade have changed somewhat with medical advances and increased longevity, so that you hear that "sixty is the new fifty," nevertheless people are considered "seniors" as young as fifty. My criterion is the decline of function.

    There is an old saying "getting old is not for sissies." I think this is a valid belief if it refers to the plethora of things that start to go wrong with the body and the mind. To mention a few, stamina diminishes, as does strength, recovery from illness and soreness takes longer, short-term memory fails, vision and hearing impairments are frequent, etc. The interactive side effects of medications take their toll in causing imbalance, drowsiness, as well as damage to internal organs of the body. Old people are much more aware about good diet and the need for exercise of the body and the mind. Some would add the soul and spirit too. People are more proactive about their health. Interestingly, while this is so, and longevity has increased, there is still a shortage of medical specialists, geriatricians, for the aged.

    In some cultures, such as Eastern ones, the aged or old people are "revered." Ancestors are almost worshipped. This is not true in Western culture. If anything, the opposite is true. Old people are thought of as "over the hill." They are not "hip" or "cool," but instead are believed to be out of touch with modernity. Popular culture with its celebrities are elevated to extreme heights of influence, while the past and history is devalued as passé. What can an old person know that is of value to a young person? After all, they need help programming their cell phone or using the DVD. Perhaps I am putting this too extremely to make a point. There are younger people who display deference and helpfulness to older strangers in public settings.

But the point is many old people who have not been afflicted with senility or Alzheimer's have lots to offer young people, a wealth of experience and often a perspective based on this that is known as wisdom. To accept this about old people is not the same as denial of the general decline that also exists. Nor do I mean to diminish the enormous creative energy of young people.

I am cognizant of the vast repository of knowledge and information that computers and the Internet makes available to us with just a click. Computers are to young people what the radio and books were to the generation of people I am calling old. But what many old people can do that a computer cannot is to engage in self-reflection about their knowledge and frame the experience in a perspective that is uniquely human with feelings. It is this that earlier generations can profit from.

Many old people accept being redundant as true, but a minority knows they have something to offer. These people volunteer their time to schools, join Boards of organizations to contribute their expertise, and even join the Peace Corps. For some who "give in" to the decline, they retreat to communities where only like-minded and like-bodied people can reside, rather than preferring to live among all the generations so as to benefit from new learning. I do not mean to be dismissive of so-called "retirement communities" which can offer multi-enrichment programs, assisted living services to help those who are physically disadvantaged, such as meals, housekeeping, and transportation, along with medical services. For a segment of old people, such communities serve a valuable function.

For some elderly, the loss or decline of some bodily functions can be very disturbing and humiliating. For men, especially, the decline of sexual prowess or interest can make some feel less masculine and even castrated. It seems less so for women in this area, perhaps because being sexual for most women is more than pleasure seeking and being feminine, but, more importantly, also being emotionally intimate with a specific partner. The intimacy can still exist without the sexual accompaniments. Incontinence is not uncommon among older women and in men who have had treatment for prostate cancer. For both genders, but particularly for men, the loss of control over urinary elimination is an embarrassment and can reduce one to feel like a little child. Some men feel less masculine if they wear a pad to absorb the leakage.

Wrinkles and graying hair seem to disturb older women more than men. "Looking their age" is to be avoided. Face lifts, long hair that is bleached or dyed, and clothes made for a younger generation are sought after to deny and disguise aging. Vanity takes over because of the emphasis our Western society places on physical beauty over personality and good sense. Additionally, looking younger supports denial of ultimately dying.

Parenting now can take a complete turnabout in some respects. The parents of old people are long dead. Old people are in some respects "parented" by their grown children. Some find it easier than others to accept this. Some, a small minority, can afford to hire help, like nurses, handymen, drivers, etc. Others who are poor, too many to allow us to be complacent about the problem, do without help and barely scrape by with some assistance from volunteers in service agencies and religious institutions.

If one's own child assists or takes care of one, an old person must accept being dependent and not feel a burden. Most grown children willingly and lovingly provide assistance, feeling they are doing for parents what they provided for them as children. Of course, there are some who resent it and feel it to be a burden and are neglectful of their elderly parents. Government help in terms of health and social welfare programs, has made a great difference in the wellbeing of the elderly.

Of paramount importance is the attitude that an old person has about a life lived and if he or she has come to terms with dying. If one feels that they have been generative in terms of contributing something of value to the world then they will feel accomplished. What may have been contributed need not necessarily be something of high monetary value like a successful business, or intellectually praiseworthy like an invention, novel, or scholarly paper. These accomplishments certainly can serve as a valued legacy. But also can a beautiful perennial garden or a reputation as being decent and honorable, and so on. Another legacy can be the family that you have produced.

Coming to terms with death is something that Mankind has struggled with forever. If you are a religious person and believe in an afterlife or in reincarnation, dying will feel less dreadful. But if you do not have such faith, then existential anxiety may be disturbing. There are, however, many old people who have come to terms with the inevitable and accept it as a fact and part of the cycle of life. They could even think of dying as returning natural matter to the Earth. Imagining a return to Mother Earth is comforting for some.

Hopefully older people can enjoy their remaining years and are able to take pleasure in the job they did as parents. One may not be a rich person, or have acquired properties, or written a book, but one will be leaving behind a legacy that is more valuable, a child and/or grandchild that one has directly or indirectly parented.

PART 3

Chapter 22
Obtaining Professional Help

We all know that in the stewarding of children from infancy to an emancipated young adult there can occur difficulties on the way. Often these developmental hurdles are just that. They look impossible to jump over when first encountered, but after some small mishaps and practice a child vaults over them. A parent can sigh with relief, and it's behind him or her. But there are other hurdles that are not so easily mastered. Some of these hurdles may be ones that a parent unnecessarily put in the path of his or her youngster. I referred to these as developmental interferences in Chapter 8. Some may be universal developmental conflicts (Chapter 8) that are difficult but need to be engaged by child and parents, with the very engagement itself and a successful outcome contributing to progression in development.

While the potential problems discussed in the paragraph above do not need always to be labeled with a diagnostic term, if even after parents speak with friends, grandparents, teachers, etc., and read self-help books, the issues remain and stress is mounting within the family, it can be helpful to seek professional help. Sometimes pediatricians are the first line of professional help about problems with children from birth through adolescence. Nowadays, their training includes behavioral issues. In some instances a child development expert may need to be consulted. My bias about the comprehensiveness of a psychoanalytic perspective leads me to recommend referral of children and adolescents to professionals trained in child analysis or psychodynamic child therapy. A consultation with such a professional may or may not involve a child directly. It may be that a focus on parenting and becoming informed about the particular developmental phase issues facing a child will be sufficient to help ameliorate the potential problem.

Not all psychological conflicts, however, remit in a quick fashion. A positive, adaptive and progressive outcome may require an extended consultation and recommendation for treatment. Some psychoneurotic conditions with their accompanying symptoms (Chapter 8) may require that a child be evaluated directly. Drug and alcohol addiction that appears unremitting also requires professional help. Additionally, delinquency with or without contrition suggests the need for expert professional help. Sudden school failure may also be a sign of serious emotional conflict. A suicidal gesture needs to be taken as a plea for help.

A disposition session, following several with parents, child or adolescent, may include a recommendation that the child or adolescent enter child analysis, being seen usually four or fives times a week, or psychodynamic therapy, being seen less frequently, with the parents being seen together weekly or bi-weekly with or without the child, usually depending on the child's age. Not all consultations with a psychoanalyst lead to a recommendation for psychoanalysis. The frequency of sessions that will be in the best interests of the family and child depends on a number of factors, most importantly, what intensity is best suited for the needs of the child to get a good response. We hope to achieve the goal of relief for the child and parents and progressive development for the child. The expected duration of treatment usually is a question that parents ask. It is a legitimate question but one that is difficult to answer. It is a bit like asking how long would it take to walk from point A to point B. You may know the exact distance but how long it takes to walk the distance depends upon the length of stride of the walker, the ability to maintain that stride, weather conditions, etc., all determinants that you may not know before hand. How long a treatment will need to last, for example, depends on factors such as the degree of motivation of the patient to work in the treatment, the intensity of resistance on the patient's part, how supportive parents are of the treatment, etc.

A child analytic treatment does not aim for perfection. The goals are much more modest. For children and adolescents, the goal is to restart progressive development. When a child or adolescent is dealing with a psychoneurosis they are unable to proceed with development insofar as most of their resources are dealing with the psychological conflicts that led to a psychoneurotic solution in the first place.

Adults seek professional help for many different reasons. Support for troubled adults who confide in family members or friends can include having them consider a consultation with a psychoanalyst or psychodynamic therapist trained to work with adults. Often but not exclusively, they are dissatisfied with their careers or work and with their personal relationships. They may feel unfulfilled, unhappy with life, given to depressed moods or anxiety, etc. Solutions that they have made can be neurotic ones that attempt to reconcile opposing forces of desire, conscience and reality demands. A good consultation with a trained professional may be helpful to articulate and focus in on what it is that they are troubled by and a recommendation can be proposed as to the treatment of choice that will be helpful to them.

I could say much more about psychoanalysis with children, adolescents, and adults. For that matter, a lot could be said about techniques that are informed by psychoanalytic clinical observations and theory, but are less intensive than child analysis or adult psychoanalysis proper. I am thinking of interventions like work with parents or psychodynamic psychotherapy with children, adolescents, or adults. The focus of this book, however, is on "normal" development and not on treatment. Referrals in the United States to qualified psychoanalysts seeing people of all ages can be obtained on the Internet from the Association of Child Analysis and the American Psychoanalytic Association. The International Psychoanalytic Association can be a referral source as well for psychoanalysts practicing in different locations around the world. Additionally, professional societies of psychodynamic therapists are present in the USA and UK. Many Institutes that train psychoanalysts maintain clinics that offer low or reduced fee psychoanalyses for people of all ages by candidates who are in training. Senior analysts closely supervise their work.

Representative List of Topics Discussed in Each Chapter

CHAPTERS

Part 1

1. The decision to have a baby. Conscious and unconscious motives.
2. The newborn. Sleeping arrangements, breast-feeding or bottle-feeding, etc. The oral phase. Self-other differentiation.
3. Psychological issues of infertility, decisions to undergo IVF, having multiples, and issues of adoption. Premature birth, miscarriage, replacement children. Death of a child.
4. Examination of toddlerhood. Issue of separation, the difference between discipline and punishment, etc. The anal & urethral phases. Sado-masochism. Action. Thought as a form of trial action.
5. The preschooler. Tolerating separation, the internal representation of the parent (object constancy), transitional objects, the meaning and value of play for a preschooler, animistic thinking, real/pretend, imaginary companions, and mentalisation, etc. The psychoanalytic model of the mind and mental conflict.
6. Day care and choosing a suitable place for a child. How to help a child adjust.
7. The psychological issues of the Oedipal years. The significance of this universal developmental conflict and its role in

progressive development. The beginning of an internalized conscience with the partial dissolution of the Oedipal Complex. Family romance and rescue fantasies.
8. Psychological disturbances of the early years are reviewed. Subdivisions include developmental interferences (including trauma); sleep problems; separation/attachment problems; toilet mastery; eating problems; learning problems; sibling rivalry; developmental conflicts; psychoneuroses; delinquency; and super-intelligence.
9. The Latency phase (elementary school years) of development is the focus. It's role as a time of consolidation and preparation for puberty. Development of a sense of competency. Mental processes used by the mind to defend against objectionable wishes, etc. Sublimation. Modern technology (e.g.,cell phones) and development is considered.
10. Helping children cope with divorce. Blended families. The arrangements that are in the best interests of children.
11. Sex education, media exposure and after-school enrichment. In each instance these areas are discussed from the point of view of child psychology and the parenting issues that arise.
12. Sexual abuse. The consequences of such an experience upon the development of children. The definition of abuse is expanded from the common one of physical molestation.
13. The Preadolescent phase is examined for boys and girls. Differences between the genders are noted. Tasks for parents to help children through this difficult time period.
14. Early adolescence and the concerns of young teenagers. Tasks of adolescence, namely, finding a non-incestuous love object (object removal) and the second separation-individuation phase.
15. Middle adolescence. The restitutive attempts of adolescents in their efforts to deal with disengagement from parents. The effects upon parents from a defiant child. Sexuality of adolescents.
16. Late adolescence is considered. A time of consolidation. "Genital primacy" is discussed.

BOOK I: INTRODUCTION TO CHILD, ADOLESCENT & ADULT DEVELOPMENT

Part 2

17. Young adulthood is discussed. The relationship with parents needs to be transformed. Parents need to realize they are dealing with young adults, not young children. Issues of young adulthood, e.g., career considerations, consolidation of character, sexual orientation, etc.
18. Homosexuality is considered. Changing viewpoints of psychoanalysts. The dynamics that may be involved in bisexual conflict are discussed alongside a homosexual orientation based upon biological determinants.
19. Issues of Middle age are discussed. Topics include the "empty nest" syndrome, compensations that are sought to deny aging, approaching retirement, etc.
20. Grandparents and what role they play in the lives of grandchildren are examined. Is there something unique that a grandparent can contribute?
21. The period of Old Age. Issues of waning health and its consequence on the psychology of elderly people is examined. The reversal of roles so that children now take care of parents is considered.

Part 3

22. Seeking a consultation. I try to distinguish between the kinds of problems that may require treatment such as psychodynamic psychotherapy, child or adult psychoanalysis, or parent work.

RECOMMENDED READINGS

Annuals & Periodicals:

Psychoanalytic Study of the Child (PSC), Yale University Press, New Haven & London, Vols 1-65.

Child Analysis, Hanna-Perkins Center for Child Development, Shaker Heights, Ohio, Vols 1-18.

Bulletin of The Hampstead Clinic, 1978-1984; renamed Bulletin of The Anna Freud Centre, 1985-1995.

Journal of the American Psychoanalytic Association – (Search www.pep-web.org for selected articles).

Psychoanalytic Quarterly- (Search www.pep-web.org for selected articles).

Collected Works:

The Writings of Anna Freud, International Universities Press (IUP), Inc., Madison, CT, Vols 1-8, 1936-1980.

The Complete Psychological Works of Sigmund Freud, Standard Edition, Vols 1-23, 1886-1939, Hogarth, London.

Psychoanalytic Theory:

Brenner, C., 1973, An Elementary Textbook of Psychoanalysis, Revised Edition, IUP, Madison, CT.

Brenner, C., 1982, The Mind in Conflict, IUP, Madison, CT.

Erikson, E.H., 1968, Identity: Youth and Crisis, New York: Norton.

Gehrie, M.J., 2011, From Archaic Narcissism to Empathy For The Self. J. Am Psa Assn 59, 313-333.

Hartmann, H. 1964, Essays on Ego Psychology, New York:IUP.

Kohut, H. 1971, The Analysis of the Self: A Systematic Approach to The Psychoanalytic Treatment of Narcissistic Personality Disorders, New York: IUP.

Loewald, H.W., 1980, Papers on Psychoanalysis, Yale Univ. Press, New Haven & London.

Nagera, H., 1966, Early childhood disturbances, the infantile neuroses' and the adult disturbances. Monograph series of the PSC, #2.

Nagera, H. 1968, The concept of ego apparatus in psychoanalysis: including considerations concerning the somatic roots of the ego. PSC, 23: 386-403.

Sandler, J. & Rosenblatt, B., 1962, The concept of the representational world. PSC, 17: 135-145.

Sandler, J. & Nagera, H., 1963, Aspects of the metapsychology of fantasy. PSC, 18: 179-184.

Schur, Max, 1967, The Id and the Regulatory Principles of Mental Functioning, Hogarth, London.

Sterba, Richard F., 1968, Introduction to the Theory of the Libido, 3rd Edition, Robert Brunner, NY.

Childhood:

Abrams, S.,2008, Transformation: Identifying a specific mode of change. Descriptive and conceptual considerations, PSC, 63, 312-320.

Bettelheim, B., 1989, The Uses of Enchantment, Vintage Books, NY.

Coles, R., 1997, The Moral Intelligence of Children, Random House, NY.

Corbett, K., 2009, Boyhoods: Rethinking Masculinities. New Haven, Yale University Press.

Decarie Gouin, T. 1965, Intelligence and Affectivity in Early Childhood, IUP, Madison, CT.

Decarie Gouin, T. 1974, The Infants Reaction to Strangers, IUP, Madison, CT.

Erikson, E., 1963, Childhood and Society, Norton, NY.

Fonagy, P., Gergely, G., Jurist, E., & Target, M., 2002, Affect Regulation, Mentalization, and the Development of the Self, New York: Other Press.

Furman, Erna, 1987, Helping Young Children Grow, IUP, Madison, CT.

Furman, Erna, 1993, Toddlers and Their Mothers, IUP, Madison, CT.

Furman, Erna, 1995, Preschoolers: Questions and Answers. IUP, Madison, CT.

Furman, Erna, 2001, On Being and Having A Mother, IUP, Madison, CT.

Flavell, J.H., 1963, The Developmental Psychology of Jean Piaget, Van Nostrand Co., Inc., Princeton, NJ.

Fraiberg, Selma, 1959, The Magic Years, Scribner's, NY.

Gilmore, Karen, 2011, Pretend Play and Development in Early Childhood (With Implications for the Oedipal Phase), JAmPsaA, 59: 1157-1181.

Greenspan, S.I., & Pollock, G.H., (Eds.), 1981, The Course of Life, Vols 1 & 2, NIMH.

Lax, R.F., Bach, S., Burland, J.A., (Eds), 1980, Rapprochement, Jason Aronson, NY.

Legg, C., and Sherick, I., 1976, The Replacement Child: A developmental tragedy. Some preliminary comments. Child Psychiatry And Human Development, 7.

Litowitz, B.E., 2011, From Dyad to Dialogue: Language and the Early Relationship in American Psychoanalytic Theory, JAmPsaA, 59, 483-507.

Mahler, M. S., Pine, F., & Bergman, A., 1997, The Psychological Birth of the Human Infant, Basic Books, NY.

McDevitt, J.B., & Settlage, C., (Eds),1971, Separation-Individuation, IUP, Madison, CT.

Nelson, K., 2007, Young Minds in Social Worlds: Experience, Meaning, and Memory. Cambridge: Harvard University Press.

Novick, K., & Novick, J., 2010, Emotional Muscle, Xliberis,

Olesker, W., & Lament, C., 2008, Conceptualizing transformations in child and adult analyses. PSC, 63, 273-279.

Olesker, W. 2011, The story of Sam. Continuities and Discontinuities in Development. PSC, 65, 48-78.

Parens, H., & Saul, L.J., 1971, Dependence: A Psychoanalytic Study, IUP, Madison, CT.

Parens, H., 1979, The Development of Aggression in Early Childhood, Jason Aronson, NY & London.

Roiphe, H., & Galenson, E., 1981, Infantile Origins of Sexual Identity, IUP, Madison, CT.

Sherick, I., 1981, The Significance of Pets for Children: Illustrated by a Latency Age Girl's Use of Pets In Her Analysis. PSC, 36, 193-215.

Sherick, I., 1983, Adoption and Disturbed Narcissism: Case Illustration of a Latency Boy. J. Am.Psa.A, 31, 487-513.

Spitz, R.A., 1965, The First Year of Life, IUP, Madison, CT.

Stern, D.N., 1985, The Interpersonal World of the Infant. A View from Psychoanalysis and Developmental Psychology. New York: Basic Books.

Tronick, E., 2003, "Of course all relationships are unique: How co-creative processes generate unique mother-infant and patient-therapist relationships and change other relationships," Psychoanalytic Inquiry, 23: 473-491.

Tyson, R., & Tyson, P., 1990, Psychoanalytic Theories of Development: An Integration, Yale, New Haven & London.

Winnicott, D.W., 1953, Transitional objects and transitional phenomena: a study of the first not-me possession. Int. J. Psychoanal., 34: 89-97.

Winnicott, D.W., 1965, The Maturational Processes and The Facilitating Environment:Studies in theTheory of Emotional Development. London: Karnac: 1990.

Winnicott, D.W., 1971, Playing and Reality. Tavistock: London.

Adolescence:

Barrett, T.F., 2008, Manic defenses against loneliness in adolescence. PSC, 63, 111-136.

Blos, Peter, 1962, On Adolescence, Free Press, NY.

Blos, Peter, 1970, The Young Adolescence, Free Press, NY.

Blos, Peter, 1979, The Adolescent Passage: Developmental Issues, IUP, Madison, CT.

Brockman, David Dean (Ed.), 1984, Late Adolescence: Psychoanalytic Studies. London: Karnac.

Browning, D.L., 2011, Testing Reality During Adolescence: The Contribution of Erikson's Concepts of Fidelity and Developmental Actuality. Psa. Q., LXXX, 555-594.

Deutsch, H., 1967, Selected Problems of Adolescence, Monograph Series of the PSC, Vol.3, IUP, Madison, CT.

Erikson, E., 1963, Childhood and Society, Norton, NY.

Greenspan, S.I., & Pollock, G.H., (Eds.), !981, The Course of Life, Vol.2, NIMH.

Katan, A., 1951, The role of displacement in "agoraphobia." Int. J. Psa., 32, 41-50.

Marcus, I.M. (Ed.), 1975, Masturbation, IUP, Madison, CT.

Adult:

Colarusso, C., 1992, Child & Adult Development, Plenum, NY.

Erikson, E., 1963, Childhood and Society, Norton, NY.

Freud, S. The Complete Psychological Works of Sigmund Freud, Vols, 1-23, 1886-1939, Standard Edition, Hogarth, London.

Greenspan, S.I., & Pollock, G.H., (Eds.), 1981, The Course of Life, Vol.3, NIMH.

INTRODUCTION TO UNDERSTANDING PSYCHOPATHOLOGY:
A Psychoanalytic Perspective

Ivan Sherick, Ph.D.

Preface

Formerly, I've written books on development throughout the life cycle, *Introduction to Child, Adolescent, and Adult Development: A Psycho-analytic perspective for students and Professionals*, and on clinical technique with people of all ages *Psychoanalytic Technique with Children, Adolescents, and Adults: An introduction for Students and Professionals*. Both of these books were written as introductions to the respective topics from a psychoanalytic perspective, with students and beginning professionals in mind as potential readers. Neither was a scholarly written book with references embedded in the text, nor with footnotes. A list of references was included at the end of these books, so that interested readers could immerse themselves more thoroughly in the topics. Technical terms were defined and the tone of these books was intended to be welcoming and not intimidating. The following book on psychopathology is written with the same goals as the above-mentioned books.

This book on the topic of psychopathology from a psychoanalytic perspective is not meant to be an all-encompassing exposition on the topic. Rather, it is meant to be an introduction. My psychoanalytic orientation is a contemporary ego psychology. Thus, it is classical but has integrated contemporary revisions that advance our thinking.

Please keep in mind that the term "psychopathology" is not meant by me to connote something ominous, malignant, or life threatening such as cancer or coronary problems. That is **NOT** what I am speaking about. The inclusion of the term "pathology" unfortunately may mean something biological and diseased to you. As a psychoanalyst my interest is in the **mind** and in **feelings, not the brain**. For example, when I talk about a depressed feeling I am **not** thinking of a biologically caused depression but one that is **reactive to a disappointment.** What is disappointing to one person is trivial to another. It is very subjective and based on one's life experiences and one's wishes, either attainable or fantastic. What I am mainly going to write about are the kinds of mental conflicts that evoke feelings and possible psychological disturbances that are common among almost all people. In fact, psychoanalysts often refer to non-patients including themselves as "normally neurotic."

On the other hand, I do not mean to minimize the degree of discomfort that mental conflict can cause many people. Obviously, it can be intense enough that an individual will seek professional help, or regretfully, contemplate suicide.

I will not be discussing the Autism spectrum, Asperger syndrome, or Psychosis. I have no experience with patients dealing with these diagnostic issues. The first two are very likely due to some kind of organicity and do not get referred to psychoanalysts. There are some analysts who have specialized in working with psychotic patients, but I am not one of them.

Occasionally, I will address a particular issue more than once insofar as it is important throughout the life cycle. Sometimes in the narrative I use the accepted contemporary convention when the gender of a subject is unknown, e.g., "parent", the pronoun "they" and the possessive "their", instead of "he or "she" and "his" or "her".

CHAPTER 1

Essential Concepts in Understanding Psychopathology

There are some essential concepts needed in our efforts to understand psychopathology. These concepts are relevant in manifestations of psychopathology across the life cycle.

We believe that a major, if not the most significant, motivator of the human psyche to be *instinctual drives*. We focus on two drives, namely, *libido* or the *sexual* drive, and *aggression*.

Both of these go through a linear sequence that we call, oral, anal, phallic, and Oedipal. In the early phases of drive development, sexual and aggressive drives are intermingled. It is only during the later phases that they autonomously distinguish themselves

Our clinical observations suggest that drives also have passive and active aims. The active aim is to achieve gratification via the expression of a drive wish towards an object and the passive aim is to have it expressed by an object towards oneself. The term "object" is used to differentiate a person from oneself, the "subject."

Examples of the active expression of the sexual and aggressive drives of the different phases follow. Keep in mind the passive expression would be where the subject obtains gratification by being the recipient of the expression of the drive by another person. An oral expression of the sexual drive is to suck, of the aggressive to bite or cannibalize. An example of the anal sexual drive is to pleasurably defecate, of the aggressive drive to mess or damage via a bowel movement. *Sadism* and *masochism* also arise in force during this phase. An example of a phallic sexual drive is to penetrate another body, of the aggressive drive to forcibly violate another body. Children express phallic aggressiveness, boys particularly, as if the body is a missile that can rapidly move though the space they occupy. *Exhibition* and *voyeurism* are also prominent sexual and aggressive drive expressions during the phallic phase. Around the same time as the phallic phase, the biological act of urination holds the attention of children. Boys will hold their penis as if it is a water hose and girls will try to stand up like boys while urinating. Before puberty, urination can be a discharge of libidinal excitement. Urethral aggression is to "piss" on something or somebody. Both genders are aware of their genitalia and frequently touch that area because it is pleasurable. It is no longer accepted theory that all girls are envious of a boy's penis because it is visible. Girls soon discover the part of their genitalia that is most pleasurable is in the interior.

Derivatives of the phases of drive are expressed in later stages of life development. I'm thinking of latency, the stage after the dissolution of the Oedipal stage and before the advent of puberty, the various stages of adolescence, the young adult years, and stages of adulthood into old age. It is more complicated than this, e.g., there are non-linear occasions, but for our purposes it will suffice to think of drive development as linear.

Drives have biological origin and seek pleasurable gratification. Gratification is a demand, not necessarily a conscious one, of the drive made upon the subject experiencing the drive. Life experience will either allow for pleasurable gratification or denial of such causing an experience of frustration, sometimes in excessive amounts.

Individuals differ in the relative constitutional or in-born strengths of the drives. A fixation occurs when during a particular phase of drive development, there is either excessive frustration or gratification of the drive. For example, if a child is born with a relatively weak need to suck and ingest milk and later foods, during the oral phase, then excessive frustration will not result in a fixation at the oral phase. On the other hand, if there is a strong oral drive then even limited frustration will result in a fixation. We call this reverse balance between strength of an inborn drive and experiences of gratification and frustration the *complemental series.*

Fixation is a concept that seems to be rarely referred to in contemporary case presentations and articles examining psychopathology. Perhaps this is because of a de-emphasis on the role of drives in contemporary thinking. I think this is a mistake.

Fixation can be thought of as a sensitivity, a vulnerability, or a pre-readiness to assert a combination of drive expressions when a contemporary experience revives memories (not necessarily conscious) of the past experiences involved in the causation of the fixation.

Regression is another essential concept in understanding psychopathology. In our understanding, it refers to the tendency to re-experience, not necessarily consciously, a past experience set off by a *psychic* similarity between a contemporary experience and a past one. It is a fixation that is like a magnet that draws the current experience back to the past (regression), so that the former is given psychic meaning, or nuanced, by the past experience. For example, if an adult is micro-managed by another adult and told how to discharge or take care of a responsibility, it could be that this interaction reminds, again not necessarily consciously, the managed adult of being told often as a youngster by their mother that they had to use the toilet even though they did not feel the need to evacuate their bowels. So, a boss is reminiscent of their mother. The response of the managed adult, depending on their past history, could be to stall or to obey immediately. Some of the expressions could be not in the best interests of the adult. For example, the employee might say, "Do it your self!" or do the task in a sloppy way. Such expressions probably will cause stress or anxiety, and could lead to psychopathology. Of course, there are many possible derivative drive expressions depending on the personal history of the managed adult.

Young children when ill or when very tired and sleepy have been observed to temporarily regress to earlier phases and manifest behavior reminiscent of an earlier time in their lives, much to the distress of some parents.

There are no children without adults, in most instances, parents. Much of the structures of a person's personality dealing with life experiences are laid down in childhood. It is the parents and other adults, such as grandparents, relatives, siblings, teachers, etc., that are important influences in a child's life.

Setting limits is an essential parental responsibility. Some parents are hesitant to do so because they wrongly equate it with expressing anger towards a child. If children have the feeling that they can act on whatever they want to then they get scared because if they can, the belief is that they can damage the adults that care for them. Also, setting limits helps a child internalize regulatory structures that helps them be in control of instinctual drives.

The foundations of later adolescent and adult psychopathology are laid down in early childhood. Adolescents also struggle with age specific puberty. Adults too, of course, have age specific issues that they deal with. However, we know when we treat adults we are treating the child and/or adolescent "within" the adult. A successful psychoanalysis of an adult is one where the adult has helped the "child or adolescent self" within to grow up. The adult has used their mature Ego resources to reassure the internal child and/or adolescent that the anxieties they dread can be withstood and that mental conflicts can have more adaptive outcomes than the ones earlier accepted. Hopefully, too, the "joys" of one's earlier age can also be re-experienced.

We know that a parent's own experience of being parented will influence or shape the parenting of his or her own children. Also, their own individual style of parenting may exacerbate things. It is inevitable, that a parent's psychopathology will enter parenting of their children and deleteriously effect their child's development. We call this the *intergenerational transmission of psychopathology*. This is an essential concept in understanding psychopathology.

Mental conflict occurs when an individual feels, either consciously or unconsciously, that he or she is in danger if expression is given either in action or thought to a wish that seeks gratification. This judgment is made by the part of the mind we call the *Ego*. Wishes are expressions of drives or instincts that originate in the part of the mind that we call the *Id*. The danger can be "understood" to be the *loss of an object* (usually mother or later representations of the maternal figure), *loss of love, injury to their body* (castration), or *loss of approval by their conscience*. The danger of loss of the maternal object is known as *separation anxiety*, something children commonly experience. Mothers serve as auxiliary egos for young children, so the absence of the mother scares a child that demands of the external and internal worlds will not be met. The sense of danger is felt as *anxiety* or, *shame* or *guilt*. We call the conscience the *Superego*, and its disapproval is felt as guilt.

Anxiety is a unique feeling that humans feel when they imagine the dangers mentioned above. There often are physical accompaniments such as an increased heartbeat and perspiration. The Ego uses it defensive resources to modify or "erase" (repress) the thought or wish provoking the anxiety. If the defensive maneuvers are not successful, the anxiety will not be sufficiently diminished in intensity and it can reach a heightened state that we call *panic*. A panic attack is very unpleasant and scary to the victim.

Children differ as to their *anxiety tolerance*. Presumably this has some connection to the strength of their Ego. With such tolerance, panic is less likely to occur unless the anxiety becomes very intense. Also, the "calling into play" of ego defenses will be delayed. If the child has supportive adults and can use his or her words then an emotional "crisis" for the child may be avoided and psychopathology averted.

Additionally, if a child has a high degree of *frustration tolerance*, the urgency to find gratification for the drive can be extended until a more acceptable expression can be found. A "melt down" can be avoided and negative consequences for the child's sense of well being can be prevented.

The part of the mind that resolves conflict we label as the *Ego*. Essentially it is the part of the mind that is in charge of executive processes like judgment. The wish that may be objectionable is then either modified or "locked away." *Symptoms* occur when the wish is modified sufficiently so its expression provides some modicum of gratification along with some degree of felt sanction demanded by the individual's internalized moral system (Superego) or by the rules and perceived demands of the external world. Essentially, symptoms are *compromise formations*. Early on, in childhood, the parents are the principle conveyers of the moral principles of the community. These are later internalized (the child's "inner policeman"), for the most part, by five or six years of age, with some modifications as the person ages.

Anna Freud proposed difference among conflicts based on their genesis, *intrapsychic, internalized*, and *external*. These three types of mental conflict are present throughout the life cycle. Intrapsychic is based on the inherent conflict between some wishes. Sometimes a person wants to be **active** in expressing a drive towards another being and sometimes they want to be the **passive** recipient of the expression of their wish. For example, an active wish to hit another person can be in conflict with a wish to be hit by the same person. Bisexual wishes can be in conflict, so that a subject may seek someone of the same gender or opposite gender to gratify a sexual urge. Ambivalence, loving and hating the same person, is another example of an intrapsychic conflict.

In an internalized conflict the structures of the mind are in conflict, i.e, the Ego feels anxiety or guilt (Superego) because a wish demands to be gratified but the Ego judges that if they execute the unmodified wish in action the Self will be punished.

External conflict is between the Ego and the external world, when the Ego judges that external rules are opposed to the expression of a wish in action. The wish must be modified to be acceptable.

Conflict cannot be completely avoided but the Ego has resources to minimize conflict in the first place so that psychopathology is not very intense and of shorter duration. This asset is called *ego strength*.

Children demonstrate individual differences in this asset. Intelligence is a favorable asset but the child has to be able to use it in beneficial ways that are more likely to exist based on good parenting and socialization. A good preschool education can help the child learn how to deal with peers in a mutually satisfying manner. Ego strength is demonstrated by resilience in the face of a stressful situation that may briefly render a child anxious and scared. A child possessing ego strength has a capacity to communicate so that adults can come to his aid. Feelings can be regulated often by the use of words rather than actions that can make stressful situations worse.

As the child ages, psychological processes develop that are able to modify objectionable drives. The outward expressions become more acceptable to other children or adults, thereby reducing external conflict. These processes are called ego defenses, and a child having ego strength has a repertoire of them. Also, he or she is cognizant of internalized moral edicts so that guilt is minimized. Ego strength will be an asset for the emerging adolescent and later for the young adult, as well as during adulthood. With reasonable limits a child might object but internally the child will feel safer and anxiety avoided.

As children age a process called *sublimation,* an aspect of ego strength, becomes a possibility. Herein, a drive wish, either sexual or aggressive, can be modified by a consolidated stronger Ego, so that the wish is expressed in a more socially acceptable form. A former unmodified aim to injure an animal may have caused feelings of guilt. Now a sense of beneficence can replace the guilt because of the expression of a more socially acceptable aim. An example could be a child that once harbored sadistic wishes towards a sib's pet, wanting to injure and kill the pet, in high school volunteers at a university laboratory doing experiments on animals to test out antibiotics. This same child that once wanted to harm pets later as an adult becomes a veterinarian.

Psychological mindedness is a trait we usually do not apply to a child, but to adolescents and adults. It is possible, however, that a precocious child may have such a trait. Having such a trait can allow someone to have insight that the unease they are feeling may be caused by some mental conflict. Consequently, they may be better able to resolve it and avoid greater distress.

Sadism and masochism are component sexual and aggressive drives arising in prominence during the anal stage. Derivatives of these two drive components continue throughout the life cycle. As mentioned above, the possibility of sublimation may play a role averting issues of unconscious feelings of inferiority, shame, and guilt that these two drives can generate for people.

Consciously, sadism involves the absence of guilt in dominating and controlling others. The sadist has a sense of being ordained with an omnipotent destiny. Masochism predominantly takes two forms, sexual masochism and moral masochism. In the former an adolescent or adult person may engage in fantasies or behavior wherein he or she is sexually humiliated and experiences pain, and subsequent orgasmic pleasure. In the latter, moral masochism, the individual seeks to suffer. This involves the relationship between the Superego and the Ego. During internalization of the parental objects in the structuralization of the Superego, de-sexualization, more-or-less, of the parental objects, occurs. In moral masochism a re-sexualization occurs. The child behaves in ways to be punished. Guilt is not experienced in most case. Depressive feelings later may accompany moral masochism. In some instances self-imposed unpleasure experienced by the moral masochist may be an unconscious way to try to win parental love, if the child believes they may be punished or that love will be withdrawn.

Trauma is another essential concept in understanding psychopathology. When an individual is unprepared to experience excessively intense incoming stimulation, they are overwhelmed. I mean that their psychic apparatus, parts of their mind, is overwhelmed or unable to process the incoming experience. This is what we mean by trauma. The effects of trauma, memories laid down in the mind, are that when the memory (memories) is re-stimulated or re-experienced by contemporary events, a feeling of being overwhelmed is re-experienced.

We think of two different kinds of trauma, *shock trauma* and *cumulative trauma*. The former refers to a single intense overwhelming experience. Examples might be, a car accident, witnessing the murder of a parent, experiencing rape, physical assault, etc. Cumulative trauma might be the result of a verbally abusive parent, experiencing racial derisive comments over the years, poverty, etc.

The effects of trauma can be delayed or manifested immediately. Some childhood traumas are experienced not until adolescence when a sexual encounter may re-stimulate memories of sexual abuse in earlier childhood. Adults who have witnessed or experienced massive terror experiences such as armed combat may return to civilian life with a post-traumatic syndrome (PTSD). For these individuals the past and present are intermingled so that a loud noise may trigger a fear reaction reminiscent from a past feeling of being near an explosion from a bomb or artillery fire. Such traumatized individuals experience a panoply of feelings like shame and anger. To get some distance from these unpleasant feelings dissociation and solitariness may follow. Difficulties sleeping and nightmares may be an affliction.

Some events for children that are planned even with supportive preparation may nevertheless prove to be traumatic. If the unexpected "negative" event has a particular meaning for a specific phase of development the interference can be experienced as a traumatic external conflict. For example, a tonsillectomy or appendectomy happening during the phallic phase when surgery is experienced as an assault on the body, can heighten castration anxiety. Psychosexual development can come to a halt and entry into the Oedipal stage might be stalled.

Narcissism is the wellbeing that is felt when a libidinal investment is directed at the self. Very early in life before there is much differentiation between the newborn and others we theorize that all libidinal investment is on the beginning self. We know better, now, that the infant seems invested in the maternal caregiver very soon after birth. Soon the growing infant receives loving expressions from the other people in his or her life. This is felt as secondary narcissism.

Acceptance later from an internalized Superego is felt as love, too. Later we will discuss psychopathology resulting from an over-inflated narcissism (narcissistic personality) and deflated narcissism (e.g., a constituent of dependency, depression, and other "bad" feelings.)

Self-esteem is a derivative of narcissism. It is the positive sense that comes from a feeling that one is a valued person, and others share this belief. Many children feeling peers do not choose to play with them on the playground, adolescents who feel unpopular or those whose girlfriend or boyfriend have ended with them, adults that are not invited to social events, etc., feel diminished self-esteem. We all seek to feel some degree of social acceptance insofar as we are social beings. However, if we are too dependent on such we are at risk to become depressed. One needs to feel good that they have achieved an accomplishment **even if** others do not applaud you. Here one's reservoir of healthy self-esteem is a safeguard. Otherwise you may be vulnerable to be hurt by the competition and envy of peers and colleagues.

CHAPTER 2

Life Events and Psychopathology

The death of a loved one almost is always experienced as a terrible loss. Grief and stress are felt. It can be a family member's death, a friend or even a beloved pet. When you love a person your self-identity includes that person. The expectation, even though, you know better, is that they will be in your life forever. For parents it is unimaginable that a child will die before you do. We now appreciate the terrible loss that is felt by parents of an infant miscarried during a pregnancy or of a stillborn infant. There is a tendency on the part of young parents to want to get pregnant again to have another child. The newborn child is a "replacement" for the one who died. To be such is a psychological burden for the replacement child. He or she psychologically "carries" the bereaved parents' expectations for the dead child. For the parents and themselves they are not a "person in their own right."

For a child, particularly, the loss of a pet is very tragic. Pets offer companionship. Like adults experiencing the death of an offspring, a child may opt for another pet to replace the one that died. After the death of a loved one or pet a process of *mourning* takes place. This is a time of remembering the lost person or pet by privately having memories of them. This is a healthy process that enables the surviving individual to "let go" of the dead person or pet. It is an emotional acceptance that they are 'gone' and that "life goes on" for oneself without them.

Regretfully, some people are unable to satisfactorily mourn and instead they become depressed. This depression can last a long time and for some it becomes part of their *self-identity*.

Some individuals need to deny the personal loss. It may be they fear grieving because they imagine that if they allow that feeling, it will be overwhelming. For others, dependency on the dead person or pet is intense and imagining a lack of gratification is unbearable.

Young children were once thought to be unable to mourn but we know better now. A supportive adult can provide the child satisfaction of his or her basic needs, and with that support a child will feel the grief of the loss of the loved one. Distress leading to psychopathology may be avoided. Parental illness can also frighten a child. The loss of a loving, comforting, need-satisfying parent can terrify a young child. An adult that "steps-in" can help such a child.

Suicide of a family member, a parent or a sib, is a trauma that "doesn't go away." Especially devastating to a parent is the suicide of a child. Often the child was an adolescent when he or she suicides. The ubiquitous expectation of parents is that our children will survive us. The survivors will think of reactions that they wish they had done differently. For example, why didn't they get the guns out of the house, why didn't they seek out an in-patient treatment facility when their child expressed suicidal intentions, etc? Often, the parents will be overcome with grief. It is very difficult to see the children of their friends growing up and progressing through life. For the child survivors of a parental suicide, self-blame is often a guilty feeling. The adult child may feel they should have been more involved with a depressed parent. The guilt generates depressive feelings. For many, they are puzzled why they were not "enough" for the parent to stay alive. Anger may follow directed at the dead parent, followed by guilt.

Many adolescents, and adults too, may have suicidal thoughts but will not act upon them. These may occur if they are feeling rejected by peers or after a relationship has ended not by their choice. Such thoughts are common although not ubiquitous.

There is a phenomenon known as *survivor guilt*. An example might be if a group of adolescents are in an auto accident and there is as fatality. A survivor may feel guilty, especially if he or she was the driver. The superego of the survivor presumably must hold a memory of some transgression in the survivor's mind and uses this to make the individual feel guilty. Such an individual may get in some kind of trouble in order to be punished.

Another traumatic experience is to grow up in a family of survivors of genocide, e.g., the Holocaust. The surviving parents do not talk about their experiences but it casts a shadow over the family. The children sense the depressive feelings of their parents. Pathological identification with the parents in different forms can occur. The surviving child, for example, may grow up with a foreboding feeling of a terrible event "lurking around the corner."

Adoption has the best of intentions but regretfully it brings with it psychological consequences for all involved. What better intentions than to provide a family for a child given up by a birth mother for a number of reasons. Also, there are the benevolent aims of a family, perhaps unable to conceive a child of their own, to allow for parental gratification in caring for a child given up for adoption.

One should keep in mind, that what follows is not meant to be applicable to all instances of adoption. There are many instances of "good" outcomes in adoption. However, starting with the birth mother, who may have conceived the child out of wedlock while a teenager, there will be eventual guilt in having given up her infant, possibly unconscious. Of course, now we have so-called "open-adoptions," where the birth mother (parents) is involved in the life of the child. I doubt, however, if this is sufficient to mitigate the guilt generated by the knowledge of having given up her child for adoption.

I have been critical of "open adoptions" insofar as I believe that a young child can only be confused by having "more" than one mother. Also, the task of early childhood is to feel emotionally connected and integrated into a family. Having "another family" can only make this task more difficult and even impossible. The adoptive parents often harbor guilt, albeit unconscious, about having "taken away" the child from the birth mother. Also the fact of adoption is often not sufficient for adoptive parents to reduce feelings of inferiority having to do with "barrenness." Infertility can be an assault on one's masculinity or femininity.

There is much variability among adoptive parents as to when and if they tell their child he or she is adopted. Most disclose it insofar as it is difficult to keep it a secret. Many speak to the infant as being "special" and "chosen" from the beginning. Of course, for an infant this has no meaning, although the positive feeling emanating from the parent likely is experienced by the infant. Others may wait to tell the child until they are older. To me it makes most sense to wait, if possible, until the mid-latency years when the child will have the intellectual abilities to understand what "adoption" means. During the earlier years it is beneficial for the child to engage in the Oedipal struggle and telling the child about being adopted is likely to interfere with this engagement.

Sometimes an adoption occurs in a family that already has biological children, but because of social, ethical, and moral beliefs, adoption takes place to provide a family for a disadvantaged baby. The biological child, in such a family, may understand and endorse his or her parents' beliefs, but, nevertheless, unconsciously, they may wonder, "Was I not enough to satisfy my mother's (father's) parental needs?"

Then there is the adoptee. As the child grows there could develop a sense of abandonment by the birth mother (father). "Why was I given up for adoption?" A child is apt to blame him or herself for being inadequate in some way. Even an "open – adoption" may not reduce such feelings.

As the child enters adolescence, assuming they have been told of their adoptive status, an interest in searching for the birth parents may start. Sometimes, the occasion of reunion can be a satisfying one for both parties but sometimes it can be very disappointing. If the birth mother gave the child up for adoption, for whatever reason, but maintained parenting with other biological children, learning that can cause an adoptee a great deal of befuddlement as to why they were given up for adoption, but siblings were not. Again, there is a tendency to blame oneself.

As I review the consultations I have conducted over the years, divorce, has been an issue for many of the patients, seeking help. This is another social-psychological event that is involved in the genesis of psychopathology. Divorce, as a factor in causing distress, occurs across the lifespan. Thus, it affects not only the children, adolescents, and adults whose parents got divorced but also the adults engaged in a divorce.

Again, the children of all ages from a divorced marriage often blame themselves, consciously or unconsciously, that if they had been better behaved then their parents would have experienced less marital tension and would not have divorced. They believe this even though they often believe they could never please one or other parent. I suppose, sometimes there may be a modicum of truth to this belief. Parents can disagree as to the nature of parenting. Some believe in setting limits and some do not. This can cause spousal bickering and the children blame themselves. Children witnessing fighting between parents feel helpless. It becomes more difficult to control anger. Sometimes, one parent, in the eyes of the child, takes the role of the "bad cop" and the other the "good cop." This befuddles the child and makes them anxious.

There is often unconscious guilt for a child because of Oedipal wishes to divide the parents and to win the favor of the positive (opposite gender) Oedipal object. When this occurs in reality, the child, because of unconscious omnipotent beliefs feels responsible.

A child of divorce often will feel divided loyalties for each parent. Often this manifests itself in the child having feelings about visitation differences between the parents. Children often hold one parent responsible for the divorce. Loyalty tensions can be exacerbated if a parent begins to date and gets attached to another adult. If the child or adolescent "likes" this new person in their lives, the loyalty conflict can be exacerbated. For adolescents, knowledge that one of the parents is engaging in sexual encounters, they may feel that this parent is "cheating" on the other parent, even though they are divorced. Of course, if the parents are only "separated" and not divorced this feeling will be intensified. The adolescents' own sexual tension may be exacerbated in ways more intense than what normally occurs due to "primal scene" fantasies in an intact family. Primal scene fantasies refer to the ubiquitous fantasies of children that involve imagined sexual interactions of their parents.

For adults engaged in a separation or a divorce there are feelings of failure about his or her own ability to be intimate and committed. Also, guilt about causing the children emotional distress is ubiquitous.

Parents involved in a divorce are often emotionally distressed and unavailable to their children. After divorce a mother may have to seek employment and will be less available for her children. Often they themselves have been the children of a divorce. Their parents' divorce may have been a reaction to infidelity. Now as married adults, adultery may be a determinant causing marital strife and divorce for them. Once again, the intergenerational transmission of psychopathology is evident.

One could debate whether marital tensions should never end in divorce for the "sake" of the children in the family. The parents could avail themselves of marital therapy and be an example for their children of their attempts to resolve tension. However, there are instances where such intervention will not be helpful and one could argue it is better for the children to no longer witness daily fighting between their parents and to have the opportunity to experience happier parents in new relationships. Divorced spouses often feel intense anger towards their ex-spouses and most children sense this. This exacerbates already existing loyalty conflicts.

Alcoholism is another frequent behavior that can tear apart a marriage. Spouses and children suffer. When these children grow up, they too may be prone to alcoholism. Some of this may be an inherited predisposition to alcohol intolerance but some of it may be an identification with the parent.

Sexual abuse has far reaching consequences that often are determinants in the genesis of psychopathology. I am considering acts as abuse wherein the child is encouraged to participate in sexual acts with the adult. This may be the result of forcible participation, but it can also be based on exploiting the child's affection for the parent. Its victims in family settings are mostly young or adolescent girls and the perpetrators are fathers. Boys are not exempt from being victims of sexual abuse. Rarely this occurs in a family setting but most often in predominantly male dominated settings such as boarding schools for boys and involvement with Catholic clergy.

It is not sexual abuse when two preschoolers explore each other's genitalia. This is very common and does not involve exploitation but rather natural curiosity. If one of the participants was much older then I would consider it sexual abuse because of the power differential. In this instance the younger child likely will be frightened by the larger size of the older child's genitals.

I also consider it sexual abuse when there is extreme immodesty practiced by parents, so that their children witness their nudity a lot of the time. Also, some parents do not take measures to be private by closing doors or waiting till the children are asleep when engaging in sexual acts with their partners. Noises emanating from the parental bedroom can awaken children and scare them.

Adults, mostly females, are also subject to sexual abuse. In almost all cultures men have privileges such as expectations to be the more assertive gender when it comes to heterosexual encounters. Regretfully, this social/cultural assignment can be distorted in an exaggerated way. This can be especially in situations of a power discrepancy between a man and a woman, e.g., in a supervisor-supervisee situation or employer-employee situation. Unfortunately, there can be real or imagined consequences for refusal to comply. Another impossible situation is when the perpetrator is a family member. It is hard for a young girl to refuse the advances of an admired father, uncle, or older male cousin. Hence, sexual abuse or more commonly sexual harassment can be the result. Feminine activism is on the rise and women are more likely to publically make known their opposition to such male behaviors and publicize the identities of perpetrators. Also, women now have the expectation that sexual involvement be consensual. Adult women have had to overcome hurt, shame and feelings of responsibility to publically express they have been victims.

The effect of sexual abuse is individually variable, although never positive. For the child victim as they mature into adolescence or adulthood, sexual inhibition or promiscuity can be a consequence of the earlier experience of sexual abuse. A relationship with a supportive partner can help a victim who is sexually inhibited to overcome this symptom.

Physical abuse without sexual violation also can contribute to psychopathology. The victim will be terrified that a beating will occur again. Often with children, my experience is that an alcoholic father is often the perpetrator. Mothers that are alcoholic may also resort to physical abuse but this is less common.

Emotional abuse can also be experienced by people of all ages. A disturbed parent may do such to his or her child, constantly undermining the child's self-worth. It is as if the child's very essence, the "soul," has been damaged. A spouse or partner in a relationship can also be emotionally abusive. The victims often *dissociate* or "escape" from their self- identity. This kind of severe emotional abuse has been labeled "soul murder."

In my view, the advent of Internet pornography has contributed to male deviant sexual behavior. It is very accessible to even preteens who have smart phones and access to the Internet. In pornographic depictions of sexual encounters between men and women, there is no emotional relationship between the two participants. The sexual act is the predominant reason for the encounter. I believe this encourages the same in real encounters and it is not healthy for heterosexual relationships to not have an emotional connection and can lead to more problems. Of course, it is also a possible outcome in depictions of sexual encounters between same gendered participants.

Regretfully, when one is a victim of abuse of any kind, there may be a tendency to identify with the abuser. This is the Ego's way of trying to master a negative or traumatic experience endured passively by actively recreating it with someone else as the victim. Earlier, this was alluded to when we discussed the intergenerational transmission of psychopatholgy.

The birth of a sibling is usually an event that a child has little influence in causing. Sometimes an "only child" can tell its parents that they wish for a sibling to play with. This can be impactful for some parents. Many children look upon a newborn sib with curiosity. Some want to hold them. Some wish they would disappear. In cases where the latter feelings are evident, parents need to be watchful because the older child's hugging can be very intense and potentially suffocating of the newborn. If a sib were to die because of illness, the surviving sib that wished the death will likely fear retribution most of the remainder of his or her life.

It can be a narcissistic injury to an existing child when a sib is born. They may feel hurt and wonder why their parents needed another child. Were they not sufficient? Was he or she lacking in some way.

They feel competitive and envious of the aging sib's talents and skills. They may perceive that the sib has a better relationship with one of the parents than he or she does. This makes them feel loved less than the sib. This can be true insofar as the child's latent angry feelings, maybe unconscious, have interfered with expressions of affection for the parent. The parent may feel this as rejection and seek closeness with another child.

These feelings of sibling rivalry can last forever. The child now an adolescent may compare themselves to the sib in a number of areas. For example, who is the better athlete, more achieving in school, accepted to a better university, has a more beautiful girlfriend or handsome boyfriend, etc?

As an adult the envy can be about the attaining of a graduate degree, the income earned on the first position upon graduation, etc. These competitive, jealous, and envious feelings all can make the adolescent or adult feeling such, either consciously or unconsciously, insecure, feeling like a failure, unloved and depressed. In some instances where a sibling has a handicap, another sib might look more inept than he or she is, because they feel the need to underplay their own accomplishments so the disadvantaged sib will feel less badly.

Many times, a parent can feel towards their own child the same rivalrous feelings they felt towards a sibling. This is an example of *psychic reality* trumping *objective reality*. If this is so they may be less loving towards the child or, defensively, loving in an exaggerated way to cover over the hateful feelings for the child and from themselves. The child who is the recipient of such hateful feelings originating from the parent's past relationship with his or her own sib, will feel unloved. If this dynamic happens early during infancy, a reactive attachment disorder could be the result.

Being a victim of racial bigotry is being a victim of sadism. I include this in this section on life events and psychopathology because the color of one's skin is not elective. People who are members of racial minorities come up against sadistic slurs frequently. It causes the victim to feel isolated, alien, and reactively angry. Having a support group is of immense benefit. Belonging to a minority religion can also evoke bigots to deliver insults and in some instances physical attacks. I am thinking of anti-Semitism and anti-Muslim feelings. Members of these groups who are observant may worry about being attacked and may make efforts in public not to wear traditional garb so as not to be noticed. Doing so they may feel badly for having compromised their beliefs.

CHAPTER 3

Basic Biological Functions That May Be Drawn into Mental Conflict

Basic functions such as sleeping, eating, toileting, locomotion, and sex can all be drawn into early mental conflict, initially external but evolving into internalized conflict as the function is drawn into intrapsychic conflict. In some instances there may be a medical cause for the problem and it is wise to first rule out such with a pediatric consultation. Once there is confidence that a medical issue is not involved, seeking clarification for the cause of the problem via a psychological explanation makes sense.

Sleeping gets drawn into conflict often because of the management by parents of sleeping arrangement of infants. Some parents espouse having the newborn, and even older child, sleep in the same bed as the parents. It feels natural and convenient if the baby awakens in the night. This arrangement can present the youngster to be witness to parental intimacy. Overstimulation from parental noises and/or visual images disrupts the sleep of the infant or youngster. The input of noise and images do not make sense to a young child. It is best to have a child sleep in a different room.

Children during the phallic and Oedipal phases have fantasies of sexual intimacy that their parents are involved in. We call these fantasies "primal scene." They erroneously interpret the noises they hear as one parent hurting the other. This is particularly during the anal sadistic phase of psychosexual development. The result can be fear and worry that a parent whom they are dependent upon is being hurt. The result could be nighttime fear and disturbance of sleep.

A few children have "pavor nocturnus" where they walk in their sleep, having no conscious memory later of its occurrence. Potentially they could injure themselves. The cause of pavor nocturnus is unclear.

As the child ages, sleep disturbances can occur because of fearful fantasies of dangerous intruders, entering their bedroom in the middle of the night. The "intruders" are creations of the child's mind that are attributed to the external world, what we call *externalizations*. Sometimes they are monsters, sometimes humans. The fearful child resists falling deeply asleep to avoid being a victim. As the child gets older, rational thinking can offer some reassurance but derivatives retreat to the Unconscious and they can persist. Disturbed sleeping can be a feature of this person. Sleep can be disrupted, too, by *nightmares*.

Ordinarily the sleeping mind is able to process wishes that are forbidden to the awake mind. These wishes, images, and thoughts are disguised sufficiently so that the dreamer can express such forbidden contents in the form of a dream. Via such *dream work* some gratification is experienced in safety. However, when the disguise is insufficient it is like an alarm going off and the sleeping dreamer is awakened by a "nightmare." This dynamic can operate throughout the life cycle.

Eating is another basic biological function that can be involved in psychic conflict. What is very common is the phenomenon of "comfort eating." This is when eating food is not because of nutritional hunger but because of "emotional hunger." That is, ingesting food is an attempt, albeit often unconsciously, to "fill up" because of an internal sense of "emptiness." It is not that the stomach is empty but rather the sense of self-worth is depleted.

The feeling of fullness after eating is meant to conceal the inner emptiness. This could be resulting from a lack of relatedness to a cherished person, perhaps a maternal figure. The function of eating often is imbued with maternal meaning insofar as it is usually the mother who provides food for the infant and is watchful that they consume a sufficient amount of food. Hence, an individual will desire a scoop of ice cream but instead they will consume the whole quart. Putting on weight and resultant unhappiness is a casualty of this dynamic. In some rare instances after overeating a person may feel "orgiastic, but soon thereafter feel depressed."

Akin to the dynamic where food has more than nutritive value is a condition known as *bulimia*. An individual will overeat likely for similar reasons discussed in comfort eating, but then the individual forces vomiting as a way of getting rid of the increased calories they have eaten. Another eating disorder is known as *anorexia*. Here, an individual reduces considerably the amount of food they eat. Unconsciously they likely wish to consume a large amount of food, but defend against this by eating little. Such individuals will appear very thin, sometimes even looking emaciated. In our culture bulimia and anorexia predominantly effect adolescent girls and young adult women. This probably is because the female gender is assigned by both genders the task of appearing thin and shapely, not overweight.

Breast-feeding is a healthy relationship building interaction between mother and infant. It usually does not exceed a duration of one year, often sooner in our Western culture. In impoverished areas of the world a longer duration has major health protection benefits for the infant. Mothers often will wean their infants when teeth start to develop for the infant. Mothers do not welcome being bitten on the nipple. In instances where the weaning from the breast or bottle is much earlier that the infant desires, an oral sucking fixation can occur, especially if the constitutional drive to suck is strong. Such infants may become adamant later about thumb sucking. When mothers breast-feed for a very long duration, e.g., for periods of two years or more, I think they do it more to satisfy something they crave unconsciously, e.g., a stronger relationship with their own mother who was emotionally distant.

The function of toileting also can get drawn into conflict. As with the function of eating where food becomes an unconscious symbol of mother, in toileting the feces can unconsciously symbolize the mother. (I say mother and not father insofar as in our culture it is the maternal figure, not the paternal figure, that mostly is involved in toilet mastery.) The child undergoing toilet training (I prefer toilet "mastery") may defy the imposed restrictions and rules about where and when to defecate, especially if the constitutional strength of the anal drive is inherently strong. Here, the aggressive drive is being expressed along with the anal libidinal one. This child could be messy and even smear the feces, much in defiance of the mother. Or they may become constipated and controlling. The child that soils may unconsciously equate the scent of the beloved or depriving mother with the scent of feces. An extreme psychopathological expression of this soiling is called *encopresis* and this can last into latency until toilet mastery is complied with. For those children who resist defecating when told to do so, some parents may resort to giving the child an enema. This can be repeated many times. This is regrettable insofar as it causes the child to feel "invaded" and unsafe and can cause or strengthen an anal fixation.

Urinating and its control over-laps with the anal phase and the later phallic phase. Some children do not obtain bladder control and bed-wetting at night can be an issue. We call this *enuresis*. Assuming that there is not a medical cause, the issue can be a psychological one. Before a child is pubertal, sexual excitement cannot be relieved through ejaculation. Instead urination seems to be imbued with this function for some children, especially boys. A child who is inappropriately exposed to parental immodesty regarding nudity, or is involved in primal scene fantasies may be sexually excited, in some instances, and the outcome could be enuresis.

Something as basic as the biological function of locomotion can get caught up in conflict. Young children, who have had to wear braces to correct some physical ailment, may have difficulties with aggression when older. The clinical conjecture is that the inability to use their lower limbs and move about interfered with the discharge of aggressive energy. The aggression is "built up" and at a later age gets discharged.

Sexual expression often gets caught up in mental conflict for both genders. For men, issues of *early ejaculation* can deprive them and their partners with full pleasure. Also, *impotence* can result in a failure to get an erection and maintain it. This reduces self-esteem for the male. For some men, intromission is scary because unconsciously they view a vagina as capable of castrating them. Women may be unable to climax via sexual intercourse, requiring the use of a dildo to engage in excessive clitoral stimulation, or need to masturbate after coitus. This may demoralize both them and their partners. Both may feel inadequate. Again, ruling out a physical cause, psychological causation needs to be explored and mental conflicts resolved.

Some individuals may be afraid of sexual intimacy and avoid it. Instead masturbation provides relief. Many issues interfering with obtaining sexual discharge and pleasure seem to be related to unresolved Oedipal issues. For example, unconsciously one's partner may represent a parent and hence an illicit relationship to be avoided because of guilt and anxiety. These issues can remain throughout one's lifetime.

For many people, mostly young adults, bisexual conflicts may be involved in sexual tension. They may believe that being heterosexual is the cultural norm but may be aware of homosexual attractions. Afraid of being exposed and ostracized they inhibit all sexuality, sometimes even fantasy. In our contemporary society there is more acceptance of homosexuality for both genders but there still is either overt or subtle condemnation of the practice. A supporting group of like-minded friends can help an individual cope with such conflicts. Also, parents who support a child who is gay or a lesbian is very helpful in relieving shame. More about this later.

Gender issues are in the forefront of contemporary society. Many people object to the binary classification of gender, male or female. Some adolescents' feel very uncomfortable with the birth gender assigned based on anatomy. As adolescents they feel more akin with the gender opposite their own or with neither. Some elect to have hormone treatment to hasten the development of the other gender's body; some elect also to have surgical interventions. Adolescents having *gender dysphoria* are very unhappy, even suicidal. A strong support group of like-minded adolescents and supportive parents is needed. More about this later.

CHAPTER 4

Natural Strengths Interfered with by Mental Conflict

I turn my attention now not to basic biological functions but to inborn talents and inherent assets. Talents presumably have a biological foundation insofar as they manifest early in life and we see significant individual differences. For example, some toddlers seem to be very adept and precocious at crawling, walking, and climbing stairs. It is as if they have a muscular balance and strength that is inborn. Such toddlers differ from peers. Practice seems to transform the talent into a skill. When they grow up the child may demonstrate athleticism.

My conjecture is that "curiosity" is one such inborn talent. Being curious is an aspect of a mind that is creative. Individual differences exist. Alas, sometimes being curious can get caught up in mental conflict. If the curiosity is believed to be "too much" involved in sexual curiosity and/or *voyeurism,* then curiosity in general can be inhibited because of a moral condemnation by the child's Superego. If so, a learning disorder can ensue and the otherwise intelligent youngster can become an underachiever, and suffer all the unpleasant accompanying feelings connected to this label, e.g., shame.

There are other non-biological functions that can get caught up in mental conflict. I will mention a couple, so you have an idea of what I mean. If a child has the inborn talent and additional learned skills that allow for athletic participation but is conflicted about competition and exhibitionism, he or she may decide not to continue involvement in the sport. These conflicts may be unresolved from the Oedipal phase. The result is a loss of a potential enhancement of self-esteem for the individual.

Another inborn talent is musical ability. A person with such a talent can become a skilled virtuoso with a musical instrument or participate in chamber music or orchestral music. All of these activities can add to their pleasure and self-esteem. But not if they have excessive "stage fright." Two major contributors to this performance anxiety are conflicts with *exhibitionism* and *competition*. The former is an instinctual component of the libidinal phallic-Oedipal phase and the latter an aggressive derivative of the same phase. Intense stage fright may not allow such a performer to engage in performances or interfere with the quality of his or her performance.

CHAPTER 5

Diagnostic Categories

The diagnoses that I will employ essentially are *neuroses, psychoses*, and *character disorders*.
As a psychoanalyst my clinical efforts have been primarily made in clinical involvement with patients dealing with neurotic issues. My experience with psychotic individuals is absent. In part, such patients were not referred to me, or if in consultation I suspected psychotic issues were a major consideration, I referred the patient to a colleague.

There are patients that are diagnosed as *borderline*, referring to those whose issues seemed to be on the border between neurosis and psychosis. Such individuals might manifest psychotic symptoms in a temporary fashion but not in a sustained way. My experience with such patients has been minimal.

I will, however, mention the major features of this disorder insofar as it is often used as a diagnosis mainly with adults. There is a continuum of severity among borderline patients, as is the case for all diagnoses. Some borderline individuals will only occasionally, and then briefly, seem to go over the boundary into psychotic functioning. The two major defenses they employ are *splitting* and *projective identification*. In the former they divide people into good and bad with the former receiving loving feelings and the latter hateful feelings.

In projective identification borderline individuals attribute negative aspects of their own personality to another person. Then, the borderline person behaves towards that person in a manner that often tends to cause the person to respond with behavior originally attributed to them, thereby "validating" the borderline's critical perception of the person. Borderline individuals have difficulty particularly with regulating aggression and with reality testing.

In my years of clinical practice, my time has mostly been spent with patients dealing with neurotic issues, most to a degree that a neurotic diagnosis was warranted. As I said earlier, we all deal with mental conflict and the majority of people have been characterized as *normally neurotic*. Those who require professional attention have not been successful independently in overcoming or compensating for their maladaptive behaviors. Presumably, all could benefit from increased emotional understanding of the origin of their neurotic thinking and behaviors.

Depressive feelings seem to be universal when an individual is "disappointed" in life. They may have not attained a goal they were seeking, or a relationship that was promising was broken off, a job offer was not secured, etc. You can see that a disappointment underlies all of the perceived causes for the depressive feelings. The severity varies and is heightened by earlier life experiences that were felt to be due to "bad luck" or self-created. The severity can be reduced if supportive family, friends, colleagues, etc., comfort the depressed individual. Often depressive feelings prompt a person to seek professional therapeutic help. The depressed person need not be diagnosed as suffering from a primary depression that is incapacitating. When it is such, the person restricts his or her involvement with life effecting sleep, eating, relationships, work, etc. In modern day psychiatry this is characterized as an *endogenous* depression, thought to be biologically caused and treated primarily by anti-depression medication. Depressive episodes caused by non-biological causes are labeled as *exogenous*. Psychotherapy or psychoanalysis is the treatment of choice. For some individuals being depressed becomes a personality type or character style.

Neuroses occur when there is mental conflict between the Ego and the external world, or the internalized "rules" of morality lodged within the Superego.

Hence some drive expression is judged by the Ego as forbidden, anxiety and/or guilt is felt, and the drive/wish must not be expressed either in thought or action unless modified sufficiently, compromised to meet with perceived approval by the external world or Superego. Symptom formation, a compromise, can result and a neurotic diagnosis may be warranted.

Character, from a psychoanalytic perspective refers to a characteristic style or behavior that typifies a particular individual. It is like a "signature" of the individual. Hence, it is a ubiquitous feature of all people. It is like a "firewall" that an individual has habitually been perceived and acted in their world. When it is so exaggerated that it becomes a "feature" of the individual we give it a diagnosis, otherwise it is characterized with terms such as "he is full of himself (narcissistic)," or "he is so dramatic (hysteric)," or "he is so rigid (obsessional)," and so on.

Developmental Interferences occur when the external world, usually, parental figures, have unreasonable expectations, regarding their children. There are many such examples, some which will be addressed below, but I will give you a sense of what is meant. As mentioned above, a mother, to gratify her own needs, may prolong nursing at her breast, into her child's third year. Prolonged nursing can cause an oral fixation and a disturbed dependence on the mother. Another example, is expecting a youngster who does not yet have anal sphincter control to conform to toileting mastery. Failure is inevitable and a consequence can be unnecessary anger by both participants and an anal fixation.

Some developmental interferences are reversible while some are not. Some could lead to psychopathology at the time of occurrence while others have a delayed effect. We may not be able to decipher the reason for the delayed effect. In the future of the child an experience occurs that has a derivative meaning related to the original earlier interference, and a neurotic symptom may appear.

Developmental conflicts are unavoidable. Such conflicts are present throughout the life cycle. For example, during adolescence, girls and boys strive to be independent of their parents but they encounter resistance from parents who do not want to "let go." In adult years, developmental conflicts are mostly psychosocial, such as "the empty nest" syndrome, decisions to retire, etc.

I believe life's major developmental conflict to be the advent of the Oedipal Complex, usually occurring between three to six years of age. During the Oedipal phase children of both genders feel both sexual (loving) and competitive (hateful) feelings towards both parents. Usually predominantly positive feelings are felt towards the parent of the gender opposite to their own, and less intense positive feelings towards the parent of their own gender. Hostile, competitive feelings are felt in the opposite direction regarding intensity. The boy feels negative towards father and the girl the same towards mother. The boy wishes to impregnate his mother and the girl wishes to be impregnated by the father.

You can see that conflict is to be expected during this developmental stage. It is more or less resolved through suppression of the Oedipal complex, insofar as the boy fears hurtful physical retaliation from the father, comparable to his own active wish (*castration*) vis-à-vis his father, and the girl fears a loss of love from her competitor, mother, for father's exclusive attention. The partial dissolution of the Oedipal complex results in internalization of the imagined and/or real parental moral demands that confront the child, and the Superego structure is the outcome. A mental structure essentially is a complex of thoughts and feelings that endure over time, i.e., they have a "long expiration date." As mentioned earlier, the internalization of parental objects is a desexualized version of them.

An internalized Superego is a great benefit to a developing child insofar as it is sort of an "inner policeman" that assists the child in controlling drives. If the Superego is weak or corrupt because of parental deficiencies the Superego will later be a determinant of psychopathology. An example of this, is with pre-adolescents and older teenagers, where delinquency is a possibility. It is because of the benefits of an internalized moral system, and the negative consequences of its absence or inadequacies, that I deem the struggle with the Oedipal Complex to be of utmost importance in limiting or encouraging future mental disturbances.

The partial dissolution of the Oedipal Complex allows for the ushering in of Latency. During Latency the strength of the drives vis-à-vis the Ego is weakened and this is a time of learning about the "real world." It is no wonder that this phase corresponds with entry into school for many children. This includes recognition by the child that there are external rules and prohibitions they must observe. When puberty occurs the latent Oedipal feelings are re-strengthened and adolescents must struggle with them and come to a resolution of the conflicts that emerge. It is a time for latent psychopathology to become more obvious.

Adulthood ordinarily means leaving the security of the family and furthering the independence that began earnestly in adolescence. Some of the major events dealt with in becoming an adult can be fertile ground for mental conflict and potential psychopathology. This will be discussed further below.

Another category of diagnoses involves the body, or soma, and hence the category of *psychosomatic* disorders. The separation of the mind and the body is artificial. As psychoanalysts we focus on the mind, not the brain but we do not deny the existence of the brain. In contemporary science the intimate connection between the two is a future achievement. Also, the connection may turn out in some or many instances to be correlation and not causal. However, we do recognize there are some instances where a somatic illness seems to be triggered by psychic conflict. Often this is the case when a diagnosis is deemed to be functional or idiopathic, meaning a medical cause cannot be found. Presumably there are some instances when a physical illness triggers a mental disturbance. For example, receiving a diagnosis of cancer is likely going to result in tension, anxiety, and depressive feelings. It is possible an individual given that diagnosis may experience guilt and consider it to be punishment for some past transgression. Somatization often seems to affect the gastrointestinal system, although pain is another symptom cluster.

It may be that there is an underlying physical issue that could not be diagnosed and because of feeling as if he or she is being accused of malingering, psychic consequences like frustration and anger can result. An example in the past decade were patients, often women, who complained of chronic fatigue who were diagnosed as being functionally depressed. Although a definitive cause has not been confidently discovered, chronic fatigue is now believed to be a result of an infection or some metabolic issue.

Somatization should not be confused with *hypochodriasis*. Hypochondriacs worry excessively about coming down with physical ailments. Usually, this is infrequent among children and adolescents, and is more common among adults. You can see adolescents in cold weather wearing only a flimsy polo shirt while adults are wearing heavy overcoats. The adolescent is making a statement of independence from parents; they own their body and they will do otherwise than dictated by parents. Parents dress children warmly.

Hypochondriacs worry that every abdominal pain is a sign of a potential serious ailment, e.g., an ulcer, or a headache is a sign of a brain tumor, etc. Sometimes such people have identified with parents who also worried excessively about illness or were afflicted by one, sometimes fatal. A child or adolescent losing a loved parent may identify with the parent in an unconscious attempt to reunite with them. In some instances hypochodiasis may be unconscious anticipated punishment for some imagined or real transgression.

CHAPTER 6

Childhood Psychopathology

In this section I will discuss psychopathology that predominates in childhood. I believe that experiences of childhood are very significant in future psychopathology. In treatment I think psychoanalysts often talk of treating the child within the adult. Adult analysands are told either explicitly or implicitly that they have to assist their child self to grow up. However, I do not mean to convey that there is no plasticity in the mind. On the contrary, while continuity is very important discontinuous experiences can occur. For example, a child may have experienced parenting that was depriving, or even abusive, maybe absent, but later during their school years they come upon a very considerate and supportive teacher and some of the adverse effects of their earlier childhood are modified in a positive growth manner. Of course, the opposite is also true. An early positive growth experience with a considerate, caring, and developmentally sensitive parent will be reduced albeit not necessarily eliminated by the loss of the parent, for example through divorce or death. Childhood is a time when emerging strengths or dysfunction can develop.

Recall, too, what I said earlier about the *complemental series* so that individuals will be affected somewhat differently by the same experience based on inherited differences in the strength of their inborn needs. So what may be a negative experience for one child may be a negligible one for another child. The impact of an adverse experience will differ for various children based on the ego resources at their disposal.

Conflicts occurring early in life before the Oedipal phase of development are classified as *pre-Oedipal*. These conflicts are seen as external insofar as the structualization of the mind is only in its infancy so that conflict between the Id and the Ego, or the Id and the Superego are not yet an issue. The infant may have been subjected to weaning before it was ready, perhaps because of a strong constitutional strength of the oral sucking drive. Perhaps the mother may have experience a lack of milk because of her own biological reasons. Maybe, the infant was starting to bite the nipple and it hurt the mother so she weaned her infant.

Interactions between parents and children that are conflictual occurring during the anal and phallic stages are also considered preOedipal. Many of these external conflicts are avoidable insofar as they result from parental demands that the child cease a behavior that is not pathological or which they are not advanced sufficiently in maturation to be able to comply with the external demand. For example, the infant with a strong drive to suck being weaned from the breast too early, or the toddler who does not yet have anal sphincter control maturation being asked to comply with toilet mastery, or the 3 year old who is harshly chastised for touching his penis and "masturbating." These are developmental conflicts that are due to misguided parenting; perhaps examples of intergenerationally transmitted pathological styles of parenting.

The consequences of such external conflicts are many and very variable based on individual differences in the persons involved. What I mean is the intensity of the frustration experienced by the child based on the strength of the thwarted instinctual expression, the degree of harshness of criticism evoked in the parent towards her or his child, whether or not physical punishment is meted out towards the non-complying child, etc. We will further explore the consequences of these *developmental interferences* and *developmental conflicts* later.

There are a whole group of infant behaviors attributed to errant early maternal relating by infants. The consequences are disturbed *attachment disorders* exhibited by the infant towards its mother or other caregivers. Reactive attachment disorders are behaviors that are peculiar to the presence of the maternal care-giving figure. The infant may show fearfulness, or perhaps disinterest, both behaviors that are contrary to the normal cheerful expressions of infants to the perceived presence of the maternal caregiver. Such infants are unable to form an emotional bond with her. Other infants may display a preference for stranger caregivers. As these infants get older, continued difficulties in the relationship to their maternal figures could be the harbinger of future psychopathology. Such children may engage in "baby talk," thereby revealing wishes to be taken care of by mother like a dependent baby.

In reviewing my notes of people who consulted with me over the years, many adults, and adolescents too, in our first meeting, convey a difficult relationship with their mothers and/or fathers. Of course, not being there, I cannot with great confidence say that some of these patients, as infants, would have had diagnoses of reactive attachment disorders. As adolescents or adults, they may display difficulties with becoming intimate with a partner, not empathic, and consequently loneliness can be an outcome for some. For others, they prefer to remain solitary. Adopted children often can exhibit difficulties in relationships with adults, often with adoptive parents. It is not surprising given that their life circumstances likely included adult neglect, sometimes in institutions, as well as fantasies of abandonment by birth parents.

Temper tantrums are a feature of some children. Their occurrence likely is due to a combination of factors, such as developmental immaturity of the brain in centers dealing with control of motor impulses, feelings, parental difficulties in setting limits, and insufficient internalization of the rule "use your words."

During a temper tantrum a child is out of control, thrashing about on the floor with his or her body, biting, throwing and breaking things, yelling and crying, etc. Upset parents have trouble restraining the child and it is best to make sure the child is safe, removing things that might hurt them, and let the temper tantrum run its course and end. In most instances, children "grow out" of temper tantrums by the time they enter Latency.

Procrastination can begin in childhood and become a habitual way of dealing with internal expectations of achieving goals. It is self destructive insofar as "waiting for the last minute" to begin to complete a task often only makes it harder to finish.

It can be a style of effort that can sabotage accomplishments in school and work. For some it begins with a sense that "no one is going to tell me what to do". A child growing up with a domineering and authoritarian parent could develop into a procrastinator. Such a person will be self-critical and vow to change but will put off doing so, only to intensify the shame they feel throughout life.

Learning disabilities affect children in primary school and can continue throughout their education. The difficulty can be limited or widespread. Only reading may be disrupted, *dyslexia*, or mathematical skills, or spelling, or writing, or the "whole gambit."

For most children who are very motivated to be like their peers, learning problems can cause a great deal of distress. Parental distress can exacerbate the problems. The cause(s) of learning difficulties are complicated and vary. Assuming no organic cause is a determinant, issues of achieving may be due to conflicts about competition, issues of diminished self- esteem based on a conviction that one is not "smart," issues of irrational gender inferiority, such as girls are not meant to master science and mathematics, etc.

Passive-aggressiveness is a defense utilized that can become a beginning character style and endure through adolescence into adulthood. Here aggressiveness is concealed in a manner that may go unnoticed by the recipient of its expression. For example, such a child reaching for the milk on the table may "accidentally" knock it over messing the table. The parent(s) may excuse it as clumsiness not recognizing it as an expression of hostility towards them. For the benefit of the child, hopefully, a parent will get suspicious that the child is expressing anger in a concealed way. Perhaps, then, the child can be encouraged to get in touch with the anger and use words to express it and the disturbed behavior can cease.

Another form of defensive behavior that can begin in childhood that can persist in later years is the use of the defense of *reaction formation*. Here too, as in passive-aggressive behavior, what is overt conceals what is felt latently or unconsciously. Affectionate behavior may be the opposite of what is more genuinely felt but forbidden, namely anger. Sometimes the opposite can be the dynamic, namely, forbidden love is expressed as anger. At some level, the child using reaction formation can feel duplicitous and guilt can be felt with little insight.

Childhood disturbances often present for the first time in a school situation. Much stress results for all the people involved with the child. Three such diagnoses are *conduct disorder, oppositional-defiant disorder*, and *attention deficiency-hyperactive disorder*. These issues can continue throughout the life cycle with different labels. The first two may be labeled delinquency or antisocial behavior in the adolescent or adult years.

A major feature of a child having a conduct issue is the impulsivity of the child. Rules of "waiting your turn," "using your words," "let someone else take a turn," do not seem to be accepted by the child. The child will be disruptive of the atmosphere of the intended calm classroom. Teachers with many children in the classroom will contact parents and with adolescents the student may be expelled.

A child presenting with an oppositional-defiant disorder, can create an even more stressful situation for all involved than a conduct disorder. This is because it is has a relational expression. The child is often "in the face" of the teacher, arguing and seeking to annoy the teacher. Presumably the child is displacing anger onto the teacher meant for someone else, perhaps a parent. The child may feel it is safer to express it outside the family.

Attention-deficit hyperactivity disorder creates havoc for the child. Learning is disrupted. In my experience this "disorder" is often a mistaken diagnosis, especially in a classroom with many children as in a public school. Many of these children are anxious and that is interfering with attention and contributing to what looks like hyperactivity. Defensive efforts against aggressive impulses secondarily interfere with concentration and learning. These children, in my opinion, need psychotherapy and not drugs to quell their behavior. The anxiety may be due to many different factors, such as those discussed above. Of course, there are children with an ADHD diagnosis that would benefit from medicine because they have a neurological problem. Careful differential diagnosis is needed.

It has only been recently that educators of young children have accepted that there is not a single learning style. Children differ as to how they learn.

This is a good example of the mind-brain synergy. Although well documented, not all school systems have enthusiastically adopted this revised teaching style. Consequently some children experience learning problems and experience the depressive and diminished self-esteem that goes along with poor school performance.

Children can find themselves being teased in school. The schoolyard bully will find something to pick on to tease. The victim will feel awful and feel alone since usually others do not come to his or her rescue lest they become the next target. Some kids who have low self-esteem because of some real or imagined "fault" may worry that it will be noticed and they will be shunned. A noticeable physical disability may attract a bully. The victim will feel scared and angry but need to suppress the feeling. A defensive maneuver "playing the role of clown" may be employed. Here one gets other kids to laugh at your antics or jokes and not at you. It often leads also to disciplinary action as a punishment and then to parental criticism, resulting in reduced secondary narcissism. The whole scenario can lead to much discomfort for the child.

In this section I will include *neurotic* conditions that usually first arise in childhood, can continue into later years, or can appear to go into remission but later reappear. Hence, these dynamic features can manifest across the entire life cycle. I include obsessive-compulsive neurosis, hysteria, hysterical conversion, phobia, and *delinquency*. Earlier, I have referred to neurotic symptomatology that compromises common life situations, everyday biological functioning, and the expression of inborn talents.

For some children who have disabilities and have suffered as a result, e.g., being teased, they can start to consider themselves as an "exception." They feel they have suffered more than they deserve and they should be exempt in the future from prohibitions that others are expected to follow, e.g., sobriety.

Obsessive-compulsive neurosis in the classical sense begins with conflict at the Oedipal phase. As discussed earlier, the child feels threatened and anxious that he will be a victim of physical injury. In a boy's case it is fear of castration at the hands of father in retaliation for his own similar aggression aimed at father in competition with him to usurp his privileges with the boy's mother. In the girl's case the fear is loss of the mother's love because of a similar competition with her to be father's favorite. A regression occurs to an anal fixation. It is in this psychic "arena" that obsessive-compulsive symptoms are formed. The child's Superego is advanced further than a younger child of two or three first dealing with anal impulses and it is intolerant of the child's anal wishes so conflict is felt and compromises, symptoms, are sought.

Obsessive thinking involves rumination and concern about details. Compulsive behavior involves repetitive actions without a sense of completion. Together, we have obsessive-compulsive behavior.

The obsessive thought and compulsive actions vary depending on the life experiences of individuals. I will give a couple of examples to illustrate what I mean. A child might be overly concerned about cleanliness, perhaps because of a wish to smear feces, but this is forbidden. However, the unconscious wish although not manifested in action nevertheless causes a sense of guilt and a feeling of physical uncleanliness and a need to wash his or her hands. But washing them once may not be sufficient and it becomes a repetitive action. The child will feel a need, felt as a compulsion to be clean. This child suffers from an obsessive-compulsive neurosis.

Another child may be fearful of an intruder at night. Perhaps this stems from its' own wish to intrude upon his or her parents because of primal scene fantasies in force during the child's Oedipal phase. When such wishes were externalized the child then began to fear a nighttime intruder. With regression to the anal phase, the child again feels unsafe at night because of anal-sadistic wishes that are externalized. The child resorts to locking the door to his room or to the street but is not easily satisfied that he or she is safe. What follows is a repetitive action of unlocking the locked door (s) and relocking them to make sure it is secure. However, the feeling of safety is not satisfied and the action needs to be repeated. This child is involved in an obsessive-compulsive neurosis.

As either of the above children age their obsessive-compulsive neurosis will likely continue although the symptoms may change as the Ego attempts to better defend against conflicted desires. Derivatives of the original wishes will be operative in the now older child as an adolescent, later as an adult, unless therapy or psychoanalysis affords them some emotional understanding and relief via a better solution to the original conflict.

In classical *hysteria* the Oedipal child is conflicted with anxiety because of forbidden sexual desires and aggressive wishes towards parental objects. Girls usually are more prone to this neurotic development than are boys. Perhaps this is because sexual expression in behavior is more culturally acceptable in females than males. A girl may be coquettish and flirtatious, especially with father, in a manner that only a five-year-old girl can express. A boy may be boastful of his strength, especially with mother, also in a manner that only a five-year-old boy can be. The Ego of both children resorts to defensive maneuvers. The forbidden impulses are repressed. Such children may regard themselves and same gendered parent as weak and their opposite gendered parent as powerful, even aggrandized. Present, too, often is an oral fixation underlying the hyper sexuality, suggesting a reservoir of dependency. This may account for the self-image portrayed as weak.

As the child becomes adolescent a "hyper sexuality" or seductiveness becomes a feature of the girl's personality. However, if responded to by a boy the girl becomes scared and retreats. It is as if the seductiveness of the girl is an unconscious maneuver to bring forth potential danger to be avoided in her surroundings. Hence, the boy who is attracted to the girl's coquettishness will be avoided.

As the hysterical adolescent girl becomes adult the features of their adolescent self will continue. They will have consolidated into a hysterical character and the behavior will be labeled histrionic. Intimacy of a sexual kind is avoided. These women may have trouble in relationships with men.

There is a manifestation of hysteria mostly in children and adolescents but sometimes in older patients that we call *hysterical identification*. A child will adopt the physical disability or symptom of a person they are competitive and envious with. For example, a latency age girl who harbors competitive Oedipal level wishes towards mother, may find herself unconsciously identifying with mother's abdominal pains that she believes are due to pregnancy. The girl may complain of abdominal pain that requires medical intervention but no physical cause can be diagnosed. This is because the pain is psychologically induced via identification brought on by envy.

Phobia is another classical neurotic manifestation that can be present in all stages of life and last for a long time. Phobic feelings need to be distinguished from objective fears. If a child has been bitten in the past by a spider, it would be expected they would demonstrate some fear in the presence of a nearby spider. A child with a spider phobia, however, has not been bitten, yet they act terrified in the presence of one. This is because the spider unconsciously represents a different "thing." The spider is like a symbol of something or somebody that evokes fear. A *displacement*, a switch from another anxiety evoking entity, has taken place unconsciously. If what is "chosen" is something usually not in close proximity to the child it will turn out to be a "good" choice. That the child is anxious about being bitten suggests an oral fixation is a determinant. Analyses of children with phobias may illuminate castration fear as a determinant. So in boys, the spider symbolizes the Oedipal rival for mother's love. The famous case of "Little Hans" written up by Freud describes these dynamics. This boy was afraid of being bitten by a horse, a displacement from father, in the streets of Vienna. Later, his difficulties with his mother were illustrated in a later publication, making more sense of his oral expression of castration anxiety.

Other Issues may also trigger a phobia. For example, a *school phobia* may result in a child refusing to go to school. This can last for an extended period of time. Child analysis might clarify that the child is really afraid of leaving home. This may be because of separation issues or anxiety about some harm coming to his or her mother. The imagined harm might be an expression of the child's own anger felt unconsciously towards the mother. Often, such a child will complain of a "stomach ache." Perhaps, the child feels that if he is "ill" the mother will take care of him or her? Hence a displacement from home (mother) to school has taken place.

There are also instances of *counter-phobia* wherein a child may participate or seek out what they are afraid about. For example, if there is a phobia of falling from a high height, the child might engage in tree climbing, without conscious awareness of the underlying dynamic.

CHAPTER 7

Adolescent Psychopathology

In this section I will focus on those conflicts that manifest themselves primarily in adolescence. Two major psychological events that adolescents contend with are increased independence from parents or other custodial adults and the advent of puberty. It is not that efforts at achieving autonomy only begin in the adolescent years but they intensify immeasurerably. The toddler when he or she starts to walk experiences beginning independence and the separation from parents causes them some modicum of *separation anxiety* and they often quickly change their direction back towards the parent for renewed comfort. The two or three year old undergoing toilet mastery will often protest the adults' directions about when and where to defecate. So called "toilet battles" can ensue. The wish for independence continues to grow with school entry but it becomes full blown in adolescence. Peer recognition and acceptance of peer rules, sometimes conflicting with parental rules, becomes a major issue for most adolescents. They want to be socially accepted and popular. Of course, that is not true for all adolescents. Friction with parents can cause family disharmony and stress for all members. In some instances, an adolescent may sense that a parent is holding onto them because of the parent's own insecurity. This could heighten the adolescent's ambivalence about becoming more independent. Intrapsychically, adolescents may feel a loss of the former security provided by an inner sense of bondedness with a strong available parental internalized image. Depressive feelings may arise.

Part of becoming independent is owning one's own body. Prior to adolescence a child accepts that the primary caregiver, usually mother, owns his or her body. They are dependent on mother to take care of his or her body, feed it and nurture it. It is not unusual to see adolescents walking around in the middle of winter in short sleeves, whereas adults around them wear a heavy coat. Owning one's own body can be a stressful situation if the child has an illness like juvenile diabetes. Mother will be protective and reluctant to relinquish control when her child becomes a teenager. The teenager will feel over-controlled and angry.

Use of drugs during adolescence can be detrimental. Recent research suggests that use of marijuana can be harmful to the developing brain of adolescents. Also, daily use of "grass" has been shown to diminish motivation to be active and deal with tasks. The adolescent will experience school achievement and learning difficulties. There can be peer pressure to imbibe that some adolescents cannot refuse for fear of being ostracized. Of course, overuse of stronger drugs can cause death.

Some adolescents will cut themselves, usually on the arm. This action, of course, alarms parents and they seek professional help. Surprisingly, most of the adolescents are not so alarmed. In my experience and that of colleagues the self-cutting is less a sign of self-destruction and, counter-intuitively, more a sign of the adolescent's proclamation of a strength of self–survival.

Puberty begins for many adolescents around age thirteen. Most adolescents welcome it but others are conflicted. Often girls become pubertal earlier than their male counterparts. It is not unusual in a beginning high school class to see girls much taller than the boys. The beginning of menses is welcomed by some girls and abhorred by others. A lot depends on the preparation provided by mothers and/or older sisters. It will be a positive sign of healthy development and future maternity for girls that have been well prepared. Regretfully, for others it could be a messy ordeal they are obliged to take care of. For some girls developing breasts and curvature of their bodies are unwelcomed and they may slouch in posture or wear baggy clothes to hide the changes. Other girls welcome the changes. For the former group sexual desires may cause anxiety, and for the latter exciting fantasies of sexual intimacy.

For boys, puberty may bring on unexpected erections at times that would be embarrassing, e.g., if called upon by a teacher to go up to the front of the classroom to the blackboard. Also, the adolescent boy often greets spontaneous emissions during sleep with displeasure and embarrassment.

Puberty brings forth sexual desires and adolescents must deal with them. Conflicts about sexual expression can be a cause of **much** discomfort during this stage of life. This can be because many adolescents do not distinguish between fantasy and action. They feel, embarrassment, shame, or guilt about both as if they are equivalent. But they are not. In dealing with conflicts about sexual desire many neurotic symptoms can arise. For example, daily masturbation, isolation, anxiety around perceived "sexy" peers, etc.

Precocious puberty can occur in girls during the latency years, usually due to some hormonal disorder. The girls and family are not prepared for it and much discomfort can be experienced. Parents are concerned and worried about the physical and mental health of their daughters. The issues diverge based on the personal psychology of all the participants. Some fathers are uneasy about a physically mature girl sitting on their lap. Some mothers, unsure of their own feminine attractiveness to their husbands, may have to deal with competitive feelings with their daughters for their husbands' interest.

Sexual desire, either heterosexual or homosexual can be a source of discomfort for adolescents. We discussed this earlier when the topic was considered of biological needs getting caught up in conflict. Of course sexual needs are not only biological but also psychological. The topic will be further discussed when we consider adult psychopathology.

When a heterosexual adolescent boy starts to feel sexual desire he notices a girl and may get an erection. Fantasies may preoccupy him and masturbation may follow. For most boys they are uneasy about the need to get up the courage to interact with the girl. Adolescents usually boys and girls together "hang out" in groups. Heterosexual girls are also anxious about dealing with boys. They feel a lot of pressure from boys in these contemporary times to engage in fellatio, a practice they may feel compelled to oblige even though they may prefer not to. For both girls and boys, there is competition with other adolescents regarding attractiveness to the other gender, and jealousy may be intense.

Masturbation, for both genders, is a normal adolescent sexual activity. However, if it becomes a substitute for relating to others, it can be a preoccupation and further inhibit personal interaction.

Younger children, particularly boys can be seen to touch the genital region. Parents best deal with this by not being punitive. They may say to the child that the activity is best done privately in the bedroom. Girls are less obvious in their masturbatory activities, such as squeezing their thighs together or pressing up their groin against a hard surface. Parents that object and insult the child may be fostering sexual anxiety. Unfortunately, this is not so uncommon.

Homosexual adolescents are faced with being "different," "although times are changing." Nevertheless, gay and lesbian adolescents must deal with isolation from the mainstream and shaming, sometimes subtle, from their peers. A support group of like-minded peers is very helpful. For some adolescents being homosexual is likely biological. Recall that during the Oedipal stage the child has sexual feelings for both parents, albeit usually those for the opposite gendered parent being stronger. Many homosexual male adolescents will tell you that they preferred to play with girls and girl's toys from earliest times, and lesbian adolescents may state they always wanted to be playing with boys and their toys as young girls. Many girls, however, labeled as "tomboys" retain their femininity and do not become lesbians.

Some future homosexuals and lesbians likely have a sexual orientation based on biology and not conflict. There are some homosexual and lesbian adolescents, however, that may be afraid of heterosexuality and this may be the underlying cause of their retreat from heterosexuality. Competition with the same gendered parent, or unavailability of the opposite gendered parent may sometimes be determinants. While sorting this out, adolescents go through a very difficult and tense time.

As mentioned earlier, in instances where the Superego was inadequately consolidated or weak, delinquency can be a problem for adolescents. This is especially so if the adolescent gets involved with a peer group where *acting-out* is prevalent. Then the norms of society are compromised. Petty thievery like shoplifting, smoking marijuana, use of drugs like cocaine and opioids, can be a frequent occurrence. Often this results in judiciary involvement and a criminal record that can be a burden for the adolescent in later years in seeking employment. Many young adults regret such past behavior, are ashamed, and will benefit from community support.

An adolescent may associate achieving in school as an acceptance of leaving childhood. They may object because of feeling dependent on adults for their sense of security. Such an adolescent may not expend effort and look as if they have a learning deficiency.

CHAPTER 8

Adult Psychopathology

Character styles are formed gradually and are consolidated in the adult years and are not easily abandoned. Character disorders or personality disorders hence are features of adulthood. We saw antecedents in neurotic symptomatology of earlier years. Thus a child who is obsessive and compulsive likely will develop character defenses consistent with such symptoms and as an adult will become an obsessional personality.

Some of the more common *personality* or *character disorders* are *narcissistic, antisocial, obsessive, hysterical, paranoid, dependent, schizoid, depressive,* and *dissociative.* Sometimes a personality type is a mixture of two types. The severity of each is on a continuum from mild to severe. This will depend on life experiences that either mitigated the need for such defenses or stimulated constant use of them to build a protective shield.

A *narcissistic personality* is someone who underneath the bravado feels very insecure. To distance themselves from low self-esteem they focus on "me" and brag about their accomplishments. They come across as knowing everything because they are "omniscient." Everything that they do is described as the "best" and they are always listening for compliments and crave applause. As children they may have been schoolyard "bullies," in a futile attempt to bolster low self-esteem. Some narcissists may have had in their youth an idealized grandparent as a model that a parent had for them to live up to. Failure to succeed in this goal, the future narcissist may compensate by acting as if they know everything and are the best at everything.

An *anti-social personality* believes in an individual moral code that benefits only him or her. The Superego of such individuals is weak or corrupt. Selfish gain to strengthen one's power over others is of paramount importance, not behavior that is aware of other's well being. As adolescents such individuals were delinquent. In instances where this personality is pervasive, criminal behavior and incarceration may occur. Often such individuals have identified with anti-social parents or peers that are delinquent.

Obsessive personality types are rigid and governed by private thoughts. They cannot relax and feel free of anxiety until they have achieved a goal. Failure to do so results in a sense of failure. Compulsive acts are in the interest of achieving "perfection." This is not accepted as an unattainable ideal that can only be approximated. Not being "perfect" leaves them very insecure. Sometimes the compulsive acts are to avoid an anxiety producing activity or fantasy, e.g., cleaning house to avoid sexual excitement.

An individual with a *hysterical personality* usually comes across as histrionic, given to dramatic story telling, with lots of emotional accompaniments. Exaggeration is the standard, covering over a sense of thinking oneself as boring and trivial. Such a woman may be flirtatious in a defensive manner insofar as this covers over a fear of sexuality and intimacy.

A *paranoid personality* believes other people cannot be trusted. They are conspiring to take advantage of you because of envy. Such suspiciousness covers over a sense of personal inadequacy. Relationships are few because they require intimacy and letting down your guard. Having fun is a rarity.

A *dependent personality* relies on the protection of another person that is viewed as strong and capable of looking after your wellbeing as well as his or her own. In some respects they are parental surrogates to make up for deficiencies of one's own. Such dependency requires that others act towards you as if they think you are worthwhile to compensate for a lack of self-esteem. In a marriage, tension and bickering can be frequent if a spouse is very dependent insofar as it is unreasonable to expect a spouse to be a parent too.

People who were loners by choice used to be thought of as having a *schizoid personality*. This term is rarely used today. It described individuals who avoided relationships likely because of latent hostility towards primary figures in the past who were disappointments. Such avoidance made it less likely that hostile aggressive behavior would come to the surface. Solitary activities are sought and occupational choices made where interaction or group participation can be avoided. A good example would be to work alone in a laboratory.

A *depressive personality* often feels rejected by others and blames him or her self because of personal inadequacies. They may always feel "empty," and lonely. Such negative feelings about the self are derivatives from earlier life experiences in childhood and/or adolescence.

"Dissociative" may be a word that you are not familiar with. Someone with a *dissociative personality* unconsciously seems to characteristically change his or her self-identity. It is as if they temporarily forget who they are. Such individuals often have been abused in the past and this defensive wall is an existential attempt to survive.

In a consultation it is not infrequent that adults will in their account of their past speak of an over-bearing, authoritative father. This is particularly difficult for males. It is as if they never felt that they pleased their fathers. Or it might be remembered that they thought a parent was not very warm so that they rarely felt cared for. With treatment this narrative might be revised for some of them. They might recognize that their memories were exaggerated and that their grandparents were not model parents either. The latter would allow some forgiveness for their parents' shortcomings. Unfortunately, in many instances the sense of having experienced unsatisfying parenting remained. Or they identified with the parenting they experienced and repeated it with their own children.

In addition to psychological conflicts that began in childhood or adolescence and are continued into later life or re-experienced later in a derivative form, there are issues that are specific to adulthood. These events are experienced by all of us and in most instances we cope adaptively with them and the solutions are favorable. When they are not we can feel anxious and/or depressed or other unfavorable feelings. Sometimes dealing with these issues re-kindles earlier mental conflicts that may have become latent. I am thinking of issues, in the usual chronological order in which they appear, such as applying to college, leaving the parental home, choosing a future occupation or career, and becoming comfortable with a sexual orientation. With increasing age, one deals with issues such as choosing a life partner, deciding on becoming a parent, dealing with an "empty nest," dealing with aging parents as one's self is getting older. Then, dealing with retirement, old age, health changes, and finally coming to terms with existential anxiety.

The above issues are *psychosocial,* as well as psychodynamic. That is, in addition to individual and familial psychodynamics, there are societal expectations, rewards or obstacles that can either facilitate or hinder the successful achieving of these goals. Let us imagine, a late adolescent African-American girl from the rural South who aspires to be an astrophysicist. Her parents have always told her that they believed "she could be whatever she wants to be." So, possessing a high degree of Ego strength and motivation she is an honor student in high school and is given a scholarship to a renowned university. The people in her new surroundings all like her because of her winning personality but may harbor private doubts about the likelihood she will be successful. They have preconceived ideas about a female Black student who grew up on a farm getting a Ph.D. in astrophysics. Outside of the academic community such doubts will exist. The doubts are preconceived biases. This is an extreme example of negative psychosocial dynamics at play that can interact with personal conflict-laden psychodynamics. Such obstacles need to be overcome by young adults, particularly young women, making life choices. You can expect that there will be a high degree of stress for most of these young adults.

Choice of career used to be decided to a great degree by what your father had chosen. It would be "Father & Son." In contemporary times this expectation is considerably reduced, although in some families it may remain and when not met feelings of disloyalty may exist, albeit under the surface. Nowadays, there are numerous choices for young adults. Women, too, have opportunities that were never normal expectations in years past. Advances in technology have created occupations that did not exist in an earlier generation. Acquiring a skill in a trade has lost its appeal in contemporary society. Hence, choosing a career can cause lots of doubts and insecurities.

Training for a career choice may mean separating from the parental home. If a college education is part of the preparation, it may mean moving a distance from parents. Having practiced in a college town for years, I am familiar with the frequent manifestation of separation anxiety, depressive feelings, and loneliness reported by college students. Suicidal thoughts also can occur. When these feelings are intense and result in poor school performance and a sense of isolation, the young adult may take a leave of absence, or hopefully, seek professional help. Presumably such intense reactions have their antecedents in childhood or during adolescence when the relationship with parents was fraught with difficulties. The possible causes are too numerous to list, but I am thinking of such family dynamics as parental divorce, an alcoholic parent, abuse by a parent, etc.

Becoming comfortable with a sexual orientation is not easy for some young adults. Many may feel comfortable to the gender they are attracted to but unable to act upon their desire. They feel a *sexual inhibition.* The cause most likely has an earlier origin having to do with self-condemnation for what they thought were illicit choices that would evoke guilt or external punishment from perceived rivals. I am thinking of unresolved positive Oedipal desires.

The binary classification of heterosexual and homosexual has proven to be not inclusive enough. We discussed this earlier in the section on adolescent psychopathology. Some young adults feel bisexual. In our observations of young children and our theory of the Oedipal complex this is thought to be universal, albeit one parent is more "sexually" desirable than the other for most children. In adolescence one inclination usually becomes much stronger than the other. For most boys, they are sexually attracted to girls, for most girls they are sexually attracted to boys. Some children seem to always have been attracted to their own gender, and here it can be attributed to a biological determinant. However, for some children such an early attraction likely was due to conflict and defensive.

It is only recently that homosexuality has been a "accepted," although on a latent level for many it is not, particularly among religiously observant people.

Gay men and lesbian women often feel ostracized and condemned from the larger community. They feel hurt and angry. A few feel guilty, stemming from early internalized moral beliefs, or because of feeling they have disappointed their parents. Some parents mourn the future absence of grandchildren, although with adoption as an option and surrogate conception this can be overcome.

Sexual perversions or *paraphilias* are sexual disturbances that some adults, usually males, experience. For these individuals sexual intercourse is not sufficiently satisfying, and maybe an experience that deprives them of an orgasm. Foreplay, in "healthy" sex is meant to arouse the participants so that coitus can occur and orgasm can be reached.

However, adults with perversions do not achieve this outcome. The feeling states vary among perverts. Some are privately and secretly planning an encounter in fantasy and/or actuality wherein the perversion can be satisfied. Sometimes a partner will comply begrudgingly in order "to keep the peace." After the experience the pervert may feel a heightened good feeling like elation, but soon there- after they may feel alone and depressed.

There are many different perversions. Exhibitionism, such as exposing one's genitals to a stranger or to a child may be acted upon. Voyeurism, such as being a "peeping Tom" looking with binoculars through the window of an adjacent neighbor's house to view an adolescent girl's nudity as she undresses. Fetishism is the required presence of a thing, usually an item of clothing such as a woman's shoe, during sexual intimacy to get full pleasure. Or it can be required focus on a specific body part such as a foot of the sexual partner. Pedophilia, or a sexual desire of children, is often the motive for sexual abuse of children. Transvestism, dressing up as the other gender during sex may be required. Sexual masochism and sadism are two common perversions. It may mean requiring bondage of oneself or one's partner to enjoy sexual intercourse, or it could involve inflicting some pain on one's partner or having it inflicted on oneself in order to get sexual pleasure.

Acceptance of one's birth gender is not a simple matter for some young adults, or as adolescents earlier. *Transgender* issues are more and more in our awareness. Such adolescents and young adults feel isolated from other youth or young adults. They can become intensely depressed and suicidal. Their parents are confused. They do not know how to respond. They want to be supportive but they may believe the child is behaving dramatically or irrationally. They feel that the child is confused and with therapy they will change his or her mind. Young adults and older adults who elect to obtain first hormonal treatment and then surgical interventions aimed at transforming their gender are more frequent in this decade alone than earlier ones. Some will elect only to be *transvestites* and dress in the clothes of the other preferred gender.

Undoubtedly, some young people who are unaccepting of their gender are feeling so because of conflict, for example, not wanting to "turn out" to be like an abusive parent, but others feel intensely that their self-identity does not correspond to the body they possess.

Choosing a life partner has been delayed in the current generation compared to mine. People nowadays do not choose to commit themselves to another until sometimes into there thirties. Also, some elect to live together but not to marry. Perhaps this is due to the decline of religious values. In any case, choosing a partner to commit to can be a source of psychological distress for some. Are they in a love that feels to be enduring? They are aware of divorce if they marry but would rather not have to go through such an event. Or is the choice made out of convenience? Two people like each other, have similar interests, sex is good, so why not live together? The choice of a partner sometimes may have unconscious undertones. What I am thinking of, is choosing someone who is like a parent, perhaps because of pre-Oedipal unmet or indulged dependency issues, or because of Oedipal issues having to do with frustrated childhood sexual desires and competitive wishes with a parental rival. It is during adolescence that the choice of a person to be connected to can be a resolved outcome of successfully severed ties to Oedipal and pre-Oedipal objects. If this has not been accomplished the marriage or partnership may be fraught with disappointment. After all, the adult partner you have chosen is not your parent and childhood wishes will not be satisfied to the level required by your unconscious desire. The outcome likely will be marital tension, fighting, and possibly divorce.

Choosing to become a parent can be met with joyful expectations. If infertility is an unexpected outcome, depressive feelings will become obvious.

Adoption, artificial insemination, and conceptual surrogacy are contemporary solutions. Nevertheless, the infertile partner may still feel inadequate and self-esteem may suffer. Infidelities in the marriage can be a reaction to the disappointment.

Becoming a parent in most instances has an emotional connection to the parenting that you experienced as a child. Will you be a better parent than your own or be unable to "live up" to the good example they put forth? If you had a "bad" parent likely you swore to be different. Unfortunately, the psychic mechanism of identification may be stronger than your vow. As a way of mastering your disappointment you may turn a passive experience into an active one and unwittingly do to your child what you endured. Here the phenomenon of intergenerational transmission of pathology is given expression.

Having children enter the family can be difficult for some men. Women seem to be more instinctively parental while men are becoming more so as our culture accepts such behavior. It is no longer believed to be un-masculine to change a diaper, sooth an infant, etc, than it once was. However, regretfully, there still will be some men who will feel displaced by their wife's attention to a child. Marital tension can result. In extreme cases, divorce can be an outcome.

For many parents, the success of their children in life brings them great pleasure. For some, they feel responsible to a greater degree than they objectively are and rob the child of its accomplishments. They own the success and they talk to their friends as if that is so. The child can become aware of this and feel anger. Some parents go the other path; they take an inordinate sense of responsibility for their child's failures in life. They are totally to blame for their bad parenting. You can see that good parenting is an asset for a child. The child, too, independently is a large factor in future success or failure.

Dealing with a so-called "empty nest" can be difficult for some parents. It is less so for those parents who have had additional interests to parenting, e.g., a career or talent that they let develop. Regretfully, for some it can lead to feelings of abandonment and depression, likely stimulated by earlier childhood losses. For some parents, mostly men, it can result in extramarital affairs as a way of reinforcing their sense of manhood diminished by no longer being a provider to a family. Others may deal with the loss by purchasing something of value that they unconsciously wish will enhance their image as a worthwhile adult, like a new expensive auto.

Retirement is something that is delayed more so now than in earlier generations. This is especially so among adults who have professional careers where physical aging has less of an impact, unless, of course, if there is a decline in cognitive functioning. When one retires, there may be diminished self-esteem insofar as one's occupation or career likely afforded the adult a feeling of competence and accomplishment as well as recognition of such from others. For some older adults, this loss of self-esteem can be intense and lead to depression. The same issues as in the "empty nest" experience are involved. Are there other interests that can be enjoyed? Can one be more involved with one's spouse?

Becoming a grandparent can be a source of great pleasure and a feeling of accomplishment for most older adults. There exists a sense of pride in the accomplishment of one's children becoming parents. When grandchildren do not exist older adults can feel envy of friends who are grandparents.

A grandparent must recognize they are not parents to their grandchildren. They can, however, impart the wisdom of their years and support the healthy parenting of their own children, and in some instances diminish the bad outcome of poor parenting by their own children. For some grandparents whose children are unable to be parents to their own children, perhaps because of drug addiction or incarceration, they are asked to become guardians of their grandchildren. This can be burdensome for those who are not physically capable or impoverished but most, nevertheless, do a needed job that benefits the grandchildren.

Older age is a time when one's own parents get ill or die. As parents' age and need the assistance of their grown up children, most children agreeably do so. They feel grateful for the care and devotion given them and they wish to reciprocate. However, for some it is felt burdensome, presumably because of a perceived history of neglect. Such older adults will be latently angry and some will feel guilty because of this.

Mourning is an experience we all endure as we age. Not only parents but also friends, who are contemporaries, die. With old age, however, we must come to terms with our own eventual death. We call this *existential anxiety*. Older adults differ as to whether or not this is a cause of anxiety. Those who are religiously observant are less bothered because they believe in "life after death," either spiritually or maybe in reincarnation. Most people who are pleased more-or-less with their life attainments are accepting of inevitable death and not anxious or preoccupied about it. They are reassured that they will be well thought of because of the legacy they have left behind. Such individuals feel they have lived a life of integrity that will be honored.

Postscript

Contemporary psychiatry is very much a discipline that views mental disturbances as diseases that can be treated with medication. Sometimes the combined use of drugs and talk therapy is recommended. The intervention of "talk therapy" is often seen in those instances as causing a change, along with the administration of drugs, in the brain effecting an alleviation of symptoms. The mind is almost never conceptualized as the site of mental conflict causing distressing feelings like anxiety, shame, or guilt resulting in compromise formations, or symptoms. It is as if "mental illness" is thought to be akin to Alzheimer's disease where plaque and tangles invade synapses leaving cognitive and mental deficiencies in their path. Another example is the brains of patients suffering from post-concussion, demonstrating cognitive and affect regulation problems. I expect that a modern day psychiatrist would accuse me of being extreme in my criticism. The mind and the brain are connected. Let us not forget that Freud started out as a neurologist but he saw the value in investigating the mind. Someday in the distant future the connections between the two will be illuminated, but I believe alleviating mental anguish will still come from emotionally understanding of mental conflicts and not from taking a pill. Plato and Socrates once said that a life not understood is a life not worth living.

In contemporary psychiatry, psychoanalysis is usually thought of as a discredited pseudo-science. The uninformed public, for the most part, has accepted this viewpoint. Or the public wants a "quick fix." If therapy is going to fix the problem it must remove the symptoms. Hence behavior modification therapy or its cousins are sought after, no matter the cause of the symptoms. Medical insurance rarely covers psychoanalysis and the fees charged can be afforded by only a few. This needs to be re-considered. Low fee clinics desperately need to be established.

Earlier, I stressed my opinion, and that of many psychoanalytic colleagues, that childhood development and problems experienced by the child during these early years lay the foundation for future psychopathology. Anna Freud, whose writings were groundbreaking, is rarely referred to in contemporary literature on development and psychopathology. The logic of this defies me. Her insights are invaluable.

All of the above distresses me and was one of my motives for writing this book. I wished to show the dynamic complexities of mental conflict, its effect on people, and the attempts to resolve them, often resulting in neurosis. I also want to show that mental "illness" can be understood, that it is not a conundrum of unexplainable thoughts and feelings that best be avoided. My hope is that I have come at least within sight of this objective.

Representative List of Topics

PREFACE
Overview of book; Style of book

ESSENTIAL CONCEPTS IN UNDERSTANDING PSYCHOPATHOLOGY
Sexual & Aggressive Drive; phases; gratification; complemental series; fixation; regression; foundation for later psychopathology; intergenerational transmission of psychopathology; mental conflict; anxiety; in trapsychic, internalized, external conflicts; passive/active aims; sublimation; psychological mindedness; sadism/masochism; trauma; narcissism; self-esteem.

LIFE EVENTS AND PSYCHOPATHOLOGY
Death of a loved one or pet; inability to mourn; suicide; survivor guilt; Genocide; adoption; infertility; Divorce; sexual abuse; emotional abuse; Internet pornography; identification with the abuser; sibling rivalry; racial and religious bigotry.

BASIC BIOLOGICAL FUNCTIONS THAT MAY DRAWN INTO CONFLICT
Sleep; eating; breast-feeding; toileting; Urination; locomotion; sexual expression; Bisexuality; gender.

NATURAL STRENGTHS INTERFERED WITH BY PSYCHOPATHOLOGY
Curiosity; Athleticism; Musical ability.

DIAGNOSTIC CATEGORIES
Borderline; Depression; Neurosis; Character; Developmental interferences; Developmental Conflicts (e.g. Oedipus Complex); Psychosomatic; Hypochondria.

CHILDHOOD PSYCHOPATHOLOGY
Preoedipal; attachment disorders; Temper tantrums; procrastination; learning disabilities; passive-aggressive; reaction formation behavior; conduct disorder; oppositional-defiant disorder; attention deficit-hyperactivity disorder; teasing; childhood neurosis; obsessive- compulsive neurosis; hysteria; hysterical Identification; phobia; school phobia; counter-phobia.

ADOLESCENT PSYCHOPATHOLOGY
Independence strivings; Self-cutting; Puberty; precocious puberty in girls; Sexual desire; heterosexuality; masturbation; Homosexuality; acting out; marijuana use.

ADULT PSYCHOPATHOLOGY
Narcissistic personality; Anti-social personality; Obsessive personality; Hysterical personality; Paranoid Personality; Dependent personality; Schizoid personality; Depressive pe rsonality; Dissociative personality; Occupational or career choice; Sexual orientation; Binary gender classification; Homosexuality;
Sexual perversion; Transgender issues; Choosing a life partner; Parenthood; "Empty nest"; Retirement; Grand parenthood; Illness, mourning; existential; anxiety.

POSTSCRIPT
Goal in writing book.

Recommended Readings

CHILDHOOD PSYCHOPATHOLOGY

(Annuals and complete works.)
Psychoanalytic Study of the Child (PSC),
Volumes 1-25, International Universities Press
Volumes 26- 27, Quadrangle Press
Volumes 28-65, Yale University Press
Volumes 70-71, Routledge Press
Child Analysis, Hanna-Perkins Center for Child Development, Volumes 1-18
Bulletin of the Hampstead Clinic, 1978-1984; renamed Bulletin of the Anna Freud Centre, 1985-1995
Journal of the American Psychoanalytic Association (JAPA) Search www.pep-web.org for appropriate articles.
The Writings of Anna Freud, International Universities Press (IUP) Volumes 1-8, 1936-1980.

(Selected articles and books.)
Corbett, K. 2009, Boyhoods: rethinking Masculinities. New Haven, Yale University Press
Decarie, Gouin, T. 1974, The Infants Reaction to Strangers, IUP, Madison, CT.
Erikson, E. 1963, Childhood and Society, Norton, N.Y.
Furman, Erna, 1987 Helping Young Children Grow, IUP, Madison, CT
1993, Toddlers and Their Mothers, IUP, Madison, CT.
1995, Preschoolers: Questions and Answers, IUP, Madison, CT.
2001, On Being and Having a Mother, IUP, Madison, CT.
Fraiberg, Selma, 1959, The Magic Years, Scribner's, N.Y.

Fraiberg, S., Adelson, E., & Shapiro, V., 1975, Ghosts in the Nursery, A psychoanalytic Approach to the problems of impaired infant-mother relationships.
J.Am.Academy of Child & Adolescent Psychiatry, 14, 387-421
Greenspan, S.I. & Pollock, G.H. (Eds.), 1981, The Course of Life, Vols 1 & 2, NIMH.
Lax, R.F., Bach,S., & Burland, J.A. (EDs.), 1980, Rapprochement, Jason Aronson, N.Y.
Legg, C., & Sherick, I.,1976, The Replacement Child: A developmental tragedy: Some preliminary comments. Child Psychiatry and Human Development, 7.
Mahler, M.S., Pine, F., & Bergman, A., 1997, The Psychological Birth of the Human Infant, Basic Books, N.Y.
McDevitt, J.B., & Settlage, C., (Eds.) 1971, IUP, Madison, Ct.
Novick, K. & Novick, J., 2019, Emotional Muscle, Xliberis.
Olesker, W. 2011, The Story of Sam. Continuities and Discontinuities in Development, PSC, 65, 48-47.
Parens, H., & Saul, I.J., Dependence: A Psychoanalytic Study, IUP, Madison, CT.
Sherick, I., 1981, The Significance of Pets for Children: Illustrated by a latency Age Girl's Use of Pets in Her Analysis., PSC, 36, 193-215.
—— 1983, Adoption and Disturbed Narcissism: Case Illustration of a Latency Boy. J.Am.Psa.A., 31, 487-513.
Spitz, R.A., 1965, The First Year of Life, IUP, Madison, CT.
Winnicott, D.W., 1965, The Maturational Processes and the facilitating Environment: Studies in the Theory of Emotional Development. London, Karnac, 1990.

ADOLESCENT PSYCHOPATHOLOGY

Barrett, T.F., 2008, Manic defenses against loneliness in adolescence, PSC, 63, 111-136.
Blos, P. 1962, On Adolescence, Free Press, N.Y.
—— 1970, Young Adolescence, Free Press, N.Y.
—— 1979, The Adolescent Passage: Developmental Issues, IUP, Madison, CT.

Brockman, D. D. (Ed.) 1984, Late Adolescence: Psychoanalytic Studies. London, Karnac.

Browning, D.L., 2011, Testing Reality During Adolescence: The Contribution of Erikson's Concepts of Fidelity and Developmental Actuality, Psa.Q., LXXX, 555-594.

Erikson, E., 1963, Childhood & Society, Norton, N.Y.

Deutsch, H., 1967, Selected Problems of Adolescence, Monograph Series of the PSC, Vol.3, IUP, Madison, CT.

Greenspan, S.I., & Pollock, G.H. (Eds.), 1981, The Course of Life, Vol. 2, NIMH.

Katan, A., 1951, The role of displacement in "agoraphobia." Int. J. Psa., 32, 41- 50.

Marcus, I.M. (Ed.), 1975, Masturbation, IUP, Madison, CT.

ADULT PSYCHOPATHOLOGY

Colarusso, C. 1992, Child & Adult Development, Plenum, N.Y.

Erikson, E., 1963, Childhood & Society, Norton, N.Y.

Freud, S.1886-1939, The Complete Psychological Works of Sigmund Freud, Vols 1- 23, Standard Edition, Hogarth, London.

Greenspan, S.I., & Pollock, G.H. (Eds.) The Course of Life, Vol. 3, NIMH

ADDITIONAL REFERENCE

PSYCHODYNAMIC DIAGNOSTIC MANUAL (PDM) 2006, Silver Springs, MD. {Collaborative effort: Am Psa Assn, Int Psa Assn, APA (Div 39), Am Academy of Psa and Dynamic Psychiatry, & Psa in Clinical SW.}

PSYCHOANALYTIC TECHNIQUE WITH CHILDREN, ADOLESCENTS, AND ADULTS:

AN INTRODUCTION FOR STUDENTS AND PROFESSIONALS

IVAN SHERICK, Ph.D.

Preface

I have decided to write this Introduction following the positive reception of a recent earlier book, *Introduction to Child, Adolescent, and Adult Development: A Psychoanalytic Perspective for Students and Professionals*, published by IP Books. That book was written in a "reader-friendly" manner. I used technical language with clear and simple definitions, did not include references, or footnotes, and it was not styled as an academic scholarly treatise. I have endeavored to write this book in the same fashion. Technical terms are italicized.

I have not divided the book up into respective child, adolescent, and adult sections. My thinking is that by not doing so, the differences and similarities in child, adolescent and adult psychoanalysis with regard to a specific technique will be more available to the reader if they are addressed together. In my opinion awareness of child and adolescent analysis is beneficial, and I would say essential, to effective work with adults. The reason is that when one treats an adult one is dealing predominantly with the child and/or the adolescent within the adult.

My focus is on psychoanalysis as a clinical technique, so I will not get involved in a discussion of psychoanalytically informed clinical treatments, e.g., psychodynamic psychotherapy. There are some similarities but also major differences. I will have an introductory section on the psychoanalytic model of the mind and developmental theory. I think this will help the reader appreciate the discussion of the various techniques because it will provide a theoretical framework or rationale of the reasons for the various interventions. The topics I have chosen to focus on are inspired by my experience completing a Hampstead Index as a requirement of my child/adolescent analytic training program.

You will notice that some issues are mentioned several times in different contexts. This is so because they have relevance for different types of analytic interventions. Psychoanalytic clinical theory and technical interventions recognize the multi-determined nature of mental conflict and its treatment and some issues reappear because they are part of this multi-determinism.

At the end of the book I will include a list of references of books on psychoanalytic technique that I have felt helpful in my career as a psychoanalyst.

I received my training first as a Child & Adolescent Analyst at The Hampstead Clinic in London, England, under Miss Anna Freud's direction, graduating in 1971. I then received my Adult Psychoanalytic training from the Michigan Psychoanalytic Institute, graduating in 1981. My psychoanalytic orientation is known as an *ego-psychological* one, derived from the *classical* technique formulated by Sigmund Freud, but I believe it is better described as a *contemporary ego-psychological* orientation insofar as I have integrated some perspectives of techniques of other contemporary schools of psychoanalysis. I will briefly mention other schools of psychoanalysis so the reader can choose to read up more on them if my brief comments raise his or her curiosity.

I am grateful to past supervisors, colleagues and patients whom I have learned from over the past years. I hope this book will be helpful to you in decisions you face regarding professional training or personal growth.

Part One

Psychoanalytic Concepts of Development

I offer this brief account of psychoanalytic concepts because later in my exposition of psychoanalytic technique you will understand, I hope, that technique and the theoretical concepts of the mind go together like "hand in glove," to use a metaphor. Our techniques have grown out of our experience in observing how patients have reacted, i.e., how their minds have reacted, to our interventions. Such observations have resulted in modifications to our theory of the mind, and to developing modifications in technique.

I will give a synopsis of the psychoanalytic theory of development, emphasizing child and adolescent development. When I discuss the aims of child and adolescent psychoanalytic technique you will have this as a context to understand the rationale underlying the interventions more fully.

As a child physically matures there is a sequence of bodily *erogenous zones* that the child experiences. Psychoanalysts call this sequence *psychosexual phases of development*. The drive involved is the sexual one; in psychoanalytic theory it is called the *libidinal drive*. The body and the mind are synergistic, i.e., the effects of the two are integrated. At first, the mouth area is the locus of oral sensations that are erogenous and the height of these sensations are between birth and two years. This *oral phase* corresponds with nursing at the breast or bottle. Next is the *anal phase* (2-3 years of age) and the anus is the focus of intense erogenous sensations and corresponds roughly with a child undergoing toilet mastery. The next phase (3-5 years of age) is a focus on the genitals and urination for each gender. This phase was called the *phallic phase* when it was erroneously believed that both genders highly valued the male genital. This has been revised as we learn that both genders value their respective genitals. Children can be observed to touch this area of their bodies. The Oedipal phase follows (roughly between three and 5 years of age) and has to do with competitive feelings with the parent of the same gender for the prerogatives of physical intimacy that the parent of the same gender as the child has with the other parent. There are wishes to make or receive a baby with the parent of the opposite gender, and feelings of threat from the parent of the same gender because this desire is considered forbidden. Sometimes the phases overlap a bit and life events such as early or delayed maturational changes and unpredictable external events may disrupt the continuous nature of development throughout the life span and be transformative. A transformation could be positive (e.g., the remission of a serious illness) or negative (e.g., identification with the aggressor). So while continuity is fundamental, it is not all-inclusive.

While the libidinal drive and its derivatives are thought to motivate much behavior, the aggressive drive and its derivatives are believed to be paramount in human motivation too. It is these two drives that psychoanalytic clinical investigation has clarified to be the major movers of human behavior.

Drives have a *source* that is the bodily zone it originates from, an *aim*, which is to seek gratification, an *economic* or quantitative intensity, and an *object* or the venue for achieving satisfaction or gratification. Implicit is a demand on the Ego to obtain gratification for the drive.

Two important life events are *fixation* to a phase and *regression* to fixation points. Later when I discuss the aims of child analysis you will understand how the techniques are strategies to help children reduce the effects of fixation and regression. We know from extensive generations of analytic work with adults about the validity of the above developmental concepts. Not to have experienced the Oedipal Complex is a disadvantage for a child, as can sometimes result in situations when parents are divorced. A consequence of the partial dissolution of the Oedipal consequence is the *internalization* of sanctions against incestuous desires, which is the beginning of the conscience (Superego). A conscience is imperative for the regulation and control of drives.

A *fixation* occurs when during a particular psychosexual phase a child experiences either too much or too little gratification from the external world with regard to drives stemming from the phase that the child is then in. A fixation on a particular phase is a "readiness" that reactivates itself, so that derivatives from that psychosexual phase strive for gratification, when a person feeling stress regresses to a fixation point. We know that there is a reverse relationship between the amount of deprivation or gratification of drive derivatives of a particular psychosexual phase and the emergence of a fixation based on the constitutional strength of the particular psychosexual phase. For example, we know that some children are born with a strong anal drive and it takes little control management by their parent during toilet mastery to result in the child's frustration and to result in developing a fixation. On the contrary, for those children with a weak anal constitution lots of control by the parent will not affect the child. We call this reverse etiological relationship the *complemental series*. A child analyst hearing examples of toilet mastery attempts by a parent, can identify a child with a strong anal constitution and advise the parent to "go slow," letting the child set their own pace in controlling his or her bowels.

Latency corresponds with beginning of elementary school and during years six to puberty the erotic desires go "under ground" (*repressed*). The relative strengths of the Ego vs. the Id are reversed in favor of the Ego during these years. Hence, the ego is less burdened with controlling libidinal drive expression. The child is learning about the external world and strengthening the repository of defenses to prepare for puberty and the regaining of ascendency of the strength of the *drives* over the executive part of the mind, the Ego.

Puberty roughly starts adolescence. During the years from puberty to around twenty years of age, the mind is dealing with mastering important issues like masturbation, sexual orientation, choosing a partner not based on a former relationship with a parent, i.e., choosing a non-incestuous relationship, becoming independent, more-or-less from parents, recognizing and accepting that one is not omnipotent and not needing to resort to self-aggrandizing fantasies and behavior, strengthening cognitive abilities so that abstract thinking is available on a reliable basis, etc. Again, psychoanalytic interventions are aimed at helping an adolescent accomplish these developmental achievements.

Adults also go through developmental stages that are psychosocially driven, as well as due to the waning of a youthful body. Thus, parenthood, choice of an occupation, dealing with an "empty nest", retirement, deaths of parents, grand parenting, and coming to terms with death, are some of the issues adults deal with developmentally. Again, psychoanalysis helps adults deal with such issues along with helping them to achieve more adaptive solutions to neurotic conflict.

Psychoanalytic Model of the Mind

Our model of the mind is that it consists primarily of an unconscious part, the *Unconscious* (Ucs), a *Preconscious* part (Pcs), and a *Conscious* part (Cs). A metaphor would be an iceberg, i.e., with the major part of an iceberg being underwater and not seen, which corresponds to the Ucs. The remainder of the mind like the iceberg is partially underwater, capable of being above water, the Pcs., or always above water, the Cs. This formulation of the mind is known as a *topographic* model. Nowadays, we think of *psychic structures*, the *Id*, corresponding to the unconscious part of the mind, and to the *Superego* and *Ego*, both predominantly conscious parts of the mind. Now we refer to them as "structures" to connote that they are mental entities enduring over time, known as a *structural* model of the mind. Most contemporary analysts prefer the structural model but some, like myself, are comfortable using both.

The Id is that part of the mind where instinctual wishes reside, from birth and evolving over the lifetime as the individual matures. These wishes are capable of being accepted into consciousness under certain circumstances, although some of earliest origin, before a child has words, may never reach the conscious part of the mind, although derivatives may. Also residing are wishes that have been expelled from conscious part of the mind because of certain circumstances. Drives make demands upon the Ego to be put into action and to be gratified. The way drives are gratified is for *objects* to be sought to gratify them. People are referred to as objects to distinguish them from the subject.

The Superego is the structure of the mind that essentially is the *conscience*. Early on its moral imperatives are unrealistic and primitive, like "an eye for an eye," but as the individual matures they do as well, becoming more relative, less absolute. An individual with a mature Superego is capable of forgiving himself or herself after he or she recognize they have felt remorse and made amends for transgressions. Once forgiving oneself, it is easier to forgive others. When a Superego "rule" is not adhered to an individual feels *guilt*. A related feeling is *shame*. It seems to have an earlier origin developmentally than guilt. The feeling of shame is that it is believed to be visible to onlookers whereas guilt is more private. The *Ego Ideal* is based on internalized images of "heroes" we wish to be like.

The Ego is the executive part of the mind. It is where so-called executive functions are carried out. The functions we refer to are reality testing, judgment, rational thinking, problem solving, perception, audition, speech, motility, and concerns about perceived safety with the employment of ego defenses to insure it.

Reality testing underscores how the Ego becomes aware of both the external and internal worlds. A child is impacted by events in the external world much more than an adult. Children are more dependent on the external world to gratify their needs. The external and internal worlds can introduce different demands on the Ego, a recipe for *conflict*. The *synthetic function* of the ego brings together these different demands and conflict takes place. What follows is the defensive functioning of the Ego.

The Ego gives meaning to exchanges between the internal and external worlds when drives demand it execute actions to satisfy the drives via objects. These meanings are experienced as *feelings* or *affects*. A theory of affects has not been thoroughly exposited; some object to defining affects as derivatives of the drives. I believe they are intimately connected via the dynamics of drive arousal.
There are primarily two types of thinking, *primary process* and *secondary process*. The former is operative in the unconscious part of the mind, the Id, and the latter primarily in the Ego. In primary process thinking things like cause and effect are abandoned, a single

event can stand for all events, what happed in the past is treated as if it happened presently, etc. This kind of thinking often enters into *fantasy*, also in *dreams*, and in a *parapraxis* (so called "slips of the tongue"). Secondary thinking includes logic, cause and effect, deductive and inductive reasoning, abstract thinking, symbolic thinking, considerations of time and space, etc. In other words, primary process thinking is "primitive" and secondary process thinking is "mature" or advanced. We also conceptualize the *Self*, a sense of one's own *identity*, a *self-image*, and the site of self-esteem, empowerment, and subjectivity. *Identifications* are an important aspect of self-identity. People modify their self-image to take in aspects of people they love, revere, frightened by, whom they have "lost" from separation, etc.

A related mental structure to the *Ego Ideal* is the *Ideal Self*. This refers to what self image an individual aspires to but seldom reaches. It is the image of narcissistic perfection. If the discrepancy is too great between the actual self and the ideal self, an individual can become despondent. *Narcissism* is a positive feeling about the self. We posit that the pleasure an infant feels when gratified, before a clear distinction between oneself and the external world, is attributed to oneself. We call this *primary narcissism*. Presumably there exists a sense of *omnipotence*. Once the external world is distinguished and gratification comes from an external source and pleasure is experienced this is *secondary narcissism*. It can be depleted if the parents become less responsive to the child's needs. We conjecture that omnipotence is attributed to the parents that reduce drive demands. Later, acceptance by the Superego enhances secondary narcissism. Human beings mature and develop, as they get older. The infant gradually develops a mature ego, but early on the caregiver, usually the mother, serves as an auxiliary ego. This is essential insofar as the child has not yet sufficiently developed and consolidated a defensive repertoire to deal with both the internal and external world. The human mind operates under a *pleasure principle* so that the ego does not tolerate "unpleasure," such as anxiety, guilt, shame, etc. Mental conflict ensues when there is a wish that a person senses is contrary to the rules of the external world or the internal world, the conscience. I say "senses" because often a conscious thought process does not occur. There occurs a feeling of anxiety followed by a sense of imminent danger, either real or imagined. If the wish is expressed in action, the sense is that punishment will follow, either abandonment, loss of love, physical bodily punishment, or feelings of guilt. Mental conflict is experienced. Hence the wish must be modified, a compromise is accepted, often a neurotic one. A neurotic symptom is such a compromise, consisting of a derivative of the prohibited wish, modified by the defensive maneuver of the Ego. The compromise formation is capable of evoking some partial gratification and attendant pleasure. Much of psychoanalytic technique, you will see, has to do with helping analysands, regardless of their age, to understand their mind and how it deals with mental conflict, the compromise solutions they have come up with, and a recognition that their automatic neurotic solutions are not in their best interest. With analytic processing of their mental life they come to accept that they will become capable of recognizing neurotic solutions in more rapid time, and choose better solutions. With younger children they recognize that they can express themselves in ways that more likely will end with their wishes being satisfied and insuring feelings of safety. Young children can appreciate that their Superego, their "inner policeman," need not be so harsh. In psychoanalytic treatment we hope that patients of all ages will be more tolerant of desires, the content of the Id, tolerate frustration better, that they will come to understand that they need to recognize a difference between a deed and a thought, and that a mature conscience, the Superego, operates mainly on relative standards and not absolute standards of right and wrong. They learn to "tolerate" anxiety more and to modify *instinctual* aims so that they are less immature and selfish and more socially acceptable (*sublimation*). In psychoanalysis we have a belief in *psychic determinism*, a concept that all mental life and behavior has a meaning, is determined by a psychological cause that may or may not be understood. (This is not to deny the causative properties of an individual's biology.)

Part Two

Referral

When an adult telephones it is a simple matter of finding a mutually convenient time to meet to learn what is being sought. Occasionally, there will be an inquiry about what your fee is and if you are on a particular insurance panel. If not, it might mean the end of the contact, unless you are prepared to offer that you would consider a reduced fee. Many prospective patients will accept that and schedule an introductory session.

With children it is more complicated. Of course, a young child, or for that matter, even an adolescent, does not contact a psychoanalyst independently. A parent usually establishes the initial contact. Sometimes, it may be a single parent but often it may be one spouse of a married couple. It is essential in cases of divorced parents to learn if both parents are in favor of an evaluation. I indicate that I will need to see or hear from the divorced spouse to get confirmation that both parents are in favor of an evaluation. Sometimes one parent has been given legal responsibility for medical decisions regarding the child. A professional asked to do an evaluation must ascertain this.

With children under the age of twelve I see the parent(s) first and then the child. With children older than this I most often elect to see the child first and later the parent(s). Children who are late latency or older are beginning to feel a need to become more independent from parents and I think it is helpful to convey support of this developmental need. Most parents understand this rationale and support it. In these cases I will answer any questions a parent might have about my fee and fee policies so they can decide whether or not to go ahead with the evaluation.

I try to schedule appointments at a time that is not disruptive of a child's or adolescent's school schedule so as not to introduce practical issues that would complicate the need to go ahead. Later, if treatment has started and the parents or child complain of competing interests after school that interfere with treatment appointments, I approach such complaints as *resistance* (more about this later).

Evaluation

In an evaluation a psychoanalyst wants to determine if psychoanalysis is the treatment of choice for the patient. We call this assessing the *analyzability* of patients. There are some diagnostic issues that some analysts consider contrary to a choice of analysis as the preferred treatment. In recent years the scope has widened of diagnostic categories deemed likely to benefit from psychoanalytic intervention. Some traumas are felt to have had irreversible consequences and not remediable by analysis. Some would say that a *trial of analysis* is warranted for all patients. This belief assumes that it is wrong to use theory to predict outcomes. Empirical results should be the criteria. There are too many false negatives. Often, patient histories contain determinants that suggest a bad outcome. Nevertheless, there are some criteria that we can employ.

Sometimes after a first meeting the "fit" between analyst and prospective *analysand* (term refers to patients in analysis) seems workable and other times it may seem impossible or doubtful. By "fit" I mean something intangible; it is a sense that this is a person I can feel comfortable with to talk about myself an/or to listen to. Both the analyst and prospective analysand should evaluate the "fit." It makes sense to me to not come to a conclusion after one meeting.

Psychoanalysis, in my opinion, in best suited for *neurotic* diagnoses that suggest mental conflict. This is so because we hope the adult does not have serious cognitive disabilities resulting from a brain illness, serious impairment of intelligence, severe distortions of the perception of reality, criminal psychopathic pathology, severe autism, and other impairments that would make it difficult for the patient to endure the relative lack of gratification that is part of psychoanalytic technique. What I mean is that an analyst is guided by a *rule of abstinence*. What is meant is that the expectation is that the future analysand will be able to deal with the frustration resulting from the analyst's not granting requests for gratification of wishes, or providing answers to curiosity about the life of the analyst, the lack of advice given by the analyst, etc. The abstinence is a therapeutic strategy that aims to re-create in a manageable way the conditions perceived by the analysand to have caused "problems" in the first place. Conflict is re-experienced, neurotic compromises occur, resistance is experienced, transference develops, and so on.

There are analysts who have worked with psychotic patients, as well as severely delinquent adolescents, who claim positive results with modifications of technique. Psychoanalytically informed treatments, namely, psychodynamic psychotherapy, will be used with patients it is felt would not benefit from classical psychoanalysis but would from the above.

Some children, such as those who have been abused, traumatized, handicapped (e.g., by blindness), or deprived as youngsters of adults who could serve as *auxiliary egos* for them, will need a form of reparative therapy, that strengthens their Ego before child analysis can be the treatment of choice. In most instances, the history provided by the parents and prospective analysands themselves will allow you to rule out some prospective patients from the start.
With an adult, an analyst might begin by asking the person "How can I be of help to you?" Adults will then begin to tell a story of who they are, what troubles them and the changes being sought. As an analyst, one listens and on occasion asks a question to clarify something. An analyst does not have a checklist of questions and I discourage taking notes. One might ask a question if you have a diagnostic issue that you wish to clarify. For example, if adults volunteer that they are depressed and have suicidal thoughts, the analyst may wish to know if a suicide plan is in effect to ascertain the seriousness of the depression. If serious, a psychiatric referral may be called for.

It may be necessary to see a prospective adult analysand multiple times. The patient is informed about this at the end of the first session. I also inquire if the patient has felt comfortable talking to me. I indicate that during the consultative time the adult can evaluate if the feel that they can work with me, feel comfortable talking to me, and that I, too, will evaluate our "fit." I think this underscores the importance of the relationship between analysand and analyst.

With adolescents, there is a lot of similarity with the consultation stage with an adult. Many adolescents are very forthcoming about their unhappiness and offer their understanding as to the genesis of the unhappiness. At the end of the consultation, which may be after several sessions, and a recommendation for treatment is proposed, I mention that confidentiality will be respected. I indicate that there will be one exception, namely, if I felt that their safety was in jeopardy, e.g., because of a suicide plan, I would notify the parents of this situation. In my experience most adolescents accept this. I also indicate that I will be meeting with the adolescent's parents on a regular basis to help them with issues of parenting. I indicate if there has been a rupture in the relationship between the adolescent and parent(s), one aim will be to restore a growth promoting one. Again, most adolescents accept this. I would not say this if I believed that a parent(s) has had a toxic effect on their child and they are unlikely to change.

With a young child, in the consultation phase with parents, I listen to the reasons for seeking an evaluation. I try to assess the correspondence between the two parents. I listen to their personal histories as younger persons. They may not volunteer a personal history during the consultative phase, and may need to feel more comfortable with me to do so. Most parents will convey the parental interventions they have tried with their child to ameliorate the problems that they come to me for help.

With parents of a young child, I ask them what they have told their child as the reasons they are seeking professional help. With some parents I learn that nothing has been said, that they were waiting to talk to me first before telling their child they are seeking help. Exploring their ideas about options conveys a lot about their parenting styles. Also, it is important to focus on both strengths and weaknesses in parenting during these early evaluation sessions. Focusing only on weaknesses makes parents feel guilty and less hopeful.

It is important for the psychoanalyst of potential analysands of all ages to be tolerant with ambiguity and uncertainty. Likely, there will be some questions in the mind of the evaluating psychoanalyst about the genesis of the issues that the adults, adolescents, and children and their parents are seeking help about. But, patience is required because the mind in conflict requires it. I will speak to more about this later.

Recommendation

A psychoanalyst may come to the belief that the patient being evaluated would best be helped by a psychoanalytic intervention. The next step is to make this recommendation to the patient, and in the case of a young child, to the parent(s). With an adolescent I will tell them first, with an understanding that to proceed, we need the agreement of his or her parent(s).

Many parents will agree immediately, but others, understandably, may ask questions, such as, "Why four or five times weekly?" Here the analyst needs to convey in an intelligible way about the essence of a psychoanalytic immersion, how it works and the conditions under which it is most effective. I point out that their child (adolescent) is dealing with mental conflict.

I then define "mental conflict" as a conflict between competing wishes and demands in the mind causing unpleasant emotional feelings such as anxiety, guilt, shame, or embarrassment. I point out, e.g., there may be a wish to express anger or a sexual desire but a part of the mind surmises that if the thought was expressed in action the external world or internal world, e.g., the conscience, would object and the unpleasant feelings would intensify. I indicate that many of these wishes in the form of thoughts or fantasies may not be conscious but are unconscious. To deal with these mental conflicts, people come up with neurotic "solutions" that are not adaptive or in their best interests; they are compromise solutions satisfying both the wish and the opposing, often imagined, force. The aim of psychoanalysis is to help an individual to tolerate thought and fantasies and accept them as non-actions, and come up with more adaptive solutions. This seems to make sense to most adults and adolescents. It is not unusual for parents to believe that if their child were more obedient then there would be no "problems" for their child. For many parents it is comforting for them to hear that their child is having worries because of mental conflict, not because of "bad" parenting or because of disobedience.

When a recommendation for analysis is made many parents and adults will ask, "How long will it take?" I respond that is a good question, and then I tell them that it is like asking someone how long will it take to walk from point A to point B? The answer is that one can give the distance but the time to walk it depends on the length of stride of the walker. The duration, then, depends on how well one works in the analysis. For some adults it seems counter-intuitive to revisit the past during which they encountered unhappiness. When they are told, however, if the past is not emotionally understood it repeats itself in the present, this makes sense to them. During analysis, both analyst and analysand become aware that "slow and steady wins the race;" change takes time because the natural resistance needs to become less formidable so that the analysand "wants" to change.

With younger children, during the evaluation I ask them what their parent(s) told them was the reason for them seeing me. Some can discuss what they were told; others say they do not know. Then I ask them for their understanding about why they were sent to see me. Based on what they say, I try to engage them in a dialogue as to whether, e.g., getting angry or not paying attention, is the best way to deal with what got them upset? Perhaps, I suggest, there are different and better ways to take care of what made them upset? I might mention a fictitious child, Freddy, I know who when he got angry about something would say, "I'm angry." This would get the attention of the person he was angry towards or the attention of a parent or teacher and they would help Freddy so he got a turn to play with a toy that another child would not allow. I tell the child that I would like to help him or her to learn ways to deal with angry or sad feeling or other bad feelings. Most children accept this.

The Frame

When the recommendation for analysis is made with adults and accepted, at that point, the *frame* of the treatment is presented. The "frame" is sort of the contract or the parameters of the treatment that the prospective analysand agrees to, or request further discussion, hoping for a modification. The frame includes the appointment schedule, my fee policy, legal holidays that I do not work, and likely vacation times that I will be taking. With children, the frame is mainly discussed with the parent(s). I will convey the appointment schedule with a young child. With an adolescent, I will discuss the frame as well, acknowledging that their parents will have ultimate responsibility about my fee but they will be asked to bring in the check.

Issues of confidentiality are part of the frame. With adults it is pretty implicit but may have to be underscored with some who question the issue. Below, when I discuss parent work I will point out the limits on confidentiality. In my work with children and adolescents I regard the child or adolescent as the patient. Parent work, however, is essential in psychoanalytic work with children and adolescents. When explaining the limits on their confidentiality to parents, they may disclose what they divulged is a secret, a *family secret*. The analyst will appreciate that much more work with the parents will be necessary before the family secret can be told to the child. The parents will be encouraged to disclose it to their child and to answer questions. Presumably in most instances the child or adolescent will bring the "secret" into their treatment.

When a recommendation for analysis is made to prospective analysands and to parents, the question is often asked about the frequency of sessions. They want to know the rationale. Why are four or five sessions weekly required? How can a child come in so often when he or she is engaged in after-school activities? The concept of immersion then needs to be explained. Essentially the analyst talks about topics receding back into defended area of the mind, if there are long time intervals between sessions. If the interruption is brief then the scary topic is less likely to be hidden away and will be more accessible to the analysand and therefore more likely to be resumed as a communication to the analyst. Most adults can appreciate this, along with older adolescents. Younger children feel less safe in talking about scary topics and worry about intrusions on their free time after school. The analyst will need to point out to the child what has been learned during the consultation that has shed light onto the difficulties the child came in with and which immersion can provide him or her with help. Some children and adolescents still balk but many welcome being rid of their distress. The analyst also hopes that the parents of the hesitant child will come to their side and support the immersion. Sometimes it is best to postpone beginning with a child or adolescent until the parents have entered into a *working alliance* (more below) with the analyst.

The "frame" is important because after adults or parents accept it (with adolescents and children mainly the frequency of sessions) if not complied with this action has an important meaning in the ongoing analysis of them or their child. It is a form of "resistance," particularly in the form of *acting out* (more later) that needs to be addressed by the analyst insofar as it suggests uneasiness about being in analysis or having a child in analysis. If not addressed it can undermine and even disrupt the analysis.

One issue of the frame merits further discussion, mainly because of the variability of position on it by different psychoanalysts. This has to do with cancellations. I indicate that analysands, or parents, will be charged for all scheduled sessions, with out regard for the reason for the cancellation. I also make it known that I will not charge them if I use their appointment time to schedule another consultation. I also indicate I will make an attempt to reschedule them if they request it. Also, when I cancel they will not be charged. I have arrived at this policy over the years experimenting with other ones, e.g., no charge if given advance warning, such as twenty-four hours, of a cancellation. My thoughts are that there are reasonable causes for a cancellation, e.g., a sick child, a flat tire, the death of a relative, etc., but I do not think it is in the best interest of the analyst or the analysand to have to make a judgment call as to what is "reasonable or not." The parameter of fee policy is part of the business arrangement or contract between the analyst and the analysand and subjectivity should not be a part of it. Another aspect of the fee policy is time of payment. I present a bill at the last session of the month and request payment by the fifth calendar day of the next month. Again, there are other ways to handle this, e.g., payment expected on the last scheduled session of the month. Late payment, as discussed above, may be a form of resistance.

The analyst's office is also part of the frame. One does not meet with an adult at a coffee shop, with an adolescent at the Mall, with a child at the playground. The office is constant and is a "boundary" of sorts for the analysis. The analyst's office is devoid of very personal things like family photos or memorabilia, in order to not interfere with the fantasies of the analysand and his or her curiosity about the analyst. Soundproofing is secure so sounds from an adjacent office are not heard, and the analysand is confident what is said will not be heard from another office. Usually, a waiting room is provided with double doors between it and the consultation room. When analysts share office space there is sometimes a common waiting area that I think is not favorable because of issues of confidentiality. I think it is ideal to have a separate entrance door and exit door so analysands are less likely to bump into each other between sessions. Analysts that elect to have a home office, as I have, are aware that the analysand is more privy to the analyst's personal tastes than an office in an office building.

Child analysts best have an area separate from the area they see adults and adolescents in, because of the scattered toys that need to be cleaned up after a session or between sessions. Also, some children do not adhere to the limit that they can say anything but not do anything in the treatment area. Hence, an analyst who also sees adults and adolescents would not want to expose a child to his office where the child may break a valuable art object or scratch furniture, or tear a carpet, or put crayon marks on a wall in a fit of anger.

I do not take notes during sessions and do not encourage supervisees to do so either. I think it distracts from your attention to the analysand and I know I would not like it if I was the analysand. What is in the analyst's mind is what will be used in interventions. In between sessions, notes can be written that are considered important to refresh one's memory. Some analysts see patients back-to-back, but I prefer a five or ten minute interval.

The Beginning of an Analysis

Psychoanalysts differ as to what they convey to analysands when they begin psychoanalysis. Some choose to say nothing about the process or procedure and wait for the analysand to ask questions about how to begin. After all, the couch is within sight in the office and there have been scores of movies showing patients lying on their backs on an analytic couch with the analyst behind them out of their sight. So most adults assume that they will lie down on the couch on their backs. But some analysands are hesitant, even afraid to use the couch. There are different reasons why this might be and after a few minutes or sessions it will usually be addressed by the analysand or the analyst. It is not imperative to use the couch if you are in analysis, but it is thought to be beneficial. On the couch, it is felt to reassure most analysands that they will not act on their impulses, e.g., hostile or sexual, and it helps them feel safer. Using the couch and not seeing the analyst behind you is believed to support a *controlled regression*. This is believed to happen because the analysand"s attention is turned inward and the pull of childhood "fixation points" leads to past memories, feelings and attitudes. Despite this regression, when the adult walks out of the consulting room he or she resumes more adult viewpoints and behavior. Analysands are chosen to benefit from psychoanalysis because they have the "ego strength" to deal with such regression. For some, the couch is like a bed and to engage in exploring sexual fantasies with another person is stimulating of erotic feelings.

Laying on one's back with your eyes looking at the ceiling or closed is also felt to encourage getting in touch with your thoughts and/or feelings insofar as you are not distracted as much by other things around you, including the analyst's face. Of course, for those analysands who are hesitant to use the couch until they feel safer, the process of analyzing fears may ultimately allow him or her to try using the couch. Some who cannot use the couch to begin with may agree to turn the chair so they are still sitting up but not facing the analyst. Some analysands close their eyes on the couch, others may not, some cross their legs, some turn their heads to occasionally look at a clock if there is one they can see from their position on the couch, others look at a wrist watch, some speak very softly, some might even turn to look at the analyst behind them, etc. All these behaviors have meaning but may not be understood for a while. Analysts must be comfortable with "not knowing," with *tolerating ambiguity*.

Then there is the issue of the so-called "basic rule," *free association*. That it is called a "rule" is a misnomer; it is more a recommendation. Some analysts elect to state the idea of free association from the beginning, as I do, thinking that analysands need some education about a process they have never encountered and unique as a form of communication.

The basic rule suggests that analysands try to allow themselves to verbalize all of their thoughts, images, fantasies and feelings without censorship as they emerge into their conscious mind, not to willfully think of things to talk about. The analyst acknowledges that this is an ideal insofar as at times there will be a reluctance to do so, but that also is encouraged to be acknowledged verbally. The analyst acknowledges that being told "this is a place where you can say **anything**" is probably the only time in one's life to hear this and it runs counter to everyday experience. The aim is to become more comfortable with one's mind and to eventually appreciate how the mind works. Incidentally, psychoanalysis as a therapeutic technique is interested in the mind and not the brain.

While free association is an ideal, it does not mean that the analysand is busy doing this and the analyst is silent most of the time. Certainly silence is a technical strategy that is useful to give an analysand the opportunity to reflect on thoughts and images. This does not mean that verbal dialogue between analyst and analysand does not take place. Often there is verbal interaction between the two. Analysts may ask a question, or an analysand may respond to an interpretation with a question or an association that takes the analytic material to a deeper level. Sometimes it may seem that the analytic process with adults is a "verbal playground." Metaphors may be spoken of, and even a joke may be told to get a point across.

Akin to the "basic rule" for the analysand is one for the analyst, although it is not called a "rule." The analyst is expected to remain *neutral* to the analysand's material and to adhere to *abstinence* and not gratification with regard to the wishes of the analysand. I will have more to say about this when I discuss the Limits that exist in the analytic process.

With adolescents the basic rule can also be stated as an ideal. I say "ideal" because analysts know that it can be sought after but rarely if ever fully achieved. This is because of how the mind seeks pleasure and avoids unpleasure. This is a universal human characteristic. Free association will be interrupted when a part of the mind we call the Ego senses unpleasure in the form of anxiety, guilt, shame, embarrassment, etc. At that point analysands will more actively think of something else to say other than what made them uncomfortable.

The basic principle in beginning an analysis is to enable the analysand regardless of their age to feel safe. This is especially essential in psychoanalytic work with young children. The analyst being an adult is believed, for the most part, by a child to be helpful and protective. Of course, with those children who have been traumatized by adults the expectation has to be gradually experienced by the child to feel safe. Children do not verbally free associate; they are incapable of doing so because of a de-emphasis on words and a natural tendency to act. Some child analysts look upon a sequence of play as free association. Many believe it is not insofar as play and its sequence is limited often by the properties of the toy being utilized or the rules of the game. For a child to voluntarily discard the controls of action, as in free association where non-control over sequences of thoughts put into words is sought, if achieved could lead many children to destructive actions. Such experiences run counter to enabling children to feel safe.

With time the child analyst helps the young child feel safe by his or her verbal interventions that convey to the child that they are welcomed and accepted, that the child has a mind that contains thoughts and feelings which can be understood. The child eventually grasps that the adult child analyst he is playing with also has a mind with thought and feelings that may be like his or her own but could also be different. We call this "mindfulness," a process instilled in most infants early on in their interactions with an empathic mother.

Establishing a Working Alliance

The efforts of a psychoanalyst to establish a working alliance with analysands of all ages, I think, is foremost in their minds in the beginning of the analysis, the early stage. Why is it so important? It is so because one wants the analysand as an ally, someone who has an initial curiosity about how the mind works so improvements can be made upon solutions to mental conflict. The aim is to strengthen this beginning curiosity so that it will help the analysand to withstand internal pressures to abandon the process once it deepens and unpleasant feelings are encountered. However, I wish to underscore, that interventions aimed at reinforcing the working alliance continue until the last day of an analysis. In a final session there might be an occasion for the analyst to support his departing analysand's comments that they are hopeful they can continue the work of analysis independently, i.e., the analyst may support the identification with the analyzing function of the analyst.

A working alliance is possible with the evolving and expanding capacity of the analysand to both "observe" and "experience" the world and the Self. These critical cognitive capacities are more developed in adults compared to adolescents and younger children. Because of limited cognitive capacities that limit ability to understand the Self and the world, *insight* potentially is not as thorough in young children. By mid-adolescence with the beginning of more abstract thinking, they, too, are capable of tolerating and being evaluative of their mental contents. With younger children, interpretations can be taken sometimes as permission to enact a heretofore forbidden impulse. So, the child analyst must be cognizant of the young analysand's capacity to control his or her desires. The structure of a child's mind may not have developed or stabilized sufficiently so that bringing awareness to an impulse, if expressed, could increase anxiety.

In working with adults, analysts soon recognize that many of the issues their analysands are dealing with originated during their childhoods. After awhile adults have insight into this as the origin of their discomfort. An intervention aimed at strengthening the working alliance is to get across to the adult that he or she will have the capacity to help one's inner child grow up to be more adult. Adult patients appreciate that the analytic process is supportive of this aim.

In working with adolescents and younger children it is imperative that the analyst establishes a working alliance with their parents. It is the parents who will be confronted by their child's threats not to continue their treatment when "the going gets tough," i.e., when the child starts to experience discomfort because of the uncovering of conflicts in analysis. The parents at that moment need to be empathic with their child's struggle and support the value of continuing by supplying hope that things will get better in the future with continued analysis. With some parents and some adults at the time of the recommendation for analysis it may be helpful to point out that there may come a time when their child or they may feel better and they may think it is time to stop, but they will be mistaken.

In psychoanalytic treatment of analysands of all ages, an important idea to point out to all is that there is a distinction between "thoughts" and "deeds." It does not seem to matter to people, even those who are not religiously observant, that the difference matters. If you have a "bad" thought or fantasy, you should feel as guilty as if you enacted it. As a psychoanalyst, if you can help those you see to appreciate the distinction, the working alliance is strengthened.

In recent times women have come forth to accuse men in past or present positions of power over them to have sexually harassed or abused them. Sometimes a period of time has elapsed between the time of the assault and the time of the public accusation by a woman. Often the woman will talk about "shame", as if the assault or harassment was her fault. Objectively, these women need not feel ashamed. It occurs, regretfully, because many women feel that if they have desired to be noticed by a man it is their fault if a man acts like a predator. I believe these women lose the distinction between a "wish" and a "want." A childhood wish to be desired by one's father likely originated during the Oedipal years, universal in Western culture, but this is not the same as "wanting" to be assaulted.

If guilt is lessened then analysands will more likely share their private thoughts with their analysts. A private thought or fantasy does not hurt another human you may even care for. One can try to understand its derivation and learn about oneself, maybe even forgive oneself and open oneself up to be more compassionate and forgiving of others.

Young *preoedipal* children often experience conflict essentially with the external world. Their own defensiveness about wishes perceived to be unacceptable to external authority makes it difficult to establish an alliance with the child analyst. It feels scary to be curious about their own minds and their role in conflict. But it does occur with some precocious children.

Resistance

Resistance in my view and that of a majority of psychoanalysts is a basic characteristic of the human mind. It is an outcome of the mind seeking pleasure and avoiding unpleasure. For example, we avoid saying things all the time in social situations if we think a recipient will be disturbed by our utterance, or we put some thought out of our mind if we think it is salacious. When this mental process occurs in the consulting room we refer to the defensive maneuver as resistance.

With our analysands we might notice a silence or a change of topic after they have said something connected to intense feeling, e.g., sadness, anger or excitement. They may have a "slip of the tongue" (a parapraxis) but ignore it, or they may be speaking of something in the present but suddenly shift to the past. Often we may make a verbal intervention but their response is apparently unrelated, without acknowledgment of this. When analysts notice this, (*close processing analysis*) they suspect that a resistance has occurred and they often choose to bring it to the analysand's attention if it goes unmentioned. The aim in making a resistance interpretation is to raise the analysand's curiosity about his or her mind and to evoke the working alliance. We hope the analysand will be able to identify the unpleasant feeling, often anxiety, that prompted the resistance, and express what the danger was that was imagined if a particular mental content was not avoided.

In addition to silence after an intervention by the analyst, resistance can take myriad forms. Joking frequently might suggest resistance. We do not expect analysands to lose their sense of humor, but if it is excessively employed an analyst might wonder if topics that elicit *dysphoric* feelings (depressive) are being avoided.

The analyst might say, "Have you noticed that you often tell jokes or laugh readily at things I say?" Another common form of resistance is forgetting of dreams. Dreaming is universal and if analysands do not bring theirs into analysis it likely has to do with resistance. Again, the analyst will wonder if the analysand has noticed that he or she almost never brings in a dream into analysis. If the analysand agrees the analyst might wonder, "Why do you think that is?" This could lead to analysis of resistance.

It is important that the analyst avoids being combative with the analysand. The analyst keeps in mind the ubiquity of resistance; the human mind seeks pleasure and avoids "unpleasure." The presence of resistance does not mean the analysand is a poor candidate for psychoanalysis.

Secrets are often kept out of an analysis until the analysand feels safe and trusting of the analyst. The basic premise of psychoanalytic treatment is that the analysand agrees to say whatever enters their mind; there can be no exception that an analyst can agree to. If the analysand discloses that they have *suppressed* a secret the analyst will acknowledge that it is progress that they disclosed this and it is important that they talk about it when they feel more comfortable doing so, because a secret can play an important role in their mental life.

Avoidance of certain topics is another sign of resistance. For example, the topic of sexual desire may not be brought up by an adult, masturbation by an adolescent, eating issues by an analysand suffering from an eating disorder, the death of a pet guinea pig by a child who does not want to feel grief, etc. An analyst will point out the absence of ubiquitous topics, or the absence of a topic that almost always follows a particular life experience, and try to raise the analysand's curiosity about the absence.

Avoidance of curiosity about the analyst is a frequent resistance. When this is eventually pointed out after some time has passed, many adults will say that they thought it was off-limits to express such thoughts. The analyst will remind them that they have been advised that they "can say anything" which would include thoughts about their analyst. One might add that such thoughts can help the process insofar as other content could emerge to further the analysis. This will make sense to many adult analysands but there will remain some where this remains a strong resistance. Adolescents and younger children sometimes can be quite vocal about their view of their analysts.

The enactment of a resistance occurs in analysands of all ages. With adults and adolescents it is most often verbal insofar as this is the way they express themselves. With younger children it is mostly in the form of action insofar as this is the way they mostly express themselves. The resistance occurs in their play. For example, the topic of the play changes after something is enacted that expresses a lot of feeling in the play, perhaps verbally (a shout) or in an impulse (something thrown), and the child does not appear to acknowledge it. With children, resistance is sometimes very overt, e.g., running out of the room, and with adolescents (and adults) it often takes the form of coming late or not showing up for a session.

With adolescents, they usually avoid the topic of masturbation. It is not an activity that they volunteer and speak freely about. This is in part an internalization of cultural mores about the topic, although over the years I have seen a greater normalization of the activity. Masturbation was once thought to be a sign of pathology but is now accepted by Western culture as universal, but still something you do privately and do not talk about. Young children of both genders touch their genitals and experience pleasure. If parents notice this, most do not chastise the child but do say they should do it only in the privacy of the bedroom. Of course, there are still parents who shame a child caught masturbating. If an adolescent can talk about the act of masturbation and the accompanying fantasy, a child analyst can reassure the adolescent that it is normal. Analysis of the fantasy can help the adolescent have a sense of normalcy about their sexual desire. Resistance is often encountered because of shame and guilt. Sometimes excessive masturbation is a sign of anxiety about interacting with the opposite sex. Overcoming resistance about the topic can lead to the open admission of such anxiety.

Another topic that analysts encounter in contemporary times with evidence of resistance, but less than a decade ago, is the topic of *sexual gender*. We used to think this was pretty much fixed by three years of age, but now we believe gender assignment is more fluid. Adolescents are more comfortable about the issue and some, albeit with much pain and social ostracism, declare they have adopted the gender identity opposite from the one they were born with. Overcoming resistance about talking about their intentions or conflicts allows analytic intervention to be of benefit to these adolescents.

The human mind employs many different processes of avoiding unpleasure. We call these processes *defense mechanisms.* The part of the mind that employs them we call the Ego. In our psychoanalytic model of the mind, the ego is the mental "structure" that carries out "executive functions," rational thinking, judgment, memory, reality testing, and defensive processes to eliminate unpleasure (e.g., feeling of anxiety, guilt, shame, embarrassment, etc.)

Insofar as our focus is on technique I will only summarily refer below to some typical mechanisms of defense, but keep in mind that the ego is resourceful and can use any mental process, thought or action, defensively to ward off unpleasant feelings.

Signal anxiety is a special feeling employed by the ego to warn a person (the Self) that either a real or imagined danger threatens the person. The danger will be experienced if a forbidden wish or its derivative is expressed in action. If the danger is felt to be in the internal world it could be condemnation by or loss of love from the superego (guilt) or in the external world some sort of punishment (loss of the object [abandonment], loss of the object's love, castration [some physical harm]. To avoid the danger the forbidden wish must be modified to be less unacceptable to the imagined or real source of the danger. Here is when defenses are called into play and the modified wish if expressed is a "compromise" reflecting aspects of the derivative wish and the defensive modifications. So instead of pummeling a younger sibling you shout that he "stinks and should be thrown away." If the defensive maneuvers are not sufficient the signal anxiety can change to *panic*, with accompanying feeling of helplessness and feeling overwhelmed.

Repression is the permanent exclusion of thoughts and feelings from consciousness and assigning them to the unconscious part of the mind. It is "the Mother of all defenses!" *Suppression* is the conscious decision not to talk about something. *Reaction formation* is when the opposite is expressed from what is meant, e.g., an expression of loving feelings when what are felt by the doer is hateful feelings, or vice versa, towards the recipient. *Projection* is when a wish or thought or feeling towards someone is felt or believed to be directed instead towards you. *Externization* occurs when unwanted aspects of the Self are attributed to others. For example, "He is greedy and exploitative of others," said by someone who typifies such a person. *Denial* is when someone ignores completely a bit of reality and acts without taking into account the reality in their decision-making. *Negation* Is when a wish or thought is allowed access to consciousness and verbalized by an analysand but negated. For example, " I have no sexual feelings for my teacher." An analyst will point out, "Who said you did?" bringing the analysand's attention to the defensive maneuver. *Rationalization* is when a person evades feeling guilty by fabricating a rational reason for their action. *Displacement* is when someone expresses a wish towards someone safer other than the person it was intended for originally. *Dissociation* is in a different category from the above defenses insofar as it is not directed at a particular thought, wish, or feeling, but at the Self. The person is so uncomfortable "being in their own skin" that they psychologically feel apart from himself or herself. *Isolation of affect* occurs when an idea or thought is expressed devoid of the accompanying affect connected to it. It is akin to *intellectualization* wherein an analysand narrates the meaning of an experience with "academic" understanding devoid of feeling. *Reversal of affect* occurs when the opposite feeling is reported from what is being experienced.

Resistance is reduced when there is a strong working alliance between the analysand and the analyst, but it is never eliminated. As mentioned earlier, with young children, in addition to endeavoring to establish a working alliance of sorts with them, a result less achievable because of their greater intolerance for unpleasant feelings, the analyst works at establishing one with their parents.

There are some defenses that have been employed since childhood and have proven effective in reducing anxiety. After awhile they are utilized regularly and become *character* defenses. We all have character styles that we "automatically" use to reduce expectations of anxiety producing situations. They become "firewalls" against expected danger. For example, procrastination, over-optimism, clowning, excessive cynicism, etc., are all example of character styles. Often character defenses are based on identification with primary people in childhood, such as parents.

Transference

As I understand psychoanalysis as a clinical technique, *transference* is another major feature of the unfolding dynamics. Transference occurs when a past relationship Is re-experienced in a contemporary relationship with another person different from the one with whom it originated. Consciously, the person enacting the transference is not aware, in most instances, of the re-experience of feelings and thoughts, and instead believes they have a contemporary origin. This is possible, psychoanalysts believe, because the *Unconscious* is timeless. That is, memories and accompanying feelings when re-experienced consciously, feel as if they are contemporary. This re-experiencing is a part of everyone's life. For example, we may experience a male teacher with the same thoughts and feelings that we once had with our father but not be aware of this consciously. In some instances we may have a thought, "He's a lot like Dad." When this experience occurs in the consulting room we call it transference. The analyst is now reacted towards, without awareness, as if they are the person from the past. We speak of *positive transference* and *negative transference*. "Positive" has to do with loving wishes and feelings, while "negative" refers to angry wishes and hateful feelings.

At the beginning of an analysis before a strong working alliance has taken hold, it can be positive transference feelings that may prevent an analysand from a premature termination. There are instances when a positive transference can have a non-beneficial effect. Sometimes it leads an analysand to be compliant with the analyst's interpretations, not thoughtfully considering its merits and noticing the feelings that are evoked, but rather simply agreeing that it is correct to please the analyst. It could be also a way to avoid examining the material further because of anxiety. The analyst with such an analysand needs to be self-aware, too, that they are not making comments with an authoritarian tone that scares an analysand who uses passivity as a defense against being assertive.

There is also the rare so-called *transference cure.* Here a patient may feel "cured" after a few consultations prior to entering analysis, or very early in the analysis. Symptoms have gone and he or she feels better. There is no need to continue. I understand this as an unconscious idealization of the analyst as omniscient, coupled with unconscious resistance to undergo analysis.

Transference can occur with analysands of all ages but is less frequent the younger the child. This is because the young child is still very invested in and involved with contemporary people such as parents in the here-and-now. These contemporary feelings may be re-experienced with the child analyst but we do not consider them transference. We consider this type of relationship a *displacement* from the parents. (Below we will discuss the different types of relationships a child experiences with their analyst.)

Transference is a valuable component of the analytic process insofar as its occurrence is thought of as a "window into the past," allowing the analyst to understand the analysand's evolution. Eventually, when the analyst engages in pointing out the origin of thoughts and feelings and begins to make interventions in the form of interpretations, the analysand gradually gets a better emotional understanding of himself or herself and the origin of conflicts. Initially, an analyst will not immediately bring the attention of the analysand to a past relationship when transference is suspected. This is because we want the intensity of the relationship experienced by the analysand towards the analyst to build up and intensify. At what point the analyst inquires about a past relationship differs with each analysand. We do not want understanding to be only intellectual but also emotional. Basically, though it depends on the working alliance and if the intensity of the relationship has begun to be fraught with such intense feelings and wishes that a feeling of safety for the analysand begins to be in jeopardy. It is then felt that an analysand will emotionally understand that there is a history to what they are currently feeling, and it makes sense.

Adolescents have to deal with pubertal changes. This causes a focus on their body. Early in childhood the mother, usually, is felt to be the "owner" of one's body. Gradually in late latency children start to take ownership of their body. When puberty "hits" many adolescents feel overwhelmed and regress in their object relatedness, at least internally. The mother is now expected again to be in charge of their body and she is blamed for the "noxious" bodily changes they are supposed to be in "charge" of but feel over whelmed by because of bodily sexual urges. Such adolescent analysands will develop a maternal transference to the analyst, feeling both the unwilling victim of the analyst but also wishing the analyst to take charge. Resistance often is expressed in 'missed" sessions, a common event in work with this age group in analysis.

In some instances, most often when the genders of the analytic couple are opposite, an *eroticized transference* can occur. The analysand will be seductive, coquettish, and is interested in a receptive response from the analyst. When this is not forthcoming, but instead the analyst responds in an empathic, compassionate, and professional manner, the analysand will feel rejected, frustrated and angry. Hopefully, the transference can be analyzed and insight gained. In instances of an erotic transference, the analyst needs to be sensitive to their own erotic feelings so that he or she does not enter into an *enactment* (discussed later) with the analysand.

Sometimes, an erotic transference can be disguised by an analysand's preoccupation with one's body, often seeming hypochondriacal, i.e., an excessive worry about the health of the body, imagining all sorts of ailments. In this manner, the analysand brings the analyst's attention to one's body.

With adult analysands particularly, and less often with adolescents, and only occasionally with young children, a *transference neurosis* may occur. This happens when the transference gets so intense it becomes the primary relationship for the analysand. It is in this relationship, then, that the analysand seeks gratifications, feels loved or unloved and expects praise or criticism. Conflicts with significant people lessen, and symptoms (neurotic solutions to conflicts) lessen. When the analysand is in the midst of the transference neurosis, again, it is an opportunity for the analyst and analysand to gain insight into the origin of personal conflicts and to gain emotional *insight*. At the height of a transference neurosis the analysand does not seek insight but rather seeks gratification. With interpretations, gradually the intensity of the transference neurosis diminishes and the analyst is no longer "all-important" as during its height. Adolescents are still involved with present day people as are children, even more so, which runs counter to the development of a transference neurosis. Hence, with these age groups, particularly young children, transference neuroses are rare. *Character transference* is what an analysand brings to the analysis from the very beginning. It does not gradually develop.

Real Object, Developmental Object, & Transference Object

In psychoanalytic theory we talk of a person as a "self" and of the person they are relating to as an "object." We do this not to objectify or dehumanize the "other" but in the interests of clarity to distinguish the two people. We have talked above about transference. The analyst in a transference relationship with an analysand is referred to as a *transference object*. As indicated above, patients of all ages are capable of responding to their analyst in this way, although the incidence typically decreases the younger the analysand. We also refer to an analyst as being a *developmental object*. Analysands of all ages may experience their analyst in this manner. When this happens the analyst has responded to the analysand in a growth promoting way compensating for an experience that the analysand has been deprived of in their earlier years, probably because of an absent parent or a disturbed caretaker. As an infant or very young child, an adult caretaker serves as an auxiliary ego providing the immature child in their charge with the cognitive or emotional support the child lacks. In some instances, noted above, this may not happen. The analyst by analyzing may provide the experience that they lacked. This experience is not a deliberate strategy and the analysand has a "second chance," so to speak, to take advantage of this growth promoting experience. The analyst has been used as a developmental object.

All analysands, irrespective of age, but predominantly by young children, may also experience the analyst as a *real object*. Young children are used to seeing adults as caretakers, and their expectation is that the child analyst will be so too. There are innumerable ways in which this manifests itself. For example, the child analyst may assist the child is maneuvering a heavy object, such as a door or table, or reaching a light switch that is above the child's reach, etc. Analysts know that they cannot be robots and only be in an interpretive mode. Hence, there are innumerable times when they say things that are real, like "Thank you," "My condolences on the death of your mother," "I hope your surgical procedure goes well," etc. Analysands of all ages appreciate this humane treatment, and it does not interfere with the analyst becoming a transference object, unless it is excessive in frequency.

Analysts are like all people and sometimes they make mistakes. I think it is best to admit the mistake if it affects an analysand. For example, I confused the return date from a vacation with the return to work date and scheduled appointments on the day of my return, which was in the evening. I telephoned the people affected, apologized for my confusion and offered to reschedule if it was convenient for them with no obligation for them to do so. I noticed no adverse effects on their treatment. I think if we expect analysands to be truthful, analysts need to be so too if it is not believed to be a burden on analysands. I introduce the latter idea because I think to share some personal events in the analyst's life with analysands can be burdensome and ought not be done. For example, a surgical procedure undergone during the analyst's vacation need not be talked about if the expectation is that the analyst will not need to cancel sessions. Also, it may be that the need for surgery or the result of it will not even be noticeable. A life event like an analyst's child's marriage or a grandchild's birth ought not be shared unless the analysand, for some reason, becomes aware of it. Then the reactions of the analysand can be analyzed.

Countertransference

Psychoanalysts are human and being so like everyone else they have "hot spots," personal issues that owe their origin to their personal life experiences. An essential part of training to become an analyst included a personal psychoanalysis. Having an emotional understanding of yourself and your emotional sensitivities will aid a clinical analyst in dealing with future patients. An analysand may bring up a topic that is a sensitive one for their analyst. The analyst may not be initially aware that they are responding to the material in a non-helpful way. They may be silent, have an angry tone, change the focus by their intervention, feel excited by the material and seductively encourage further details by their manner and words, etc. The above may also not be noticed initially by the analysand. We speak of the interaction at this point as an *enactment*. Eventually, hopefully, one of the two will notice and an analysand may comment about a change in the analyst's tone, for example, since she has brought up erotic fantasies about her male analyst. If brought to his attention, an analyst may agree to the observation. "I think your observation has merit and I will think more about it." In my experience if an analysand makes mention of an enactment, for me to acknowledge its likely presence, has always advanced the treatment in a positive way. Analysands like to hear confirmation that the analyst is human, not a robot, has an Unconscious too, and he or she can have an effect on the analyst. An analyst may note the change before their analysand, may not say something openly but may ponder the experience. If nothing is said, the analyst makes a judgment that the analysand may not benefit from an admission and may feel unsafe but will likely benefit from a change in the analyst's behavior. The analyst will undergo some self-analysis to gain more insight as to why they were effected so by the material. Another way that an analyst may unwittingly be affected by an analysand's material about a significant person in their past, is to behave in a manner that we call *role responsiveness*. Here the analyst unwittingly enacts the behavioral mode of the significant object from the past of the analysand. I understand it as an unconscious identification with the object, a form of countertransference.

It used to be thought that countertransference was always detrimental to a psychoanalysis, that the analyst should keep its occurrence to their self, and in some instances seek peer supervision or further personal analysis. This attitude has been changed so that now we believe that countertransference is inevitable and it can be useful in understanding not only oneself but also one's analysand. Most analysts are now not ashamed of having countertransference but think of it as a tool in their bag of technical "instruments."

Freud encouraged analysts to listen with "free floating attention." By this he meant they should allow their attention to go freely towards the analysand's associations and towards their own reveries in reaction to the analysand's material. In doing the latter an analyst who is tolerant of his or her own thoughts or images can be alert to uncomfortable feelings they may be experiencing while listening to their analysand's associations. Countertransference can then be analyzed. Analysts now accept that both their own personality and their theory influence interventions and consequently the shape of analysand's material.

An issue that is recent in psychoanalysis is "love." Can an analyst come to "love" his or her analysand? This will be asked or be implicit in analytic material. Often it arises after expressions of love are voiced from the couch and the analysand asks or it is implied that he or she is curious if the feeling is mutual. Analysts have been reluctant to answer this question. They have dealt with it with an analytic posture. "Notice you ask me this after professing your love for me. It took courage to tell me you love me, and it would be very hurtful to you if I did not tell you I feel love for you too. I am committed to your best interests and hope you achieve your goals.

If that isn't love then I don't know what is." The analyst who feels this way does love the analysand, but it is different from "romantic love" or "erotic love." In my opinion, either of the last two, if felt, would be countertransference and very burdensome to disclose to an analysand.

Interpretation

Another fundamental aspect of psychoanalytic treatment is the making of an interpretation. An interpretation is a verbal intervention that is meant to provide some modicum of insight that in turn will deepen the material, i.e., allow the analysand to access additional mental content heretofore repressed. Insight is sought. An interpretation based on the *topographic model* of the mind, makes conscious what was formerly unconscious. Based on the structural model of the mind, an interpretation expands the ego's understanding of some mental content unknown up to that point, albeit the site of feelings like anxiety and/or guilt associated with the repressed content. An interpretation is aimed at expanding an analysand's self-understanding, both intellectually and emotionally. It is also a way ultimately of helping an analysand reclaim a sense of *self-agency*. This is so because with greater tolerance of instinctual drive, an analysand gains a greater sense of control over their decision-making and actions in the real world.

An *interpretative process* is more than a declarative statement from the analyst. It may include clarifications, confrontations, questions, initial steps at working through, even supportive comments, all aimed at helping the analysand gain insight. Essentially the process describes a dialogue between the "analytic couple."

Analysts try to use vocabulary that is easily understood, not requiring a dictionary, and use words evocative of feeling, e.g., " scared" instead of "intimidated." The aim is to reach the scared "inner child' whom the analysand can help to feel safe to grow up. Such an intervention can be delivered to analysands of all ages.

An analyst does not want to take on an authoritarian manner so that an analysand feels that they are being lectured about what is right or wrong by an all-knowing authority. It is best to convey interpretations as conjectures so that the analysand does not feel lectured to and can feel comfortable to refute an interpretation. "I wonder if you may have been feeling…" Sometimes interpretations can be made in a playful way and the analysand responds back with a similar tone. "You're hoping Prince Charming will put the glass slipper on your foot." "Yes, but with my luck the shoe probably will be a size too big."

An analyst does not make interpretations from the start. One waits until there is confidence about the meaning of material being brought by the analysand. The analyst is hopeful that an analysand will be curious about the workings of their mind. If made too soon, an interpretation could increase resistance. A general principal in making interpretations is to work from the *surface* to the *depth*. The analyst judges the analysand's readiness to hear an interpretation. Usually, both analyst and analysand are aware of the uncomfortable feelings of the surface content.

From the above you can understand that the readiness is based on the strength of the working alliance, the intensity of resistance, and the quality of the transference. The weakened intensity of the resistance will bring attention to mental content that at the moment has the most affect attached to it. It is the mental content at this surface that the analyst will judge to be most ready to be interpreted. This is a strategic technical choice. An interpretation when made by an analyst carries the hopeful expectation that the analysand will be identified with the *analyzing function* of the analyst.

For example, the analyst might say, "You seem to be uncomfortable, judging from your silence, about what I just said about your apparent discomfort being invited to your parents' home for Thanksgiving." This interpretation is meant to bring attention to defensiveness about conflicted feelings and thoughts about the invitation. An intervention might be, "I wonder if what I just said about your attitude towards attending a family reunion is reminiscent of what your father might say?" Such an interpretation is meant to bring attention to transference feelings and thoughts that could be elaborated upon by the analysand. Some interpretations underscore a feeling evidenced by the analysand. A question might be asked, "What are you feeling about what you just said?" Naming a feeling often will allow the associated thought to be brought into consciousness and to be felt and connected thoughts to be verbalized.

With adolescents, the same judgment used with an adult, is employed as to timing of an interpretation. It might be said, "Your account of your noticing the girl sitting at the desk across from you suggests that you felt excited because of the physical closeness of such a sexy girl." The analyst notices the adolescent recognizes his excitement but is uneasy about it. This interpretation to an adolescent is meant to bring his attention to sexual feelings and to convey he can talk here about anything he chooses to. Or, "Do you notice that your attendance here has become more irregular ever since I commented about your conflicted desires to masturbate?" The aim here is to underscore the adolescent's struggles with masturbation, with the hopeful expectation that he might feel less inclined to keep it a secret. There is the *act of masturbation* and the accompanying *masturbation fantasy*. The latter can tell both the analyst and the analysand a lot about the status of the sexual drive, its psychosexual level and its aim, if it can be examined analytically. Noting the adolescent's anxiety and offering the empathic intervention that the act is universal may allow further exploration.

An interpretation is aimed at the Ego, although all mental structures, such as the Superego and Id will be affected too because of the *multiple determination* of mental conflict. What this refers to is how complex mental processes can be and how many structures of the mind can have in-put. For example, if there is a wish to pull the pony tail of the girl sitting in front of you in the fourth grade of elementary school, you may feel anxiety because the hostile/sadistic wish (Id), is opposed by your conscience that lets you know it is not a "nice" thing to do (Superego), and you know that the girl may yell out and the teacher will get involved and you may be punished (Ego).

There are some interpretations that are *reconstructions* of past experiences that influence the present world view of the analysand. For example, "I get the impression that your view of how men and women deal with one another so that men are dominant and women are submissive may be based on how your father controlled your mother." Reconstructions are based on a psychoanalytic tenet of human dynamics that contends that unless you understand the past it repeats itself in the present. Reconstructive interpretations with young children seem to be less used insofar as they are more involved and influenced by present external and internal reality.

Reconstructive interpretations are used with analysands who have been traumatized in the past. *Trauma* occurs when an individual is unprepared for some experience that scares them immensely so that the ego feels **overwhelmed and helpless**. With the passing of time this terrible experience may be repressed or the individual dissociates from any derivative of the memory so it is as if it never happened. A gap in memory results from trauma. When helping adult and adolescent analysands to process the trauma it occurs to the analyst that the memory may be fact or may be a fantasy. Freud originally thought that hysterical woman often were seduced by their fathers but later came to recognize that this was a fantasy that satisfied a libidinal wish. Eventually, with analytic processing of the trauma, what is referred to as *working through,* one becomes more confidant that the trauma happened or that it was a fantasy. It can be difficult sometimes to distinguish the two because of the use of denial by the victim and the perpetrator. It is significant to distinguish one from the other because it is therapeutic for the traumatized individual to confront the perpetrator of the abuse. With young children who have been traumatized it may be necessary to confront the perpetrator(s) or remove the child from the home temporarily or permanently until the parents can be worked with and change their parenting. For example, some parents believe it is good for young children to be exposed to nudity or even to witness sexual intercourse. They believe it makes the child more comfortable "within their own skin," and to accept their sexuality. This rationalization covers pathological *exhibitionism*. It is not in the best interests of young children to be exposed to parental nudity or to sexual intimacy (*primal scene*). It is too exciting to a child to be constantly observing parental nudity (cumulative trauma) and the child has no way to discharge the feelings. A young child, also, may interpret the sounds emanating from the parental couple during sexual intimacy as the sounds of one parent beating the other.

Analysts do not only make reconstructions of the past; analysands also may reconstruct the past as they gain insight. Also, more than one revision may take place as resistance is weakened, insight is gained, and more unconscious memories are allowed into consciousness.

The traumatized individual sometimes employs a *screen memory* defensively. A screen memory is a memory of something that happened but without the traumatic quality. For example, a memory of two dogs copulating may be a screen to cover over the anxious memory of witnessing the primal scene.

Children experience some traumas that are avoidable and some that are not. Some traumas happen once, *shock traumas*, some happen more than once over stretches of time, *cumulative traumas*. Child abuse, either physical or emotional, sexual molestation, exposure to parental sexual intercourse are examples of cumulative trauma. The death of a parent or beloved grandparent, being bitten by a dog, having unplanned emergency surgery, are examples of shock trauma.

In some instances a trauma experienced may be a danger that is in synchrony with the psychosexual phase that is ongoing at the time of the experience. For example, surgery during the phallic phase may be experienced as castration. This could strengthen the trauma or cause a regression. A traumatic experience could result in disruption of progressive development. In child analysis, it is important to help the traumatized child to work through the trauma so that progressive development is not hampered.

In some instances, the cause of a behavior might have a physiological origin, but, nevertheless, the meaning of the behavior may be psychological. We endeavor to make this distinction clear to our analysands. The skeptical analysand might comment, "Sometimes a cigar is a cigar." Here the "meaning" of reference to a cigar is being noted. What I have in mind is different. For example, an adult male analysand might need to interrupt sessions a couple of times to urinate. While the cause of this might be a benign enlarged prostate or some drink ingested prior to the session, a physiological determinant, the meaning may be psychological. The meaning, however, based on the dynamics of the analysand and the timing of the interruptions can be the analysand's way of reassuring himself that his penis is still intact after experiencing *castration anxiety* on the couch, in the transference.

With analysands who are depressed it is important to discern if the depression is biological (*endogenous*) or reactive (*exogenous*). The latter refers to those occasions when someone has a normal grief reaction if someone you care for dies or if you are disappointed about the outcome of some event that you are very committed to. This is normal and not pathological; analysands will benefit from this being interpreted. We now know that women experiencing miscarriage have lots of grief that needs processing. It used to be believed that the best remedy would be for another pregnancy soon thereafter. A *replacement child* was thought to be a good way to deal with the earlier loss. Now we appreciate that the grief needs to be felt and processed. Replacement children are also burdened with issues of identity confusion; are they who they are or someone else who once was?

Another example is distinguishing between *normal guilt* and *neurotic guilt*. When one does not live up to an ideal then it is normal to feel guilty. In neurotic guilt one feels guilty about something they fantasized and did not act upon. An interpretation aimed at helping them to understand the difference between a fantasy or a wish and an act is helpful. An example of normal guilt might be a woman dealing with postpartum depression who feels guilty she has not been attentive to her newborn infant. This is normal guilt insofar as she has the ideal of caring for her offspring but could not because of a biological condition she had no control over. She can be helped by an interpretation that is aimed at relieving her of neurotic guilt.

With children, it is sometimes useful to make an interpretation about an imaginary child in order to allow it to be listened to. For example, "I once knew a boy named Johnny who always said "Yes" when he meant "No," because he was afraid an adult would not like him unless he did whatever he was told to do." In this manner a young child might understand the defense of reaction formation. He might follow this up with a belligerent comment that he does not like to be told what to do, opening up a new topic for discussion. Or a child analyst might say, "Ugh, that was hard." This simple expression of displeasure might allow a child to openly express similar degrees of distaste.

With adolescents, becoming more independent from parents is a developmental need. Severance from parents is not beneficial but more autonomy and confidence about it is beneficial for adolescents. For a while they may feel lonely, feeling bereft because of the diminished intensity of involvement from the real and *"inner" (below)* parents. We call this the *second individuation phase*, the first one occurs when the young child has *internalized* the caregiving parent. Doing so, they achieve *object constancy*, experiencing comfort and attachment from the internalized parent *imago*. This is a subjective sense of parents being within one-self. The toddler now can walk away and separate from the mother and not experience intense separation anxiety. Much interpretive work with adolescents is to help them to process feelings of insecurity about increased autonomy from parents. Often support is obtained from being a member of a group of other adolescents. Sometimes the choice of a group might involve joining an anti-social one and acts of delinquency need to be addressed by the analyst.

With the advent of puberty, many adolescents have a difficult time. They must come to terms with a new body image that integrates a mature sexual body with a body image that prior to puberty did not include the capacity to be a mother or father. The body image now is a sexual body image that often feels to them to be uncontrollable. There is an urge to masturbate. The urge can be very strong. The *central masturbation fantasy* must integrate childhood immature fantasies that seem "out of tune" with a mature sexual identity. This conflict affects all of the structures of the mind, the Id, Superego, and Ego. Freud postulated that the Ego is first and foremost a "body ego" suggesting the need to regulate bodily needs. It is this conundrum of feelings, desires and conflict that an adolescent analysand often presents to the analyst. With time, and the adolescent feeling safe, conflicts about their sexual body, gender identity, and their masturbation fantasy may be brought into analysis. The latter will be a mixture of past neurotic compromises and present day solutions.

Interpretation of the central masturbation fantasy will be gradual and reconstruction of the past antecedents integrated into the current adolescent fantasy will need to wait until the adolescent feels less anxious and more in control of sexual urges. Otherwise the adolescent might retreat from their contemporary conflicts about sexual expression and resist further efforts to deal with pubertal upheavals.

Analysis of identifications must take into account that the analysand's perception of the person identified with might not be valid. Careful analysis might help the analysand distinguish what was so and what they wished was so. Sometimes *identification with a perceived aggressor* takes place, and the analysand can process this and be reassured that they are capable of *dis-identifying* with this person. Also, an analysand who has been "wronged" by a significant figure from the past, such as a parent, with whom they feel estranged from, can consider through interpretations that the parent may have some redeemable features too.

Two other verbal interventions, not considered interpretations, are *clarification* and *confrontation*. Clarification occurs when an analyst is confused about something said and asks a question for greater clarity. For example, "Why is it you just said Jane is not a sibling although in the past you've included her as one." The analysand might respond, "That's because she is only a half-sibling and doesn't count." Of course, this could lead to further inquiry. Confrontation in common usage refers to an angry interaction, but that is not meant here. I use confrontation when an analysand is using denial and I have a sense that the "bubble" of denial is strong and can only be burst by a confrontation. "Do you notice that you repeatedly act with resignation to many instances where your spouse is hurtful to you, telling yourself that she cannot change?" This type of intervention may help the analysand to reconsider their pessimistic conclusion about their spouse, and even to explore further their passivity vis-a--vis their spouse. Or one might say to an adolescent, "Have you considered the consequences of being involved with a group of delinquent boys?"

With *pre-latency* children, the child analyst must keep in mind that interpretations take into account the particular developmental level of the child. One doe not want to increase the child's anxiety beyond a level that they can cope with so as not to illicit a *regression*. One assesses if there are adequate defenses so the child will not respond with a *temper tantrum,* a form of *acting-in* that they cannot control.

The issue of how does an analyst know if the interpretation made is correct or incorrect is not easy to answer. If correct, the analyst may expect to see some change in the transference. The change might follow the meaning of the interpretation, e.g., after interpreting how the analysand as a child felt his father to be uninterested in his after-school activities, it might be noticed later in the session observations are made about the analyst's interest in a particular event, a movie, seen by the analysand. It might be said, then, "Unlike your father who seemed uninterested in your after-school activities, you notice my asking questions about the movie you saw. Perhaps, you wished your father to be more inquisitive about your interests?" Sometimes, if an interpretation is correct, associations are offered by the analysand that goes deeper into details about the topic of the interpretation. A wrong interpretation might elicit resistance. For example, after an interpretation, there is a long silence, or a change of topic, or an equivocation such as "I don't know about that." A complicating factor, however, is that a correct interpretation might elicit resistance. This is likely to happen if the interpretation was made "too soon," i.e., before the analysand is ready to hear it. In such situations, time usually clarifies the issue.

Acting Out

Acting out is a term that often is misused to describe behavior that is impulsive, but if properly used the term has another meaning. If strictly used, it describes behavior that is a transference manifestation that occurs outside the consulting room. An adult male analysand may have an angry memory involving their father about an incident involving a school project that he led that took place years earlier but it cannot be accessed because it is repressed. At work, unexpectedly he has an angry verbal outburst towards his male boss who in praising the efforts of the office staff in completing a project does not specifically mention his leadership. With analytic work soon thereafter, the analysand is able to process the incident and link it to the analyst whom he feels neglected to praise him when he related a recent success at work, and then remember the childhood memory.

It is not uncommon in the case of married adult analysands where the spouse who may or may not be in analysis themselves asks partners to tell them what transpires in his or her analysis. While the query may be motivated by good intentions for intimacy, it encourages a form of acting out insofar as in the retelling of a session feelings and thoughts belonging in the consulting room may get "lost."

The analysand is aware of his or her behavior, although the analysand does not label it as "acting out," but is unaware of its meaning. Therefore it can be considered a type of resistance. Violations of the frame are often expressions of negative transference, e.g., coming late or payment made after the agreed upon date for submission of a check. In general, it is easier for analysands to verbalize positive transference than negative transference. Erotized positive transference is often acted-in the transference, e.g., a female analysand wearing a "sexy" outfit to her session.

With adolescent and child analysands, acting out will follow the same dynamic sequence, namely, transference, resistance to the transference, reoccurrence of the transference to a person outside the consulting room, followed, perhaps, by a report of the unexpected event and analytic processing of it leading to insight.

As mentioned earlier, when talking about countertransference, enactments can be understood as a unique form of acting out by the analyst, at least until the time of the analyst's recognition of the transference to the analysand. The one major difference is that it occurs inside the consulting room, but it could be acted outside too.

Limit Setting

There are not many occasions where limits need to be set in adult analysis. Most adults accept the implicit limits put forth in discussing the "frame" of the analysis. Of course, violations of the parameters of the frame often occur, and the analyst will make verbal interventions that bring it to the analysand's attention, with the expectation that the incident will be processed. For example, if payment of the fee is late the analyst will notice when payment is received if the analysand does or does not remark about the late payment. " You haven't remarked about late payment." The analysand may come up with a simple explanation such as, "I forget. Sorry." Or, assuming they have established a working alliance and are curious about their behavior (mind), they may remark, "I wonder what it means that I was late in payment." There are myriad meanings that are possible, e.g., it might be understood as an expression of the current state of the transference. The analysand may feel the analyst to be "withholding," so he or she dispense a little of the same "medicine" to him.

Sometimes the analysand may invite the analyst to an event, performing perhaps in a play or as an instrumentalist in a concert. This can occur with analysands of all ages. The analyst may elect to indicate appreciation of the invitation but in his judgment it is in the best interests of the analysis not to confuse for the analysand the role of the analyst. With young children an analyst expresses appreciation for the invitation but declines pointing out that he or she and the child have a very special relationship unlike any other. The analyst is their "worry doctor" and a friend but not like other friends. They meet in the office and not away from it. In my experience, a child may be disappointed but having a 'special' kind of a friend is compensatory and acceptable.

In a small community, it may be that the analyst and analysand are in the same or overlapping social circles. Both may get invited to a small dinner party. At such an event, other guests may direct personal questions to the analyst within "ear shot" of the analysand. The analyst may feel that the answers could burden the analysand and interfere negatively in the analysis. Openly discussing this with the analysand is helpful and one of the two may elect to decline the invitation. If this happens often the two can decide to take turns in declining invitations.

Again, in a small community, the analyst's spouse may interact with his analysand, not knowing this because of confidentiality. I think if this happens it is the responsibility of the analysand to indicate that he or she is in analysis with the spouse so that an intimate conversation is "off limits." Another limit setting may occur when after experiencing intense stress and adult analysand may request a "hug" from the analyst when exiting from the consulting room. The analyst empathizing with the stressful condition of the analysand politely declines and expresses physical contact of this type could burden the relationship of the two.

Related to limit setting is the basic premise of *neutrality* and *abstinence* followed by the analyst. Strictly speaking, neutrality refers to the analyst "positioning" understanding equidistant from the Ego, Superego, and Id. What this means is that the analyst listens with an "open mind" trying to listen for the influence of all the structures of the mind on the material the analysand is bringing into a session. It is an appreciation of the over-determination of mental processes, content and conflict. The analyst prefers the role of observer and not participant. We know, however, being an observer affects the process being observed especially if human beings are involved.

Abstinence refers to the non-gratification of the wishes primarily expressed in the transference. This is **very** important insofar as the lack of gratification encourages the continued and deeper expression, i.e., formerly repressed, of thoughts, fantasies, wishes, feelings, and conflict. It also contributes to increased feelings of safety because even though the analysand wishes to gratify his or her repressed wishes, and not only understand them, such an occasion would lead to guilt and anxiety too.

As valuable and essential as the concept of abstinence is, it is more complicated than total adherence to the principle. With the widening scope of psychoanalysis applied to more than neurotic patients, there was recognition that these patients could not tolerate high degrees of frustration due to a lack of gratification. There are some situations when, I believe, the analyst does not engage beneficially in one hundred percent abstinence. These occasions are referred to as *parameters*.

Some analysts do not offer to shake hands before a vacation, while I do so. Also, some decline to wish a patient well before a surgical procedure, or to express condolences when a relative dies, or to say "Happy Birthday." They have conviction that this is being too much of a "real person" and being so will interfere with being a transference object. I do not accept this. My thinking is, as expressed earlier, the analyst must be humane is dealing with analysands in a thoughtful way and that this will not interfere with the transference. I used to never answer questions of analysands about my vacation destinations, but now I do so. If they know, some will still express regrets about the interruption and some may even dare to say in a disquised fashion that I do not enjoy myself. I think that as the analyst gets to know more about his analysand, he or she learns what the likely consequences might be for answering or declining to answer. Early on and maybe never is there one hundred percent confidence that you understand your analysand. As said more than once, the analyst must tolerate ambiguity. So, an analyst might apologize for misremembering a bit of family history. The analysand could understand an apology by the analyst means he or she does not tolerate anger. But then not to apologize for an egregious mistake could be understood as the analyst needs to be complied with. Every analyst tries to consider what the consequences of gratification might be but there is never certainty. An assessment of the narcissistic vulnerability of the analysand helps the analyst gage the degree of abstinence tolerable.

In principle, the need for abstinence makes good sense if not rigidly ascribed to. Early in the analysis if a question is asked, the analyst might say, "Why do you think you are asking me this question now?" or "I'm going to choose not to answer your question insofar as I feel this might deter us from learning more about why you are asking the question now." The analyst might add, "Once we are confident we understand why you are asking me the question, if you still wish to know the answer I will provide it." This is assuming the analyst believes that the answer will not burden the analysand.

My impression is that analysts first trained to work with children before training to treat adults, are less rigidly committed to abstinence. This is because working with children who have a lower *frustration tolerance*, has taught them that answering some questions or saying "Thank you" or " Hope your vacation goes well" does not derail an analysis. Nor does it prevent the expression of anger towards the analyst. The *real object relationship* affords children gratification. But adults are not children and more abstinence can be tolerated for the most part.

With some adult and adolescent analysands, the analyst must judge whether or not to limit food and drink in sessions, e.g., soda or coffee brought from outside. They may see it as interference. After several such instances, I prefer to wonder aloud about the meaning of the behavior and pose that to the analysand to ponder. I think an exception is with young children. I remember at the Hampstead Clinic the receptionist would provide cookies and milk in the waiting room to the children coming directly after school for their sessions. It is customary for parents to provide children with after school snacks, and children expect it. If a child brought a snack into a child analytic session I did not comment on it.

Setting a limit has to do with not violating the *boundaries* of either the analyst or analysand. By a boundary I mean the "personal space" of either so that the analyst will not feel his or her privacy has been violated, and the analysand will not feel pressured or encroached upon to reveal something before they are ready to do so. In contemporary times with the Internet the privacy of the analyst is often intruded upon by people either looking for a suitable professional to consult or by patients already in treatment who are curious about their analyst. Such intrusions do not irreparably impair transference development.

Some analysands prefer to be called by first name and to address me by my first name too. In a majority of instances this request came after a couple of years of analysis or after a former analysand returned for further treatment. It was suggested that after so many years of intimacy it felt it too formal to refer to me as "Dr. Sherick." I did not object and called them by first name too, putting aside the limit regarding acceptance of boundaries. The decision did not seem to cause unwanted results.

With young children, sometimes limits need to be made verbally and sometimes with physical restraint to stop destructive behavior towards the things in the consulting room play area, or towards the person of the analyst. The point is made maybe even in the first session, depending on the child's personal history, "In here you may say anything but you cannot do anything. You will not be allowed to hurt me, the things in the room, or yourself. I want you to feel safe." This is necessary because sometimes in an angry outburst a child may knock over a lamp or mark wallpaper with a crayon or even physically attack the analyst. With young children, too, they sometimes like to play "doctor" and want to examine the body of the analyst. I set limits, pointing out that a doll (I had a "Dr. Sherick" doll) represents me and I prefer it be examined rather than me. Rarely, did a child strongly object. Very young children may want to sit on the analyst"s lap. I think most child analysts would gently limit this, believing that it could get too exciting for the child. The feelings of safety for the child, and the analyst's own comfort level are the guiding principals in such limit setting. For each child there is an optimal distance for the child analyst to sit in proximity to the child. Some younger child analysts choose with young children who often play on the floor to sit alongside them on the floor.

Young children need to be told at some point that the play room needs to be left in the same way it was when they entered.

This is because children may wish to hang up on the wall a drawing they completed. The child analyst points out that what he or she and the child do during their time together is private, not to be shared with other children. That is why the child never sees drawings from other children in the room. This limit supports confidentiality and likely helps some children to feel special, a not uncommon childhood aspiration.

Earlier, in my comments about work with parents I spoke about conveying to them the confidentiality that will be abided by an analyst's in the work with their child, and the "limits" of confidentiality in work with them. The confidentiality of the child will not hold if the child's wellbeing is in doubt, e.g., if suicide is a strong possibility. If an analyst seriously is concerned about suicidal potentiality in an adolescent or adult, it is advisable to ask the analysand to "promise" to try to telephone the analyst if they are worried they may act on a suicidal thought. Of course, a promise is not binding, but most analysands respect the commitment.

As a non-physician I do not have requests made to me by analysands for medication of any kind, e.g., a sleeping pill, a tranquilizer, an anti-depressant, etc. There are psychoanalysts who are MDs and their analysands sometimes make such requests. I believe if these requests are complied with it complicates the relationship between the two. A limit should be made on such requests. In one instance they are acting as an analyst and in another as a physician. The analysand acts in one way towards their analyst and in another way towards their physician. It makes more sense to me to refer the analysand to a psychiatrist for a consultation if it is believed that analysis has gone "as far as it can" in alleviating *psychosomatic* symptoms.

Ways of Bringing Material

Analysts rarely have an agenda as to what should be the focus in a particular session. Suggestion is not a technique, nor is manipulation. Analysands decide the agenda in their own analysis. The understanding of a person's mind is based partly on the gradual peeling off of layers until you get to the core conflicts, much like peeling a piece of fruit. Occasionally, the analyst will introduce something at the beginning of a session, usually having to do with the frame, e.g., a schedule change, such as the analyst's vacation. It is introduced at the beginning in order to give the analysand time to react to the news. Sometimes an analysand has to miss a session or has some other bit of news and may delay mentioning this until they are ready to leave the hour. Presumably there is some meaning to this and a reluctance to deal with the associated feelings. If this happens regularly with a particular analysand the analyst will introduce it into a session.

With adults and adolescents, the major way material is brought into sessions is verbally. Occasionally, a photograph will be presented of someone or a pet that is often spoken about. With the advent of smart phones a text or email from someone will be read rather than reliance on memory. In contemporary time, some analysts have regular telephone or Skype sessions. I have not regularly had long-distance analytic sessions. I believe that there is a different quality in a session when analyst and analysand are present together. Occasionally, when reality intrudes I will have a telephone session, e.g., if a person is travelling a distance by car to get to a session and traffic is stalled because of an accident making it impossible for the analysand to arrive during the hour, we will talk on the phone. Some analysands will write down a dream in the middle of the night. While

I do not prohibit reading of notes, I point out what is in their mind is important and that forgotten details will return to memory once they try to associate to the dream.

It is not unusual for free association to be in the form of a metaphor that conveys a lot of meaning. For example, an adult male analysand said she "cut it off," referring to the verbal dispute he and his wife were having. After a moment he referred to his choice of words and commented about his castration fear of injury to his penis. What followed were childhood memories of similar worries.

Analysands of all ages have difficulty speaking about memories of traumatic experiences. It is very difficult for adults and adolescents to talk about trauma in sessions, and for young children to enact it in play. It is much too upsetting. They may feel dissociated whenever a memory of the trauma is "glimpsed" by the Ego. Analysts know that analysands cannot be "pushed" to talk about trauma; they must feel safe and allied with their analyst and feel hopeful that processing the traumatic events will be helpful to them. Talking about a past trauma allows for some *abreaction*, but while emotional discharge can be helpful, analytic processing of it, i.e., emotional understanding of it is more so. It is helpful when analysands begin to feel empowered and can confront their abusers.

Dreams and dream interpretation have had a significant history in psychoanalysis. Adults and adolescents, less so with younger children, may bring material in this manner. Dreams were once thought to be "the royal road" to the Unconscious (Ucs.). Nowadays we consider dreams as a road to the Ucs, but not the only road. A dream occurs during sleep when the *censor* between the unconscious and conscious part of the mind relaxes enough to allow repressed mental content access into the conscious part of the mind as long as it is disguised. Perhaps the sleep state makes it less likely that the repressed wishes will be expressed in action, and hence the censorship is not as strong. An experience of the day of the dream, the *day residue,* is seized by a repressed wish, perhaps because of a related meaning. A *latent dream* is constructed in the Ucs. Primitive primary processes of thinking, such as condensation, displacement, reversals, and substitution, form the latent dream. After more revision so as to be acceptable as a *manifest dream*, the Ego allows it to be recalled in a wakeful state. Freely associating to details in the dream and recognizing the meaning of the day residue, along with the current state of the transference and resistance, may allow the analytic couple to begin to understand the dream. Such processing of a dream often deepens the analysis.

Some analysands rarely bring dreams or say they dream but cannot remember them. Some may ask if it is helpful to record their memory of the dream after awakening or write down their memory. When this is asked there is likely a resistance to remembering and this is the primary focus. The analysand may admit preconceived notions about dreams based on movies or fiction and be afraid to reveal dreams. If a dream is reported early in an analysis it is helpful to give some education about the process of understanding the latent meaning from the manifest dream. It is important to impress upon the analysand that the meaning of a dream is dependent upon associations. The analyst is not a "mind reader." I think adult analysands appreciate knowing about this partnership, although, of course, some may use it to thwart the understanding of dreams. More analysis of resistance follows.

There are some common features of dreams. Reversals are often present, so that the representation of something in the present is really depicting something that happened in the past and vice versa. Dreams can employ phrases, words, and expressions or images that convey meaning. For example, an image of a "hail Mary pass " in a football game, might portray a wish for a miracle to change their life situation. Symbols are often used. Again, it is imperative to get associations to the symbol and not for the analyst to assume understanding of the meaning of the symbol, metaphor, or aphorism used by the analysand. Sometimes the symbol is meant to represent the dreamer's body or sexual intercourse.

A dream may have something to do with the analysand's feelings about the analytic process or about the analyst. For example, there may be a nurse in the dream who "thinks she knows everything, even more than the doctor." In this instance the nurse may be the analyst and the doctor the analysand. Sometimes there are multiple dreams in one night that the analysand reports. Such multiple dreams are usually related. The analyst is always alert to the possibility that an incident in the previous session is represented in the dream, lending continuity to the analysis.

There are "common dreams" such as punishment or rescue dreams. One common dream is an examination dream wherein the dreamer is failing an exam. The dreamer awakes and is reassured that he or she has not failed and has progressed in their life. There are some dreams that occur over and over separated by time in the dreamer's life. The repetition signifies some important event in their psyche.

A *daydream* is a daytime fantasy that a person deliberately playfully constructs, often to engage in a pleasurable, often reality denying, activity. An example is being capable of flying.

Often a symbol may convey important meanings. A older patient was fearing a decline of his mental and physical capacities. He had a dream that included the insect "slugs." Via associations we discovered the slugs represented both his fear of "slowing down" and his wish that his decline be slow. This understanding came only with my introducing the adjective "sluggish" into our analyzing the dream.

I have had a child who brought in a pet dog. A good part of the analysis centered around her behavior with the dog and/or my occasional displacement of interpretations to the dog when I thought doing so would allow her to hear my comment. Her behavior with the dog allowed her in a displaced way to express her feelings and thoughts about significant people in her life.

Younger children predominantly play. The material is in the story that is implicit in the play or explicitly narrated by the child alongside the play. The child is like the playwright or director of a play and the child analyst may be assigned a role. The child describes the analyst's part in the play. "You play a boy on the playground but be like a bully." "Be a strict teacher and I will be the smartest kid in the class." Sometimes children by themselves play out all the characters in their dramas.

Play is a mental activity like other mental activities and shares commonalities such as associated affects, defensive modifications, symbolism, etc. While it seeks gratification of the drive derivative being expressed, immediate gratification may not be sought.

Children also may elect to draw or use playdough, use a toy brought from home or use toys provided by the child analyst. For example, children build with blocks or Lego, use puppets, use toy soldiers, arrange miniature furniture in a dollhouse, and play with board games such as Snakes and Ladders, checkers or chess. The fundamental characteristic of play is *action*.

The analyst chooses toys based on the chronological age of the child. Toys are chosen that are capable of being creatively used in play, i.e., ones that do not have to adhere to rules, such as a board game. Sometimes, however, a board game serves a useful purpose for a child that is anxious. The rules allow the child to retreat from disclosing something at that moment which is making them anxious and could escalate. A child analyst will have a community of toys that all the children in his or her practice can use, while also having lockers or boxes in which toys selected for a particular child and those brought from home are used exclusively by the owner. Puppets, dolls of both genders, toy animals and soldiers, a doctor's examination kit, a doll house, etc., are examples of toys that can be selected. Baby dolls with appropriate genitalia of both genders allow young child opportunities to express thoughts about parental care and sexual identity. A child can use blocks at times when he or she needs to be uncommunicative, much like silence with an adult or adolescent. The analyst can address the silence of the adult or adolescent in an empathic manner, "You seem to wish to be within yourself today, judging from your silence." With a young child, I might say, "You are very quiet today. You seem to be building a wall behind which you hope to be safe, instead of playing."

Some child analysts believe play can be therapeutic even if no interpretations are made. Perhaps a distinction can be made between "therapeutic" and "analytic." The former can result from play because a discharge of feelings might take place and the child gets pleasure from the play. If a child has experienced a scary event, such as a medical procedure or a barking dog that jumped up on them, they may repeat the experience in their play. We call this turning a *passively* experienced event into an *actively* experienced event. The child often assigns the role of "victim" to the child analyst and he or she assumes the role of the perpetrator. Often, the child may not verbalize memory of the event, but the child analyst will have been told of its occurrence by the parents. The enactment of this passive experience into an active one probably has a therapeutic value. To have an analytic outcome, I would prefer to have play result in a partial resolution of a conflict, a diminution of anxiety, etc., which is more likely to be accomplished by the aid of interventions on the child analyst's part.

Adolescents also play. By the time adolescence is reached the cognitive abilities have matured from early concrete ways of thinking, to mature deductive reasoning, so that play moves, for the most part, from action to *playful thought*. Thought now becomes *trial action* wherein immediate gratification is less imperative, and fantasy is adopted as a major way to obtain satisfaction, at least partially. The child analyst working with an adolescent will follow the sequence of speech, much like free association. If there seems to be some resistance noticed using "close process analysis," this will be brought to the adolescent's attention. "Did you notice, your slip of the tongue?" or "Did you notice the long silence after you told me about your walking up the steps at school alongside a girl, you did not know, that you found to be very attractive?"

The child analyst with a young child observes the child's play, listens to his utterances or spoken words, tries to decipher the meaning of the play, may intervene to label a feeling being expressed by the child by attributing the affect to a character, deconstruct or decipher a symbol to get at the child's pre- or unconscious meaning. The analyst will watch to see if the play changes in ways that can be attributed to the impact upon the child by the interventions. If it does and the play is elaborated the deeper meaning might be inferred by the analyst. If the child seems ready in the child analyst's judgment to hear an interpretation about the meaning of the play, one may be offered and the child's reaction carefully noted.

Adolescents often talk about musical groups and songs that you have never heard. It seems to me that each generation of adolescents likes and has allegiance to music that is undecipherable to their parents' generation. I think it is one way that they seek independence. The child analyst expresses interest and asks to have the words spoken or sung or played on a smart phone and together with the adolescent seeks to understand the affinity of the analysand to the song. Analytic meaning can be learned in a fun way.

Comings and Goings

Arriving for an appointment and leaving at the end of an appointment essentially are part of the frame of the treatment, the essential aspects of which were introduced earlier. Prospective patients agreeing to enter psychoanalysis implicitly accept that they are expected to arrive punctually and leave when the time scheduled has expired. We know that the exigencies of life sometimes interfere with punctuality. Adult analysands usually offer an explanation for the cause of the lateness, e.g., an excessive unexpected amount of auto traffic. Adolescents are often late and may decry punctuality. When lateness becomes a characteristic of a particular adult or adolescent the analyst likely will conjecture that it has a meaning and will pose a comment to the analysand, "Have you noticed that you rarely come on time?" The hope is that the analysand will become curious, too, about whether there is a meaning to their lateness? Of course, the stronger the working alliance the more likely they will seriously consider that there may be a meaning. As a "rule of thumb" an analyst will not express that there may be a meaning about a particular manner of "coming" with one single instance, but wait to see if the analysand independently raises curiosity. Analysands differ as to whether or not they offer a greeting upon entering or being picked up in the waiting room. Some simply say "Hello", while some might say "How are you?" We presume there may be a meaning beyond social convention but likely not to be understood until later in the analysis or until the analysand raises it or has a free association to it.

With children "comings" are more complicated. After all, their parents bring them usually, so punctuality or tardiness may not be due to them, unless you learn that the child delayed meeting the parents at a designated place for the departure to a session. Some children greet the child analyst with a hug, others run ahead into the consulting room, while others eagerly accompany the analyst. If the location of the office lends itself to it, a child might play "hide-and-seek" and exclaim with joy or regret when you "find" him. Again, the meaning of the beginning of a session for a particular child may have to wait awhile until the child's *dynamics* are better understood. But at the first few episodes the child analyst might say, " You seem to want me to either find you or not find you at the beginnings of our time together. I wonder why?" As with older analysands, the intervention is aimed at arousing the child's curiosity about their behavior (mind).

Departures at the end of a session also likely have meanings that will take time to understand. Some adults say, "Thank you," others simply say "Goodbye," or simply leave without consistently saying anything. In some cultures, an adult may shake your hand on coming and going because this is the polite thing that adults do with one another. Young children may join you in the request to clean up the room, i.e., put toys away, in compliance with the limit set at the beginning of the analysis. "We will try to keep the play area looking at the end of a session as it looked at the beginning." Most children comply although there are some who do not because of their particular dynamics, e.g., *anal expulsive* issues. Some children wish to hang up a drawing of theirs in non-compliance with the request that the room be the way it was when they started the session. Often this is motivated by exhibitionistic or competitive feelings regarding other children seen by the child analyst. For some children, the request to bring something home from the session is an expression of a preconscious wish to extend their time with the analyst, a wish that the analyst can make conscious if there is confidence in its meaning.

Role of Education

The early history of psychoanalysis involved a debate about making the patient as "free" as possible to talk about the thoughts on this or her mind. Thus any intervention or instruction by the analyst that involved suggestion was frowned upon. Free association became the ideal way for analysands to bring psychic material with the analyst maintaining a position of *neutrality*. Classically, what this meant was that the analyst would not favor the Id, Superego, or Ego in listening or in interpreting. The analyst was to listen in a non-biased manner "equidistant" from the instinctual desires (Id), the moral commitments (Superego), and the reality concerns (Ego) of the analysand. Imposing values onto the analysand was unacceptable, although we now appreciate that countertransference is ubiquitous so that the analyst's values do influence, to some degree, how things are heard and responded to by the analyst.

Educating the analysand was held to have no or very little place in psychoanalysis as a technique. Essentially it was thought that a consequence could be an imposition of a viewpoint upon the analysand and in some way compromising the neutrality of the analyst. While I accept this, I think there are times in an analysis with analysands of all ages, especially children, where education has a beneficial value. With an adult, at the beginning of an analysis when the analyst explains the "basic rule" of free association and answers questions as to why the couch is recommended, an educational intervention is being made. Some analysts choose to refrain from giving the "basic rule" or suggesting the value of a supine position on the analytic couch. They prefer to let the analysand proceed as they choose, addressing resistance to speaking freely and use of the couch on the occasion when the analysand notes curiosity of its presence.

A quasi-educational intervention with adults and adolescents that I often use when early origin of conflicts is noted by the analysand, is to point out that we all have a child within us, so to speak, and that we can help the child grow up to be an adult or adolescent, using the resources we now have that the child did not have. Sometimes, I have found it useful to point out the universality of a conflict, such as the Oedipus Complex, or that of the mind that seeks pleasure and avoids "unpleasure," to help them emotionally understand "resistance." This educational imparting of a bit of psychoanalytic clinical theory, used judiciously, I have found to have beneficial value.

Earlier, I referred to interpretive interventions that deal with reactive depression and normal guilt. I made the point about how it is important with some analysands to "normalize" both these feeling states. While such interventions are interpretive they also contain an educative component, namely, distinguishing "normal" from "pathological."

I find it helpful to point out the potential value for analysands who have been "abused" to confront their abuser. They need to be prepared that an apology may not be forthcoming but that they still might feel better regarding their sense of self-agency. Another "educative" intervention is to point out the value of "self-forgiveness" after feeling remorse and making amends about a transgression.

Distinguishing between anger and assertion can be extremely important for some adult and adolescent analysands. It often is an intervention that is educational as part of interpretive work focusing on the use of *passivity* as a defense against anger. The analysand is afraid that if they set limits or are critical of a spouse, e.g., that they will be destructive. It is as if they feel such an expression will get out of control. After processing the anger, it can be helpful to distinguish the difference between anger and assertiveness. I think this is an educational intervention. The self-empowering feeling that can follow when one sets limits on someone who has exceeded the limits of civility gives an analysand a sense of hopefulness that they can protect themselves in an adult manner.

With young children, it is natural for them to look to an adult to guide them and to help them understand novel situations. This being so, the child analyst is helping them to feel safe both with their inner worlds as well as the outer world. This lends itself to occasional comments about how some of the child's actions cause him or her to feel unsafe, either because of worry the "inner policeman" (the superego) or mommy, daddy, teacher, etc., will disapprove. There are other times when the child analyst needs to impart or correct misunderstandings about, e.g., how babies are made, the different external and internal anatomy of males and females, what "divorce" means, etc. Of course, education is not given without first hearing the child's own understanding of the issue. What one is providing is a correction to clear up confusion. Earlier, I referred to a child analyst being a "real" and or "developmental" object to a child analysand. With young child I would use a plastic doll that had internal organs that could be seen. I also had baby dolls of each gender with the appropriate genitalia. Ideally, sexual education is best learned in the context of a parent-child relationship, but, regretfully, this is often not the case because of the absence or inability of a parent to do so.

Work with Parents

It used to be that child analysts did not believe that it was essential to see parents conjointly when one was seeing their child or adolescent in psychoanalysis. This attitude has changed drastically in the past thirty years. We once thought that we only needed to get the parents to support their child's treatment, to pay the fees and to transport the child to his or her sessions.

Partly, this was based on the model of adult analysis where the analysand is the sole person in treatment and the analysis proceeded on the basis only of what transpired in the consulting room. Another issue was the lack of confidence of child analysts that they were truly practicing psychoanalysis and not play therapy as some of their only-adult trained colleagues were contending. Hence, they treated child and adolescent patients as mini-adults. With adolescents there existed the observations that a developmental need of that age group was to achieve independence from parents. To support this developmental need child analysts did not include parents in the process.

With preoediplal children, sometimes they cannot separate from their mothers. She will have to be in the consulting room for a period of time until the child can feel safe alone with the child analyst. This could be a matter of a number of sessions or even weeks. Sometimes, the child refuses to leave the lap of the mother. With time, however, the child will allow the mother to leave. The mother or the child analyst may initiate this permission from the child.

We now know better. We recognize that there is no child without parents. Also, we realize that child analysts need to build a working alliance with parents as well. We do this for more reasons than they pay our fees. We know that a child or adolescent in analysis will reach a point when there is a wish to quit and it is the parents' support of the treatment that keeps the child or adolescent in the analysis. With adolescents, while we support them in their wish to become more independent from their parents we do not believe that severing ties with parents is in the best interests of most adolescents. Rather, except in some cases of abusive parents, we try to help the adolescent and his or her parents revive the healthier and growth promoting aspects of their former relationship. We state this openly to both parties.

With adolescent patients and some older preadolescents when we see their parents we offer them the opportunity to attend the parent sessions. Most opt not to attend. I do not believe this choice is a sign of psychopathology but rather an intuitive recognition of the need for privacy. Child analysts are not in favor of keeping secrets but are in support of privacy.

Initial work with parents is to help them understand that their child's "problems" are not because of disobedience or personal choice but because of neurotic conflict. Once they appreciate this then they are much more allied with the child analyst. Sometimes, a child analysis may have to be delayed until the parents can accept this formulation. It is essential, too, that parental self-blame for their child's issues and aspiration to be "good" parents not be over-looked in the initial contacts. "Strengths" need to be focused on along with "weakness" in parenting.

My understanding is that working with parents is not the same as viewing them as patients. It is more focused on issues of parenting. I believe that if the parent work becomes psychotherapy with the parent couple or with one of the parents, issues can arise that will undermine the analysis with their child. One parent may develop transference to the child analyst and become competitive with his or her child as they once did with a sibling. Of course, this can happen in parent work too, but it is less likely if the kind of controlled regression in a treatment is not encouraged.

Analysts are now very aware of the *intergenerational transmission of psychopathology*. Hence, in parent work we want to get a picture of the parents' respective childhoods and their relationship with their own parents. Doing so we can help parents understand if they have identified with their own parents' style of parenting, or if they have identified their child with one of their own siblings and have a transference to them based on their past dealings with a sibling.

Parents can appreciate that the child analyst's work with their child is confidential, except if it is necessary for them to be notified that their child, usually an adolescent, is seriously considering suicide. First, the adolescent would be encouraged to share this with their parents before the analyst tells them this. The child analyst also tells parents that what they talk about will not be treated confidentially. The child analyst will, at his or her discretion, tell the child or adolescent what the parents have shared with him or her if it is believed to be in the best interests of the analysand to be told. Parents are encouraged in such instances to share with their child what they have told the analyst at an opportune time. Of course, there are some parents who have trouble not knowing details about what transpires in their child's treatment. When this is noticed, work with a parent such as this deals with the psychic dynamics of his or her "need to know."

What does the child analyst do with extra-analytic material obtained, e.g., from a teacher? Presumably, the analyst has obtained permission from the parent to talk to the teacher, and from an older child as well. I think each analyst will use judgment about what, how, and when to share the information with the child.

With very young children, their belief in the *omnipotence* of their parents, appears to run counter to efforts to assure them of confidentiality; after all, their parents "know" everything. Nevertheless, there will be occasions when this belief will be weakened and confidentiality will emerge as a concern.

When working with parents, as with analysands, a child analyst needs to be aware of countertransference. Sometimes, a child analyst may feel they could do a better job parenting than the child or adolescent's parents can accomplish. He or she may become competitive with the parents.

Parent work with mothers and their infants or toddlers is a specialization of some child analysts. Fathers can also benefit. We know that parenting is a difficult endeavor. Parents can provide nurturance but also they can burden a very young child with their own psychopathology. Above, I have pointed out intergenerational transmission of psychopathology. Hence, a mother might react towards an infant or toddler son that has an outburst of angry feelings as if he was her father. Here a mother is putting aside, unconsciously, her *objective reality* and responding to her *psychic reality* wherein there is an equation between her son and her father. With an infant, an analyst might intervene with an anxious mother by offering interpretations about how hard it seems to feel her infant is separate from herself, insofar as the infant was once inside of her. A mother coming out of a postpartum depressive episode can be reassured that the guilt she is feeling for having neglected her infant is not pathological and underscores her devotion to her baby. It can be pointed out that her comforting ministrations hereon will go a long way to helping her infant develop normally.

Sometimes, educative interventions are helpful. An analyst might help a parent to distinguish between different types of outbursts from their young child, e.g., anxiety or fear, from frustration. A parent can benefit from knowing the likely developmental trajectory soon to unfold based on their child's chronological age. A father can be helped to deal with his envy when his spouse seems overly attentive to her nursing infant and he feels ignored.

Goals of Psychoanalytic Treatment

Psychoanalysis does not claim to "cure" people of mental distress. Nor does it claim to "eradicate" mental conflict. Mental conflict is universal and ubiquitous. A psychoanalytic treatment is successful if it makes an analysand more aware of his or her conflicts, so that the conscious mind can allow into awareness what was once forbidden. With greater tolerance for anxiety a less neurotic solution than one formerly used can be achieved. Insofar as the reaction time is reduced when the person becomes aware of the conflict, a more rational, adaptive solution can be affected than the usual neurotic one. Analysts focus less on goals and more on the process of analysis.

The initial goals of analyst and analysand often do not correspond with one another. Patients enter analysis often with life goals that have been elusive, e.g., to find a compatible life partner. All patients wish to be relieved of symptoms, e.g., an eating pickiness. Also, they seek to be happier in their life, less depressed and cynical. An adolescent or younger child may want to be more popular, less shy around peers.

While analysts would hope that these goals would be achieved during psychoanalysis, they focus less on life goals, symptom relief, and social success, and more on *intrapsychic* changes. That is, modification in the way the mind manages conflict. An analytic aim would be a Superego that is more mature and relativistic in its moral compass, a Self that is more secure in it's self-esteem, not needing external "applause" to feel valued, an Ego that in its judgment recognizes that a deed is different from a thought or fantasy, an Ego that is more tolerant of the desires and feelings of all kind so that defensive maneuvers are not immediately necessary. Insofar as desires and needs are not always gratified, the heightening of frustration tolerance is a goal of psychoanalytic treatment. Also, greater tolerance for anxiety is also a goal of analysis. It is hoped that the analysand has examined core conflicts and that neurotic solutions are not sought but rather more adaptive ones. *Sublimation* of the aims of the expression of instinctual drives is also welcomed. We mean that more socially acceptable aims replace ones less so. For example, for a child, anal-explosive impulses to mess are replaced by a wish to paint colors on an easel. With an adolescent, a wish to hurt a rival by drawing blood is replaced by a passion to become an expert fencer, and later to become a surgeon. At the end of an analysis it is hoped that the analysand has identified with the analyzing function of the analyst and will carry on with self-analysis after the treatment ends.

An analyst endeavors to educate an analysand that personal conflicts are not eradicated by psychoanalysis, that mental conflict is ubiquitous and universal. Most analysands can accept this, including young children. A child can be told that there will be times when he or she will feel scared (anxious), and that is alright because he or she now knows that the "inner policeman" will not seek punishment for only a "naughty" thought.

With adolescents an aim of the analyst is to help them and their parents resume a healthier relationship wherein the former feels supported by the parents, while also feeling more independent from them. Most adolescents welcome this as an outcome. They understand that severing ties with parents is not sensible except if the parents are abusive and unwilling to change.

With younger children, the analyst aims to return the childs' development on a progressive trajectory. You will recall the discussion above about fixation points, which cause development to halt, sometimes in a partial way but sometimes in a major way. The child analysis hopefully undoes the fixation by an emotional understanding and *catharsis*. Having an analysis as a child does not prevent later neurotic issues but it can help the older child deal with it more effectively.

In psychoanalytic developmental theory, reaching the Oedipal phase and dealing with it is believed to be a beneficial experience for an individual. Hence, a goal of work with children dealing predominantly with *preoedipal* issues is to resume progressive development and hope that they will struggle with the Oedipal Complex. Regretfully, in some instances a two-parent household may be non-existent. While this makes it more difficult for the child to deal with Oedipal issues it does not make it impossible. Kids are resourceful and a relative, teacher, or community leader can be employed in their psyche to play the role of the absent parent.

The internalization of parental authority in the form of the Superego, results in an internal "inner policeman," albeit a "harsh" one to begin with. Over time the Superego becomes more mature. The struggle with the Oedipal Complex often results in a de-idealization of the parents and eventually a more realistic image of them as people with faults but also redeeming characteristics. The internalization of a Superego and the partial dissolution of the Oedipal Complex allows for Latency to begin. We call this *infantile amnesia*. Now less burdened by strong *instinctual wishes*, the child can begin to deal with and learn coping skills to adapt to the external world. It is no wonder that formal education begins the advent of Latency. The strengthening of the Ego vis-à-vis the Id will allow the child to be prepared with a better defensive armamentarium to deal with the advent of puberty and the re-strengthening of the sexual and aggressive drives. Child analysis has as an aim the strengthening of the child's ego.

With older adults, dealing with *existential issues* is very beneficial. They are ubiquitous but not everyone grapples with them. Hopefully in an analysis, the analyst, who also has such issues, has been able to help the analysand deal with them.

Working Through

Every analyst has had the experience of having an analysand, usually adult but also adolescent, react with an "Ah,ha" sense of relief about a breakthrough insight after the analyst has made an interpretation. The analyst will be pleased but also note, privately, that the same interpretation has been made countless times before without the profound sense by the analysand that they have had a major insight. What accounts for the change? Perhaps one should not look a "gift horse in the mouth." I think it is helpful for an analyst to comment on "progress" that the analysand is showing, commenting on the analysand's own words until now that they "seem unable to get out from under" a particular self-defeating behavior. Such comments strengthen the working alliance. When there are frequent "ah, ha!" type expressions by the analysand, termination may be forthcoming in the near future.

We call the above phenomenon *working through*. It underscores the persistence of neurotic solutions to mental conflicts. What has reduced anxiety in the past for the neurotic individual is accepted as a valuable tool even if it is self-defeating. The resistance or dynamic process has to be interpreted many times before the insight is convincing. It is as if what is required is the cumulative effect of multiple insights to weaken the resistance of the unconscious ego, and effect a structural change, i.e., an effect that is not time-limited. There seems to be a tendency on the part of the mind, most likely a characteristic of the Id to engage in a *repetition compulsion*. This characteristic could be considered an Id resistance. This type of resistance is also encountered with the Ego regarding character defenses. As mentioned earlier, these are defenses that have proven their neurotic usefulness countless times so they become like a personality signature.

An adult analysand after four years of analysis, had a stomach ache and worried that he might have an accident and soil. A memory occurred of a childhood soiling incident wherein he felt ashamed. Father took him home from school to clean him up and did not shame him. The analysand had just concluded a successful business venture and was feeling adult and masculine. I commented that in the Ucs money and feces are equated. He immediately responded with memories of "dirty money" from his childhood. This money was obtained by relatives from exploited customers and not reported as income. I said he has transformed soiling to spending money on commercial ventures that benefitted himself and the community, giving him a sense of pride and accomplishment, different from the shame he felt as a child, adolescent, and young adult when he felt he disappointed his father. Additionally, I said this was a sign of progress. Working through displays progressive steps of progress. Defenses are loosened, even given up, and feelings of self-actualization occur.

Termination

Analysands often wish to know during a treatment, how will they know or how will the analyst know when it is time to end. This topic was considered earlier when we discussed the aims or goals of analysis from the analysand and analyst perspectives. This is a legitimate question with no easy answer. Putting aside the unilateral ending of an analysis because the adult moves to another state, or the adolescent goes off to an out-of-state college, or the family of the young adult or child analysand incurs unexpected debts and the cost of analysis is prohibitive. Of course, regarding the latter, the fee can be reduced permanently or temporarily. Nowadays, if an analysand moves away, some analysts via telephone or via Skype practice long distance analysis, with occasional in-person visits by the analysand. Sometimes, the best-made plans cannot be achieved.

In some respects an analysis does not ever end, insofar as one of the aims of the analyst is that after termination the analysand will continue to identify with the analyzing function of the analyst and engage in self-analysis.

Eradicating all mental conflict cannot be the criterion insofar as eradication is not possible. With adults we aim before stopping to have analyzed to some degree the entire major conflicts that have been identified during the analysis. The key word here is "major" insofar as minor ones may not have been able to "compete" with major ones for attention. Again, here is where we hope the analysand will feel confident that he or she can do some self-analysis.

When the analyst is thinking of termination, a consideration is the quality of the transference. Once the adult analysand is reacting towards the analyst as another adult and not as a special kind of adult like a parent, then he or she is feeling less regressed and "the child within the adult' analysand has "grown up." A major aim of the analysis has likely been achieved.

With young children and adolescents, termination is considered once progressive movement in development has been reinstated. This presumably will be possible, as with adults, once the core conflicts have been sufficiently analyzed. The same criterion is a determinant in the decision to stop analysis with some young adults who are essentially prolonging their adolescence. If we think of adult stages of development, we can also think of progressive development being restarted, e.g., if an adult who was once afraid of becoming a parent now can consider that status, or even look forward to it.

Once the analyst and analysand agree to terminate, a termination date is set, and the termination stage begins. The termination period varies in length depending on individual cases, but I would say the average length of time is at least three to six months. Some analysts ask the analysand to assume a sitting position facing the analyst. Some analysands request this too. It is done because the transference has been more-or-less resolved and two adults of "equal" status can now talk "face to face." Some analysts also reduce the frequency of sessions from four or five to two or three. It is to discourage regression. I believe, however, that the frequency and the use of the couch should be maintained until the last day, except if the analysand wishes a change. My thought is that there are termination issues that best be talked about and the maintaining of the frame best encourages this to happen.

The major issue that needs to be talked about is the analysand's feelings about the ending. Are they sad because of the ending? Does it remind them of significant losses from the past, e.g., the death of a grandparent or the relocation of a friend to a distant city, or moving from elementary school to middle school, etc.

With many young children and adolescents, they will express pleasure that with the ending of the analysis they will again have more free time after school. With some of these analysands, the analyst may elect to continue with their parents. The feelings of these children about that prospect need to be considered.

There may be some voiced expression of whether the analyst will agree to be seen again after the ending on an as-needed basis. Often this request is not followed up on, but analysts may hear from a former child patient when they have become older, sometimes with a request to resume analysis. Almost no analyst will contact a former patient for a follow-up to see how he or she is doing. It is believed that this would be an intrusion.

Termination is a " leave taking," of sorts. It is likely reminiscent in the Unconscious of other "leave takings" in development. I'm thinking of the toddler who beginning to walk toddles away from the arms of its caregiver or the sight of this person. I presume the toddler, when he falls, at some level, regrets leaving the arms and sight of the *omnipotent* adult. The oedipal child who de-idealizes his parents and internalizes them as structures in his mind, I presume feels a loss of the "perfect" parent, and may regret this "leave taking." The adolescent during the *second-individuation* phase must feel lonely or bereft to some degree that the bond with protective parents is weakened, another "leave taking." All of these prior experiences likely re-trigger the feelings of leave-taking connected to termination. During this phase the analyst and analysand will have occasion to connect contemporary feelings with earlier ones, and this will help in the processing of feelings of loss. This process may facilitate identification with the analyst's analyzing function akin to the oedipal-latency child's identification with the rule-giving parent of the same gender at the time of the partial dissolution of the Oedipal Complex.

At the termination of an analysis the expectation is that the transference will have been more-or-less resolved. One sign of this, mentioned above, is that the analysand acts and feels as if he or she is the equal to the analyst. The adult analysand will no longer feel like a child or adolescent vis-a-vis the adult analyst.

Some children may choose not to contact their former analyst later in life, even if they need more analysis, the reason being that the former analyst in their memory is in the context of "childhood" which they wish to leave behind. Adults may contact their former analyst when life's circumstances make them feel a brief return would be helpful. In my experience this is not uncommon. They may or may not choose to use the couch.

Part Three

Brief Clinical Illustrations

Below are illustrations of the clinical process of Psychoanalysis with two children, an adolescent, and two adults, followed by work with parents. Regretfully, a complete account of the analyses is not possible in the context of the aims of my book. I will give illustrations of the beginning of our work, the middle, and the end. First sessions can be very meaningful. It is as if a first session gives as preview of what is to follow. I have made the necessary biographical changes to insure confidentiality and anonymity.

Case #1)

A 4 ½ year old boy separated from his mother without apparent difficulty the first session and the rest of the week. He was referred because of anxiety and eating difficulties. He asked me what I would like to do. When I returned the question back to him he said, "It's your room." Thus, he took charge. He told me he was "strong" when it came time to remove the lids from the jars of playdoh. Towards the end of the hour he pretended he was a doctor and cared for my injured finger. Earlier he had told me of injuring his finger in the car door and was wearing a band-aid. Just before telling me of his injury, he told me how he and his father had "horrible fights at night." He lined up all the animals so that all but the last one, the "smallest" one, a lamb, had its tail bitten by the animal next in line. Then the soldiers shot the animals and each other. The animals then gathered around a fallen soldier and consumed him. He whispered the parts of the body being eaten (the analysand only ate meat contained in Heinz baby food). The material at the beginning of this analysis strongly suggested a boy dealing with phase adequate castration anxiety colored by an oral fixation.

Approximately six months later, he was disappointed because I saw what was in the bag he had brought. He complained about having no "surprise" until his mother reminded him of something in the bag. On the way to the room he had me guess what the surprise was. It was a "spy face" - by means of a magnet one could move metal shavings into different positions to make an indeterminate number of faces. He discovered it needed cellophane tape on it and went into the waiting room to ask his mother to fix it. I pointed out how his mother was the "fixer" like I was the previous session. We then played with cars he also had brought in. We enacted a television show that had to do with a car crash. The police wanted to shoot the guilty person and he asked me to decide if they should. I said it was a frightening thought to him that a naughty person should be shot but part of him thought it was a just penalty. He decided to shoot the man. After some more crashes I was a nighttime robber and the police (the analysand) chased me on a dangerous highway. He ran over a ghost but it was all right because he was the President. After awhile, I said he tells me about the nighttime and how exciting and frightening it can be. I pointed out how nighttime is a frightening time for many children because of the sounds they hear and other things they imagine and because it is dark and their parents are in another room. He said it isn't frightening in a car and told me how a friend's grandmother saw a lion from her car in Africa and she wasn't frightened. At the end of the hour he didn't want to tidy up or carry anything into the waiting room. I commented about the big boy-little boy conflict within him- he then helped. He wanted us to use different routes to the waiting room and I commented about separation and reunion and connected this to separation feelings during a recent holiday separation from me.

After three years of analysis termination affirmatively was decided upon. Progressive development had resumed. Our ending revived death wishes and guilt feelings connected with separations from his parents when they went on a vacation, as well as rivalrous Oedipal feelings with father (I learned from mother that her husband was traveling outside the country on business.) He requested to play chess. I reminded him how in a recent session he pretended to be an older brother to a younger one (me). They played after school, and did no home work. I spoke of his impatience to learn the skills of older children like his brother who seems so far ahead that he feels he'll never catch up. He switched the material to Oedipal rivalry. He pretended to be like father, an expert chess player, playing chess blindfolded and winning over three men (me) who joined together as a team. He wanted me to let him win so he could duplicate father's feat.

He was late for his final week of sessions. I learned father was home again from his business trip. I commented about his scary dream the previous week as "haunting" him because of his inner policeman and loving feelings in conflict with angry ones directed at father. He told me to "fuck off" and to stop speaking. At the end of the session he told me he would leave the Lego house we built earlier in the session intact for a "long time." I told him I recognize he has good feelings too. The next day we played a board game that I won but he pretended that he won. I was a silly younger brother. Within my role I spoke about my envy and the hardship of being the youngest member of the family. As a treat I got to go to school with my older brother. Fighting broke out between the older and younger boys. I spoke about my fear that if I did well an older boy would hurt me. I was told to "Shut up."

At our next to last session, he repeatedly said "I'm sorry to say…" He did not finish the sentence. I told him there was a song that goes "I'm sorry to say I'm on my way, won't be back for many a day…" He then killed an insect. I said he felt safer killing it than me or his parents and brother. He smiled and called me a "fart." At our last session he was teary but stoic. I shook his hand and said "Goodbye." Near tears he said, "I'll never forget you," and I said I would never forget him. Given an opportunity to take a toy home from his private drawer he chose a pistol. He said he could not find his pistols at home but if he found another he could play cowboys and Indians with a friend. We walked to the waiting room together. Before we ended I met with mother. I learned that she thought her son was much less anxious and less restricted in his appetite for foods.

Case # 2)

In our first analytic session, a nine-year-old girl who brought in a drawing, sat down on the opposite side of a play table. She was referred because of separation issues. She looked about the room. For the first three quarters of this session she was not spontaneous; I broke periods of silence. Throughout she smiled, a bit forced, and did not seem to be too uncomfortable. I asked about her drawing. It was of a squirrel walking across a fallen tree. The sky was very blue with a bright sun and the grass was very green. She likes to draw but most of the time in school is spent on arithmetic and reading. I wondered, after a silence, if she was wondering what sort of person I would turn out to be? She decided to draw another picture like the one she brought in but was dissatisfied with the outcome. We talked a bit about her unhappiness that an older brother was moving on to a different school than the one they were both attending. I explained the schedule I was going to propose to her parents later in the week. After another silence I asked if she likes to draw animals. She commented she liked "all" animals. I said I thought she brought a drawing of an animal to our first meeting to show me her fondness for animals. From here on she was more spontaneous about her interest in animals and her affect seemed more real. At the end of the session mother had come to pick her up and brought along her pet dog. I petted the dog. I felt at the end of the session that she looked forward to return.

Approximately six months later, she ran to the play room on her first day back following her school break and family vacation. She was silent, smiled, stuck her tongue out, and twirled the key to her toy drawer while humming "around the world in eighty days." Later she opened the window but closed it because she asked and learned I preferred it open. I commented she was angry with me. Later she asked if I took my dog on vacation with me and if I did not I would be cruel. I said she may feel I was cruel for not taking her and it may have seemed as if I was around the other side of the world. I related this to similar feelings as a younger girl when her parents were away on vacation or out for the evening. She rejected this; her family is "one big happy family." Then she told me it was her mother's anniversary but she would not say more because I do not tell her about my marriage. I spoke to how excluded she felt from a part of my life as she does from her parents' life. We then played a school game, with her as the teacher, for the remainder of the session. I said she copes with feelings of loss by wishing to control things.

In a meeting with her parents, they expressed pleasure with the changes over the past three years. Their daughter was more mature emotionally, coped better, did not panic when anxious, and no longer had stomach aches. In the sessions in the next to last week she played a bossy controlling teacher and I was a young child. Via this game she reversed roles and defended against feelings of helplessness connected with our ending. In my role as the child, I verbalized how I was being scolded because of my "naughtiness." She said I was an old man. I said she felt childish sometimes and thought I was too old to like. She smiled and wished me a horrible weekend. Underneath her façade of insults I sensed her fondness and love for me and I pointed out how it was difficult for her to express the good feelings openly. In our last session her tears were expressed in displacement. Her teacher cried at a meeting with parents and students. The teacher was moving away. My analysand expressed gratitude towards the teacher and bought her a gift. She worked on a watercolor painting and left the water faucet on for most of the session (symbolic crying?) and wet the picture till it was "sopping." She expressed curiosity about other children I see while she picked plaster off the wall. After setting a limit I expressed how she felt excluded and perhaps she thought we were ending because she does naughty things with her hands. She called me "stupid" and left the room but returned. She wanted to know what I would do with the contents of her private drawer. She refused my offer to take something home. She smiled and said she might send me a photo of her mare and foal (a recent family acquisition) and then left.

Case #3)

In the first session with a 13 ½ year old boy, he could not think of anything to say. He had been referred because of feeling "the odd man out at school." His father had unexpectedly died about a year earlier. I said that people find it helpful to say whatever comes into their minds. "Mathematics?" He said he always thinks of mathematics but did not wish to speak about it. I suggested he should not select what to speak about. He complained about all the television shows he would miss because of appointments. He again complained of nothing to say. I said perhaps he does not know where to begin and suggested he begin anywhere. He grimaced and looked about the room. I said it was natural for him to feel a bit uncomfortable and not sure about what to speak about since I was a stranger. I recalled to myself that the first time we met he was reading a book titled "In the Silence of the Night." I wondered if he was anticipating silences. He corrected me; it was "The City and the Stars." "Everyone gets things wrong, especially my mother. You say one thing and people say another thing." I said, "And now I got something wrong." He said he was tired and remained silent and uneasy. I said silence was fatiguing to him. A little later I wondered aloud if I recalled the title incorrectly because a part of me was responding to what he said the first time we met, namely that he found speaking difficult. I may have been anticipating that silence would make him feel uncomfortable. He was relieved when our time was up and said as he left, "Not an eventful day."

Approximately six months later, he was very late for a Monday appointment. He asked what time he arrived and said "Ugh" when told. He said I looked annoyed. Later a lot of birds flew over-head and he wondered why such a group is not called a "crowd" as with humans. The next day he was late again, although not so late as the prior session. When I queried him about the reasons for his lateness I learned he waits for his brother. He doesn't like to walk to the bus stop alone as it is getting dark because he passes a church that has a large crucifix in the front. He is afraid the figure will come alive, although he knows this cannot actually happen. He felt his fear was because he has not fully accepted the finality of his father's death. In death the body is "inert" but the brain and mind are still operating. If the latter could contact the former the person would be alive again.

There was a silence and a comment about a "sunrise." I said I thought he was hoping his father could reappear. He confirmed this notion. I said perhaps he also thought that some telepathic communication was possible. He said he never thought of this between a dead and living person but has thought it could happen between two living people. Later he noticed that some furniture in the consulting room had been moved. I said he was "observant." He responded he feels uncomfortable otherwise. He could not sleep in a room he does not know about; he opens up drawers, looks in cupboards, and locks drawers. What was he expecting to find? "What we were speaking about before," but he did not want to go further with this. He expects the usual contents to be in a cupboard but...I said only a part of him expects to discover something unusual. Later he imaged a woman in high heels sitting in the tree outside in the garden; he imagined this from the formation of the branches. I linked such imagined content to the idea that his father might reappear. He replied he could imagine anything. I said he has control over his mind and does not permit some images to emerge. I said the hope but fear that his father would reappear may put him off. He agreed.

After approximately two years of analysis we had a forced termination because my analysand and his mother moved to another state. After dealing with his resistance he was able to express some anger about our ending. He invited me to a concert and I accepted insofar as we were ending and I believed it would be a narcissistic injury to refuse. He did not see me at the concert and had doubts that I attended. He then talked about a movie he had seen where US cavalry slaughter native-Americans. He was surprised about having enjoyed the film, along with depressive feelings. He felt guilty. He accepted he had sadistic thoughts like other people. My attempts to connect such thoughts with doubts that I attended the concert did not evoke a reply from him. The week before we planned to end, he told me about a party he went to the night before and danced in group dances and enjoyed himself. It was nearing the end of the school year and some of his classmates would not be returning the next semester. I said August was a difficult month for him. He agreed and said his father "left' in August too. There's a book titled "August Was a Difficult Month" which he doesn't intend to read. I suggested after he gets settled in his new residence he contact a colleague and arrange a meeting. (We had both agreed he was not ready to end.) He said, "Not right away." When he finished a book he does not want to start another immediately. It would be "disrespectful" to do so. I said I appreciated his feeling and reminded him of his loyalty conflicts about father and me, and that both of us, I was sure, would not think him disloyal if he formed a relationship with another person. I said maybe he will feel different in a few months. We shook hands. He put his head on his hands resting on his elbows resting on his knees. As we left I told him my colleague liked music (a passion of his). He smiled and said that would help. He did meet a few times with my colleague but ended unilaterally soon thereafter.

Case# 4)

The analysand was a self-referred 32year old Caucasian female graduate student in Social Work. She referred herself because of anxiety that she attributed to the competitiveness of her graduate program. She also reported feeling "regressed" in terms of self-feelings, feeling depressed and "deviant." She was accepted for a low-fee analysis.

In our very first session, her fantasy of expecting to be abandoned was manifested. She came a couple of hours early for her first session, having gotten the appointment time confused. Her confusion seemed to indicate turning a passive expectation into an active possibility. Later, before assuming a reclining position on the couch, she indicated that her boots had mud on them and wondered if she should take them off. In a session during her first week she reported a dream where she was in a garment bag, and later associated to a garbage bag. Her feeling was that I would reject her and throw her out. She was a potentially attractive looking woman, but her appearance had a peculiar quality about it, a "second-hand Rose" touch. She gave off an impression of having "street sense." She had an older brother and sister. Father required hospitalization for a paranoid state and committed suicide when she was in her mid-twenties.

Resistance was initially manifested in the form that she had to be refined and have no feelings. Early in the treatment she was taken by surprise about feelings that seemed to be emerging about me. It was no coincidence that a relationship with a young man started to intensify as she entered analysis, and this was pointed out to her. A major resistance was externalization. A fear was that I would diagnose her as hysterical with an interest in older men. A fear of going crazy was also underneath her initial resistance. The initial transference was an expectation that she would feel violated by an interpretation. (Much later I learned that a former male therapist alluded to sexual feelings for her.) My precise verbalizations reminded her of mother. I was grim like mother, too. A paternal transference then emerged; I would abandon her and not protect her. Just prior to our summer vacation, six months into our work, a positive paternal transference began to emerge. Although potentially violent, father was not phony or pretentious like mother.

Our working alliance strengthened as we worked on her anxiety in dealing with her own patients. Conflicts about her femininity and masculine identification entered the analysis. She felt she would "lose" something in a relationship with a man. There was a beginning recognition of projection of her own castrating wishes onto men. The transference changed into predominantly a negative maternal one. She thought I was disdainful of her and directed much anger at me. She worried I would feel burdened by the lability of her moods. It was helpful to get her to appreciate that by focusing on how she processed external reality I was not denying the relevancy of it for her. She became more accepting of her externalization and more allied with me. After one year she realized how easily she felt provoked, and how "over-the- top" her anger was. She recognized she feared a lack of crises.

There was an enhancement of her feminity and she expressed gratitude for her analysis. She now recognized that feeling anxious did not mean going crazy. She began to see me as a good father figure but expressed no curiosity about me. I wondered if this was so because she felt excluded from my life. After I brought her attention to a parapraxis having to do with sexual gender, she threatened to quit, to make me "skittish." Countertransference emerged and I dismissed her ten minutes early one session. She experienced my behavior as due to a seduction on her part reminiscent of sex play with her brother. Insofar as I was able to openly discuss our enactment, I was experienced as more "real" and she became more accepting of sexual resistance. She was defending against shame and guilt in feeling responsible for both brother's and father's emotional issues because of her sexuality, e.g., sitting on her father's lap. Sitting in my waiting room was like sitting on father's lap. I began to point out when she got angry I temporarily lost her as a patient. I learned mother insinuated she was crazy and this evoked murderous rage that was then projected.

There was a linking up of her enemas, surgery and castration beliefs. She externalized the belief that her body was her enemy and the external world seemed malevolent. Mother was held responsible for father's fate; she worried she was like her mother, a sadist. She would avenge her father and absolve her guilt by destroying her mother/analyst. She suppressed loving feelings towards me because she worried I would misconstrue them as erotic. She had a dream where she was the mistress of the President and I could interpret the positive Oedipal implications. Soon thereafter for the first time triangular Oedipal material came to the fore. A female supervisor, linked to me, served as a bad mother, a displacement from my wife. When she missed sessions because of illness, she forced herself to come in because she wanted to tell me she really missed me.

She agreed with my interpretation that she was acting out erotic feelings towards me by becoming attracted to a male supervisor, a friend of mine. She talked about leaving town once she obtained her degree. A dream pointed to maternal aspects of her relationship with father that she was attracted to. I became the mother/witch analyst that would kill her. She knew it was irrational, but missed sessions without cancelling. She would imagine my suffering. It was her sadism that made her anxious. Paranoid-like terror followed after projecting her sadism onto the external world.

After obtaining her degree she accepted a job in another city. She asked to sit up in our last week. She had been in analysis for nearly four years. While attending a conference in another city she fell in love with a married man. She realized she was acting out a fantasy that was linked with her ending with me, and one where she could be very disappointed because of his marital status. She became more realistic about the limits of her new relationship, and recognized an attitudinal change about further analysis. She wondered if she could write after feeling more settled. I never received any correspondence.

Case #5)

The analysand, a Caucasian male, was in his mid-twenties working as an occupational therapist for the past five years. He was experiencing life long envy of his younger sister. His therapist, who was leaving town, referred him to me for a low fee analysis. He was overweight, with a boyish appearance. He had been living with a woman for a number of years, with an intention of someday marrying. His grandmother was a major caregiver when he and his sib were separated from his parents because of father's hospitalization for an illness. Both parent were in health professions.

The initial transference was a displacement of unresolved feelings and thoughts from his previous female therapist. He expected me to be sarcastic, impatient, scrutinizing, and humiliating. By the fourth month a paternal transference seemed to be developing. Father had an avocational interest in psychiatry. We discovered a hidden agenda was to try to confuse me as he did father and thereby feel power over me. With this understanding there was a reduction in resistance, less externalization of his Superego, so he became more accepting that his conflict was internalized. A countertransference issue during this early part of his analysis was my impatience in reaction to his attempts to "stump-the-expert" via tedious repetitiveness and passivity. I interpreted how he seemed to experience my "rules" such as charging for missed appointments, as similar to father's prohibiting his masturbation. This allowed him to bring competitive feelings into the paternal transference. Anxiety and guilt appeared about not conforming to the ideal patient/child that he felt his analyst/parents wanted. He forgot to attend a panel for nurses, an acting out of a fear that in my absence he would take the analyst/father's place with the nurse/mother, as he felt he had done as a five-year-old boy when father was out of the home convalescing.

After I returned from a vacation, he took one. He was doing to the analyst/parent what was done to him, namely "abandonment" (22 months and 5 years of age) when mother left to be with his convalescing father. I interpreted his "reversal of roles," wanting me to feel helpless, rejected, and angry while he was feeling like a powerful, self-indulging adult/parent. I represented the voice of reason and prohibition. After fifteen months of analysis he fantasized mother as a sexually aggressive woman who shot (castrated) her husband in the chest. More tender feelings for father emerged. He began to play a competitive sport, the first time in six years around this time.

When he saw me downtown he did not look at whom I was with because if it was my wife he might find her attractive and he would feel like a competitor. The solution to all this was to be loved by the father/analyst in a way that father loved his sister, namely, a helpless, dependent girl. He tried to exasperate me with pleas to be taken care of. He was amazed that he was feeling all this at a time he was also feeling outside of analysis more autonomous and independent, which suggested a transference neurosis was established. He felt he had to remain overweight so as to not overpower father. He saw me downtown again, but this time he felt a kinship insofar as we lived in the same world, but he also became aware of how little he knew me. Instead of destroying me to obtain my status, he wanted it conferred on him. A passive-feminine position was safer. He became discontented with his willingness to be castrated. His use of identification with me as defense against destructive impulses was interpreted. It was his sexual greed regarding his mother that he felt threatened his father. He felt me to be adult and himself to be a child. There was masochistic pleasure when he felt he was not being cared for. Hidden in each experience of defeat was a victory.

After our second summer vacation, he grew a mustache. He was more accepting of his masculinity. He recalled as a five year old having sexual play with a girl who later married father's friend. It felt as if father stole his girlfriend. I reconstructed positive Oedipal fantasies. For the first time he expressed anger at me for not "making him better." He felt humiliated doing "woman's work" as an occupational therapist. This belief was a defense against competitiveness and destructiveness against father.

Sex was an undercurrent in the analysis. He wanted me to "prod." He used to worry about being homosexual. Childhood fears of castration came to the surface. He no longer felt intimidated by his girlfriend and he proposed marriage, which she accepted. He the made an admission of his most carefully guarded secret, namely, that since the age of thirteen he had been cutting out magazine pictures of women with guns or drawing such women, which he then used to masturbate. This material entered the transference. He had a fantasy of discovering me shot by the previous patient, a female with a gun. There was an unconscious part where the woman with the gun has come from killing his father. He succeeds then in convincing the woman not to hurt him.

As a boy he identified with his male pony that showed dominance over his sister's pony by eating its food; the parallel was that the analysand overate too. He assumed the missionary position during sexual intercourse with his wife. However, he ejaculated prematurely. Talking about this to me made him feel humiliated as he felt as a boy seeing father's bigger penis. He felt himself to be an assassin. He had a fantasy of pushing me off the road with his car and my car ends up in a ditch. If I got angry the next session he'd punch me in the face. As a child he vowed not to live up to his potential as a way to "get even" with his parents. He'd do the same with me by being a failed analysand.

Following this there was a major shift in the transference. He felt the wish to displace father in status and the wish to be taken care of had come together; he wanted neither and felt nearly ready to terminate the analysis. He recalled as a child he was frightened that father could not set limits, and that mother was stronger than father. He soon thereafter accidentally cut his finger. Within the paternal transference I could convincingly point out the passive-into-active defense. What followed was understanding that the gun in his masturbation fantasy was a "penis." I interpreted his construction of an image of his mother as a "phallic" woman. This was impactful. He said the only thing he needed to fear was self-castration.

We set a termination in three months time. Material about his beloved and feared grandmother emerged. The little boy part of him felt abandoned by the ending of our work and pre-Oedipal issues emerged. In the transference the battle was his stubborn refusal to grow up, whereas earlier as a child it was around toilet mastery. He began to see my flaws that made me less than a perfect analyst. Psychoanalysis, he came to believe, was no guarantee to happiness without conflicts, a myth he had held to. He and his wife decided to become parents. He felt different; now he wanted to become an adult. As we approached ending he felt sad but felt strong and recognized that work remained to be done, e.g., losing weight and career planning, but felt confident he could do it independently.

His devoted grandmother was present for both separation from his parents, one at a pre-Oedipal age and the other when he was in the Oedipal stage. This facilitated the prior separation and its consequences to be organized into his dominant phase, the Oedipal Complex, and this made the pre-Oedipal conflict much more amenable to resolution. This plus his high intelligence, and psychological mindedness, once his resistances were reduced, were assets in our work. Once he became aware of the costs to him of being neurotic he was very motivated to grow up. I think these factors account for the short duration, three ½ years, of his successful analysis.

When I trained as a child and adolescent analyst, we had not yet revised our thinking to recognize that parents needed to be seen regularly to work on their parenting, to forge a working alliance with the child/adolescent analyst, etc. So I do not have process notes of parent work from this era. Because of this and reasons of anonymity and confidentiality of my more contemporary parent work done conjointly with analysis of their children, I regret I cannot illustrate such work. I do, however, want to give a vignette of work in "parent guidance" with a mother of a two year old, and a "follow-up" meeting with the parents of a latency boy I saw whose parents were seen by a social work colleague in a day treatment setting.

Case #6)
A mother of a two year old having outbursts of anger that made mother anxious was seen a total of twelve times. I explained there were different causes for temper tantrums and this helped her to realize her son was anxious. She recognized she became angry when interrupted by her son. Next she recognized she was fearful of the intensity of her own feelings so she could not help her son with his anxiety when he experienced her anger. We explored the origin of her fear of the intensity of her feelings. She delayed my meeting her son until she delved deeper into her own feelings. Soon we understood the intergenerational transmission of psychopathology across three generations. We saw how her son's anal phase with all the associated aggressive derivatives made her anxious because of experiences during her own childhood anal phase.

Case #7)
I saw the parents of an adopted latency age boy I had seen for just over three years, a month after I had ended with their son. They wondered if they needed to lower their expectations of their son who was not living up to them. They described his behavior in an extreme way, but my impression was that it was not extraordinary. Basically they seemed worried he would not be capable of becoming an independent adult. Privately, I wondered if their own anxiety about ending work with the social worker they saw regularly was exacerbating their worries about their son.

I pointed out that they temperamentally were reflective while their son was more action oriented. I indicated when their son is interested in an activity he exercises more control. He shows lack of control especially at Sunday School. Father related an incident where his son misbehaved at a religious education program organized by father that caused father to cry. His son apologized and made great effort to have his parents proud of him. Father used this example to illustrate his disappointment in his son. I emphasized how the incident was significant, as it seemed to be their son's genuine attempt to inculcate their values, show empathy, and wish to please them. Mother wondered if he would have done this if her husband had not showed his feelings so openly. I said that what her husband did was positive and perhaps more open expression of feelings with their son would allow the nature of their relationship and the bond between them to be more genuine.

I also raised the issue of adoption. They always denied this as a problem area for their son. I said he struggles with it, perhaps silently, and his rebellion may be reflected in his conflicts about accepting their values and life style. In adolescence there may be intensification about this issue. I told them he had an average IQ and that his educational goals would have to keep this in mind. At the end they spoke of the many positive changes they have seen over the time he was in day treatment and analysis. They recognized the areas of interest that do enhance his self esteem, e.g., athletics and musical instrument training. I encourage them to share our meeting with their son.

Part Four

Other Schools of Psychoanalysis

I will mention four other schools of psychoanalysis. My comments will be very brief and succinct. My aim is to bring their existence to the reader's attention. If what is said interests you then you can follow it up with more reading. The reader should keep in mind that I am not in any way an expert about these orientations. I have not practiced them and nor have I immersed myself in the scholarship written about their theory and technique. It is possible that a practitioner of one of these schools will criticize my focus as incorrect. Nevertheless, I will give my impression of the shortcomings of these schools based on my attendance at presentations and discussions. Despite this, I believe these schools have made valuable contributions. I believe that contemporary ego psychology, the more classical theory and technique I have written about above, has integrated some of the theory and technique of these methods. It is also my belief that several of these schools have in their efforts to revise the classical school have, so to speak, "thrown out the baby with the bathwater." Particularly, several have de-emphasized the significance of the instinctual drives, which, in my opinion, is a mistake.

First, I mention the Kleinian school of psychoanalysis. Here there is an emphasis on the significance of the preoedipal years of children. I think the theory demands more cognitive maturity to account for the dynamics of the period than I think exist in very young children. Nevertheless, it has brought more attention to these early years of development and has raised the awareness of ego psychologists that while the Oedipal Complex is very important it is not the only significant period of development in early childhood. The Kleinian focus on *projective identification*, a concept that postulates that an analysand projects or attributes something of themselves, e.g., a conflicted wish, onto the analyst who identifies with it and believes the origin of the wish to be within his or her own psyche, in my opinion, laid the foundation for interest in countertransference. I believe this is so because projective identification focused on the effects of analysands on their analysts to cause behavior imposed on the analytic material by analysts.

Secondly, mention should be made to the Self psychologists. They focused on the importance of deficiencies or deficits involving narcissism in personality development. This school has elucidated the varied kinds of transference that seriously disturbed narcissistic personalities evidence in the analytic situation. They seek an omnipotent object that they can merge with to heal the damaged Self. This is called a *selfobject*. Self-psychologists underscore the importance of *empathy* as a strategy. Ego psychologists have become more aware of these various transferences and hence are more sensitive to narcissistic issues in their analysands. Empathy is valued but not as a technical strategy; it more a way of relating with compassion to people who seek our help. Interpretation is, rather, our main technical strategy.

Thirdly, there is the relational school of psychoanalysis. Here the relationship between the analyst and analysand is held to be the venue or site where a "psychoanalytic cure" takes place. I agree that psychoanalysis is a procedure involving two people, not only a patient and an authoritative analyst. While I think there is much merit in thinking of psychoanalysis as involving two people, I feel that this focus has minimized the value of emotional understanding of instinctual drives and conflict involving them and the effects on the individual. Conflict experienced about the expression of wishes in the relationship seems to be lost and focus is on the analyst's interaction with the analysand. Focus on anxiety and guilt because of conflict is not a focus.

Finally, I bring attention to the inter-subjective school of psychoanalysis. Here the idea is that both analysand and analyst together create the subjective *analytic field*. The analyst is a participant-observer and he or she influences the analysand and vice-versa. It is as if there is no distinction between the analyst and the analysand. Each affects the other. The analyst's vulnerabilities enter the subjective field and impact on the analysand, and vice versa. My observation is that there is too much self-disclosure by the analyst. I think that this is burdensome to analysands, except in some instances. In my observation it is difficult sometimes to discern who is the analyst and who is the analysand. I mentioned earlier, focusing on enactments as a contribution of the inter-subjective school of psychoanalysis. This is a valuable contribution. In enactments the analyst's countertransference enters into the analytic field. The analyst is unaware of this happening and often it is the analysand who brings it to the analyst's attention. My opinion is that the analyst is wise to acknowledge its presence, assuming it's a valid observation, but not to do self-analysis and self-disclosure at the scene. After understanding what happened the analyst may elect to say something that is not too burdensome to account for the enactment. For example, "I think that when you were talking of your mother's death when you were young it reminded me of a grief reaction of my own that was painful. Your eventual observation was correct that we got off the topic of your grief about your mother's death. I think that's why I changed the subject." Most analysands respect this limitation of self-disclosure and appreciate knowing that the analyst is human too.

Part Five

The widening spectrum of Psychoanalytic treatment

Work with psychotics of any age, in my opinion, is treatment that is psychoanalytically informed. Again, my self-admission is that I have no experience treating this diagnostic type of patient. Colleagues who work with psychotics might claim it is a travesty to exclude such work as psychotherapy, albeit psychoanalytically informed, and not as psychoanalysis proper. There are analysts who report some remarkable positive effects. Because of delusionary thinking, hallucinations, paranoid beliefs, and defective reality testing, it would seem to me that a period of psychotherapy would be required before a more interpretive approach would be effective. The patient would need to feel safe and this would take time. I assume every patient is different in the severity of these symptoms and the duration of a more supportive and educative psychotherapy will vary.

Work with delinquent adolescents is another diagnostic category that I lack experience with. The delinquent adolescent has had a deficiency of being educated about ethical community behavior. The delinquent's Superego and Ego Ideal are ill formed or pathologically formed because of "bad parenting." It would seem to me that the analyst/therapist must first develop a trusting relationship with the adolescent with the expectation that a period of re-education will follow. A trusting relationship I presume will be an outcome of varied strategies based on the different histories of the adolescents in treatment. A positive transference will likely take time to build up. Once achieved, identification with the analyst might occur and an ethical adult imago will be internalized and a new Superego and Ego Ideal can be structured. Perhaps then, in some cases more traditional psychoanalysis can be helpful.

Part Six

Dealing with Illness & Death

Existential anxiety issues are always there for everyone but often do not surface until older age, or if one has a serious, sometimes potentially fatal illness. In young children, death may be a theme, but they often do not recognize the permanency of death until age eight or nine. Adolescents often do not think of it because the issues of puberty and becoming more autonomous individuals takes "center stage." But for older people who recognize that more of their lives are behind them than ahead of them, death is an issue.

Religiously observant people struggle less with dying insofar as they often embrace a concept of the soul and eternal life. But for the majority of adults dying is recognized as inevitable and some put the fact out of consciousness, while others deal with it or struggle with it.

In analysis when an analysand talks about thoughts and feelings about dying, the analyst, too, must deal with their own corresponding feelings and thoughts evoked by the analytic process. An analyst must empathically and compassionately point out that the analysand seems to have death on their mind. The analyst will convey that this is something that can be talked about, and that thinking about it is not pathological. Hopefully, the analysand will proceed to reflect on the subject. The analyst, too, will do some self-analysis about how the subject affects them.

If an analyst is due to have a planned surgery and will need to cancel some sessions, should this be disclosed to an analysand? I think that it depends upon whether it will be obvious or not, e.g., using crutches. The issue of boundaries and consideration as to whether such a disclosure will or will not violate the existing boundary is paramount here. But consideration of boundaries is relative. I think crossing a boundary is not done casually but done with forethought and carefully. Of course, if an analysand cannot attend sessions and is in hospice at home, boundaries will be put aside and a session will be conducted in the analysand's home or via Skype.

A Professional Will

It is professional, ethical, and the responsibility of every analyst to draw up a professional will. In this document there will be instructions to a colleague chosen and agreeing to execute the will, about how to identify one's patients and supervisees and their telephone numbers, to inform them of your unexpected death. Further instructions might be where folders on patients are kept, putting an announcement on your phone that the practice is closed, how to identify the balance of outstanding fees owed by patients and analysands, etc. Additional instructions will be given about the destruction of files. The executor of your professional will now will decide with the patients as to whether or not they would like a referral to talk about the unexpected ending of their treatment, your death, and their grief, etc.

Planned Retirement by the Analyst

Analysand's, I think, best be given sufficient time to plan and react to their analyst's planned retirement. What is sufficient time? I think one year suffices as a reasonable amount of time. An analysand's reactions when told will be immediate and then recede and then resurface, as the date of the forced ending is close. Some analysands will regret learning about the retirement; others may be pleased but suppress saying this. In either case, learning about one's analyst's retirement likely will trigger memories of other "endings." What I have in mind are endings such as going off to college in another city or state, leaving the parental home, moving out of state where you spent your childhood for a job, etc. Then there are also grief reactions to endings such as a grandparent's death, the divorce of parents, etc. Hopefully, during the ensuing year these thoughts and feelings can be analyzed and worked through. Some analysands may elect to end the analysis before the planned ending, thereby turning *passive-into-active*, a defense, to leave rather than be left. With each analysand consideration as to whether or not a suggestion of continued work with a colleague should be made. Some analysands will raise this possibility. If this possibility seems feasible, a referral can be made. I think it best be made before ending so the analysand can have a consultation prior to ending and have the possibility of talking about their reactions to their analyst.

As one ages, one may develop cognitive impairments and this eventuality can also affect analysts. Hopefully, the analyst does not utilize denial and he or she notices the diminished effectiveness on being an analyst. One's analysands often do not bring this to the attention of the analyst. A planned retirement is the sensible option.

Negative Therapeutic Reaction

Rarely in an analysis that is going well, where the process seems to be deepening, suddenly an interpretation is made and there is a worsening of the analysand's condition. It can be bewildering to the analyst. It would seem that "things were going too well." The analysand maybe feels guilty that he or she is undeserving of feeling better, experiencing less guilt and anxiety. It is akin to "survivior guilt." It may be that there is an underlying masochistic streak that went unnoticed up to this point. With more analytic work and insight on the analysand's part, hopefully, the treatment can renew a progressive trajectory.

"Soul Murder"

There are some patients that have been so traumatized by an abusive past, perhaps by a disturbed parent, that it would seem that their very essence has been damaged, their "soul." There is no joy in their lives. These patients dissociate from the Self that has been "destroyed." They lose their identity. Like with some children who need ego strengthening psychotherapy before child analysis is embarked upon, such adult patients will need to build up a sense of trust in psychotherapy before they will risk "getting in touch" with their Self and exposing it to another. It makes sense to me that the analyst be consistent and that a change of professional not take place.

Diversity

Psychoanalysis has not had a long history of treating people of color, so having the analyst and analysand be of different races is a relatively new experience. Psychoanalytic Institutes in the United State only in the past two decades have been training non-Caucasian candidates. As a result, analysts are becoming more sensitive to the need to pay attention to their analysands' feelings about racial differences between the two of them. Also, countertransference sensitivities need to be attended to. Analysands may be reluctant to speak openly about their perceptions and feelings, being apprehensive that they may be seen as accusing the analyst as being racist, or by their disclosures revealing their own racist predilections. Analysts can intervene, by pointing out that everyone has some racism as part of their psychology, zenophobia, that regrettably is inculcated by one's social culture, a form of vestigial tribalism.

Part Seven

Postscript

Why did I decide to write this book? I am sure that there are multiple motives for writing this book. The one that I would like to speak to is the following. Psychoanalysis will never be popular. This is because it deals with a subject that most people would prefer not to think about, and certainly not talk about. The idea that civilized human beings unconsciously have base instincts like other animals is an abhorrent idea to many people. That Freud focused on the sexual and aggressive instincts made matters even worse for civilized and religious people. They did not consider that Freud was not advocating the free expression of basic unconscious drives. He was all for self-control and sublimation of aims.

In popular Western culture when psychoanalysts are portrayed in movies or in drama, often they are fools or corrupt. It used to be that they were shown to be silent and busy taking notes. But this misrepresentation or caricature of analysts, I think is a way of demeaning the goals of psychoanalysis, self-actualization, understanding the past so it does not repeat itself in the present, learning to forgive oneself for transgressions so you can forgive others, etc. It also gets back to an uneasiness that another can know more about you then you know about yourself. I am hesitant to disclose that I am a psychoanalyst when invariably asked at a social gathering, "So what kind of work do you do?" Some people openly say, "Oh, I better watch myself." I let them know that, "I'm off for the day."

Anna Freud is seldom mentioned any more in child studies about development or pathology. Why is it that her valuable contribution is neglected? Also, new schools of psychoanalysis have started originally to revise the field but they seem in some respects to be trying to replace the "classical school." They have valuable contribution to make but what was indispensible in the classical school seems to become dispensable.

The "zeitgeist" in contemporary psychiatry is a biological orientation. Indeed, the mind and the brain are connected and someday in the future we will know how. But, in my opinion, this is not in the near future. And even so, if by "tweaking" the brain we could change the mind I would still want to know why the mind worked in the way it did before the biological intervention. "A life not understood is not a life worth living."

Medication is the treatment of choice in most Psychiatry departments in the States. Residents are not taught to listen to their patients but instead have a questionnaire to be asked in order to arrive at a diagnosis so that a drug can be prescribed. Very young children are given diagnoses requiring medication that often have dire side effects. Diagnoses in child psychiatry become popular and are over-used. Kids who are anxious are diagnosed as hyperactive with attention deficit disorder. Instead of drugs the more appropriate disposition would be psychotherapy for them and their parents. But when you are dealing with almost thirty children in a classroom, a teacher wants quick results and medication to "numb" such a child is sought.

Patients want quick results. Understandably, when you have symptoms that burden you, impatience is to be expected. But symptom removal is not sufficient. Patients need to be educated that a symptom is a neurotic "solution" to a "mental conflict." The conflict needs to be processed lest the symptom reappears or another different one will appear. Insurance companies, too, want quick results so that the period of paying out benefits is shortened. One consequence of this has been the development of treatments such as "Cognitive Behavior Therapy." The claim is that the goal should be symptom removal not resolution of conflict. Under the mantel of being "evidence based treatment" CBT has become popular. Statistics can be used to point out that the symptom has gone and has not been replaced. Psychoanalysis is said not to be evidence based. But the results of a treatment such as analysis cannot be assessed by a simple questionnaire. Also, there is statistical evidence to show the effectiveness of psychoanalysis as a treatment. Besides, there are many "testimonials" from former analysands attesting to the value of their analysis. Skeptics will say that after a lot of cost and time, what else would you expect a former analysand to say. I am pleased to say that I have heard sincere testimonials from former adult patients and parents of children and adolescents I have seen.

The above accounts for why I wrote this book. I hope to make more understandable a process that is private and misrepresented. I hope, too, that more people will consider consultations for themselves and their children to learn if an analysis is the "treatment of choice." For this to happen on a larger scale, psychoanalysts need to reduce their fees whenever possible. I know one needs to "make a living" but if money is the reason for choosing to be an analyst then going into a "helping profession" is probably the wrong choice. Psychoanalytic Institutes need to establish clinics staffed by candidate analysts and supervised by graduate analysts. Reduced fee treatment can be an option as well as insurance covered treatment.

Representative List of Topics

Preface
Psychoanalytic Concepts of Development
    Psychosexual Phases,
    Characteristics of Drives,
    Fixation & Regression
    Complemental Series
    Adolescent Development
    Adult Development
Psychoanalytic Model of the Mind
    Ucs., Pcs. Cs.
    Topographic Model
    Structural Model
    Characteristics of Id, Superego, & Ego
    Ego Ideal/ Ideal Self
    Ego Functions
    Self, Identity & Identifications
    Mental Conflict
Referral
    Initial contact with Adult
    Seeing Parents First with Young Children
    Initial Contact with Adolescent
Evaluation
    Analyzability
    Trial Analysis?
    "Rule" of Abstinence
    Reparative Therapy First

- Initial Face to Face Contact
- The "Fit" between analytic couple

Recommendation
- Procedures with Different Age Groups
- Common Questions Asked

The Frame
- Issues of Confidentiality
- Immersion
- Cancellations
- Office Setups
- Note Taking

The Beginning of an Analysis
- Use of Couch
- Free Association
- Feeling Safe

Establishing a Working Alliance
- Self Observation & Self Experiencing
- Helping Inner Child in Adult to Grow Up
- Alliance with Parents of Adolescents and Children
- Distinction Between Thoughts & Deeds
- Lessening of Guilt

Resistance
- Ubiquity of Resistance
- Examples of Resistance
- Signal anxiety
- Ego defenses
- Absence of Dreams
- Secrets
- Topic of Masturbation with Adolescents
- Avoidance of Curiosity About Analyst
- Young Children and Resistance
- Sexual Gender Issues and Resistance
- Use of Defenses in Resistance
- Character Defense

Transference
    Positive and Negative
    Transference Cure
    Transference with young Children
    Timing of Interpretation
    Transference with Adolescents
    Erotic Transference
    Transference Neurosis
Real Object, Developmental Object, Transference Object
    Definition
Countertransference
    Manifestations
    Enactments
    Free Floating Attention
    Love in the dyadic relationship
Interpretation
    Definition & purpose
    Interpretations as Conjectures
    Surface to Depth
    Adolescents and Interpretation
        Struggles with masturbation
    Reconstruction
    Trauma
    Adolescence and Separation
    Masturbation
    Clarification & Confrontation
    Interpretations as Conjectures
Acting Out
    Definition
    Acting out and Resistance
Limit Setting
    Violation of the Frame
    Answering Questions
    Boundaries

- Children and Limits
- Requests for medications

Ways of Bringing Material
- Deciding on an Agenda
- Traumatic Memories
- Telephone sessions
- Dreams
- Bringing a Pet
- Play
- Toys
- Playful thought with Adolescents
- Music

Comings and Goings
- Punctuality/Lateness
- Departures

Role of Education
- Neutrality
  - Departures
- Normalizing some feelings
  - Depression
  - Guilt
- Confronting an Abuser

Work with Parents
- Value in Work with Children & Adolescents
- Difficulties
- Defining a child's "problems"
- Issues of Confidentiality
- Parents and Infants

Goals of Psychoanalytic Treatment
- Analysand's Goals
- Analyst's Goals

Working Through
- Repetition
- Overcoming Resistance
- Repetition Compulsion

    Eradication of Conflict
    Progressive Movement
Termination
    Analysis of Major Conflicts
    Quality of Transference
    Issues
    Sadness/Grief
    Follow Up
    Earlier Leave-taking Experiences

Part Three
Brief Clinical Illustrations

Part Four
Other Schools of Psychoanalysis
    Revision of Classical School
    Kleinian
    Self psychology
    Relational
    Inter-Subjective

Part Five
Widening Spectrum of psychoanalytic Treatment
    Work with Psychotics
    Work with Delinquent Adolescents

Part Six
Dealing with Illness & Death
    Existential Anxiety
A Professional Will
    Definition
Planned Retirement of Analyst
    Telling the Analysand
    Cognitive Impairment of Analyst
Negative Therapeutic Reaction
    Definition

Soul Murder
    Definition
Diversity
    Racism as ubiquitous

Part Seven
Postscript
    Reasons for writing the book

Representative List of Topics

Recommended Readings

Recommended Readings

Child Analysis

The Psychoanalytic Study of the Child, Vol 1-67, International Universities Press, NY 1945-70
Quadrangle, NY 1971-72
Yale University Press, CT 1973-2015
Routledge, Phila, PA 2016-

Bulletin of the Hampstead Clinic, Vol 1-7, 1978-83

Bulletin of the Anna Freud Centre, Vol 8-18, 1984-1995

Child Analysis, Vol 1-18

Child Analysis & Therapy, John Glenn (ED.), Jason Aronson, NY, 1978

The Psychoanalytic Works of Hansi Kennedy, Jill M. Miller & Carla Neely (Eds.) Karnac: London, 2008

The Many Meanings of Play, Albert J. Solnit, Donald J. Cohen, Peter B. Neubauer, Yale University Press, New Haven & London, 1993

Studies in Child Psychoanalysis: Pure and Applied. Monograph Series PSC, #5, Yale Universities Press, New Haven & London, 1975

The Technique of Child Psychoanalysis: Discussions With Anna Freud, Joseph Sandler, Hansi Kennedy, Robert L. Tyson (Eds) Harvard University Press, Cambridge, MA, 1980

Rosenbaum, A.L. The assessment of parental functioning: A critical process in the evaluation of children for Psychoanalysis. *Psa Q.*, 1994, 63: 466-90

Working With Parents Makes Therapy Work, Kerry Kelly Novick & Jack Novick, Jason Aronson, NY, 2005

Adolescent Psychoanalysis

The Psychoanalytic Study of the Child, Vol 1-70

The Analyst & the Adolescent at Work, Marjorie Harley (Ed), Quadrangle, NY, 1974

Developmental Breakdown and Psychoanalytic Treatment in Adolescense, Moses Laufer & M. Egle Laufer (Eds), Yale University Press, New Haven & London, 1989

The Suicidal Adolescent Moses Laufer (Ed) International Universities Press, CT., 1995

Adult Psychoanalysis

Freud's Rules of Deream Interprtetation, Alexander Grinstein, International Universitites Press, CT., 1983

On Beginning an Analysis, Theodore J. Jacobs & Arnold Rothstein (Eds), International Universities Press, CT, 1990

Psychoanalytic Technique and the Creation of Analytic Patients, Arnold Rothstein, International Universities Press, CT., 1995

The Interpretation of Dreams in Clinical Work, Workshop Series, American Psychoanalytical Association, Monograph 3, Arnold Rothstein (Ed), International Universities Press, CT., 1987

The Technique & Practice of Psychoanalysis 1, Ralph R. Greenson, International Universities Press, NY, 1967

The Technique & Practice of Psychoanalysis 2, Alan Sugarman, Robert A. Nemiroff, Daniel P. Greenson, (Eds), International Universities Press, CT., 1992

The Patient & the Analyst, Joseph Sandler, Christopher Dare, Alex Holder (Eds), International Universities Press, NY, 1973

www.ingramcontent.com/pod-product-compliance
Lightning Source LLC
LaVergne TN
LVHW011927070526
838202LV00054B/4514